LAYERED

Layered

BAKING, BUILDING, AND STYLING SPECTACULAR CAKES

TESSA HUFF

founder of *Style Sweet CA*

ABRAMS, NEW YORK

For Everett James—Dream big, baby boy.

CONTENTS

It's a Sweet Life

WHENEVER ANYONE ASKS ME how I got started baking, there's an expectation for me to describe myself with flour-dusted chubby cheeks, a mini apron, and admiring eyes watching my grandmother bake from heirloom recipes in a cinnamon-scented kitchen. This was not the case. It wasn't until my last year of college that I made my first cake, with canned frosting and a plastic zip-top piping bag, but I have always wished for a more enticing story.

However, if I really think about it, food and cooking have always been an influential part of my family and culture. I come from a family with diverse backgrounds. My father's strong German roots and Midwestern upbringing mixed with my mother's Hawaiian ancestry and Puerto Rican flair resulted in a colorful and creative household for both me and my older brother. Driving many of my parents' stories and teachings were lessons of ambition, community, and cuisine.

Even though I don't have the coveted memories of baking with Grandma as a child, her culinary influence found its way into many of my recipes anyway. Rich in culture but not in purse, my maternal grandmother was an original DIY-er, not because it was trendy, but because she had to be. She cooked, sewed, taught herself how to reupholster furniture, and balanced a job while being a mom with a husband attending night school. Although they were not exceedingly wealthy, my grandparents were very generous. The neighborhood kids knew that if they showed up to the house in the afternoon, my grandmother would make them a treat. She saved the good ingredients for special occasions, leaving my mom with many memories of cookies made with orange extract because it was cheaper than the pure vanilla. But with birthdays came homemade, deep-fried corn dogs and extravagant cakes—giving my mom and her siblings something to look forward to.

Almost all of my memories from my maternal grandfather's side of the family revolve around food. Fittingly, my great-grandfather first came to Hawaii from the Philippines to work at a sugar mill. My grandfather was born and raised in a tiny rural village on the North Shore of Oahu. Although he left the islands at age eighteen and raised his family in California, our Hawaiian roots run oceans deep. With three small kids, he went to night school and worked toward becoming a civil engineer in order to fly them all back to Hawaii each summer.

My parents kept this tradition alive, and I plan to teach my children about their culture rich in food, family, and tradition.

Although my brother and I are the *hapa* (half-Caucasian) cousins, every time we visit Hawaii we quickly fall into the island rhythm. You may be thinking umbrella drinks and resort pools, but my Hawaii is another story. My summers were made up of eating Kahuku watermelon at the local beach, *haupia* (coconut pudding) pie, salty skin, sunburns, and potluck dinners spent in the carport because no one had air-conditioning. I learned hula from my cousins and would string leis with my aunties—all while sharing stories, laughs, and memories of how our family came to be. The island life explains my appetite for passion fruit- and mango-inspired desserts, but it also taught me a lot of respect for unique flavors and unfamiliar foods.

My father's side of the family is much different. He was born to affluent, well-educated parents working in the motor vehicle industry of Detroit's heyday. The photos of his childhood home, the extravagant holiday parties, and my paternal grandparents' elaborate seven-tier wedding cake were picture-perfect. And while everything seemed flawless, they had more than their fair share of tragedy. My grandmother passed away when my dad was only a teenager. While I never had the chance to meet her, I did inherit her entrepreneurial spirit. She graduated from the University of Michigan in the 1940s before founding her own company. I thought I was ambitious when I started the Frosted Cake Shop when I was twenty-four, but that does not compare to how brilliant my grandmother was in business. While this part of our family history is tragic, had it not been written this way, my father may not have accepted a job across the country, where he met my mother.

Beyond my annual experiments decorating Christmas cookies as a kid, I only went into the kitchen to practice pirouettes and tap routines on the hardwood floor. While I had the dedication to spend hours each day at the ballet barre, I never had the patience for baking or any interest in cooking. However, I was being immersed in different types of food and global cuisine without even realizing it. My dad traveled a lot for work and found it important to introduce us kids to different cultures. In Tokyo we discovered chestnut paste "noodles," in Sydney I first tried Turkish delight, and at Harrods Department Store in London I was mesmerized by the fruit-shaped marzipan. These influences gradually seeped into my culinary toolbox, but it wasn't until college that I started using them to manipulate ingredients and create my own flavor pairings.

The only entertaining television programs that aired between my college classes and dance team practice were cooking shows. I started watching and thought, "I can do that." I began writing down recipes and testing them out on my roommates. As it turns out, I was pretty good at it. The first cakes I ever made were for Christmas in 2005. With finals approaching, none of us had the time, money, or insight to go out shopping for thoughtful gifts. Instead, I bought my first set of cake pans and planned to make individual cakes for my friends. I used boxed cake mix and canned frosting, and steadily wrote their names in icing with a piping bag made from a plastic zip-top bag. There was something special about those cakes. My roommates and I were already pretty close, but as we sat digging into the chocolate frosting, laughing, and relishing one another's company before winter break, I saw the power that cake had on community and knew that it was the start of something new.

With rich family ties rooted in food, coupled with the discipline of my ballet background, I suppose it's no coincidence that I found passion in pastry. Requiring a similar level of dedication and attention to detail, cake design became my new creative outlet after I quit dancing. While many of my peers were becoming doctors, therapists, and nurses, I was playing with buttercream and sugar. I quickly became "that girl" with the cookies, cupcakes, and pastries at any celebration, holiday, or even weeknight gathering. I took the night shift at a local bakery, filling and icing layer cakes, before pursuing my dream to start my own custom cake boutique.

I opened the Frosted Cake Shop in Sacramento, California, in 2008, where I serviced an array of loyal clients, weddings, and community events. With only the help of my family and husband, it was pretty much a one-woman show. The business was small and intimate, but I wouldn't have had it any other way. I enjoyed working with my clients from concept to completion and seeing what joy cake can bring to someone's life. I will always cherish the rewarding memories of giddy brides seeing their cakes for the first time.

Today, I feel very fortunate to have lived such an enriched life and am grateful for all of the people and places that shaped my culinary point of view. My frugal side has pushed me to creatively develop new recipes from ingredients already in my pantry that I would not normally pair together. On the other hand, the opportunity to travel has helped me discover the luxurious and exotic flavors used in some of my recipes, like the tin of matcha powder I picked up in Tokyo, hardly even knowing what it was used for.

I now live in Vancouver—an international city with dozens of different types of cuisine and specialty food shops within a two-block radius of my doorstep. Whether I am cooking a meal for my husband and our son, Everett, or working on a new dessert, the wide array of spices and fresh ingredients from around the world at my fingertips generates unlimited inspiration for new recipes. It is my hope that the recipes here encourage you to think outside the (cake mix) box when it comes to your own cake creations.

Reach for New Heights

Layer cakes are the ideal vehicle for both creative expression and deliciousness. Whether you are an experienced baker or a complete novice, *Layered* can help you take your creations to the next level. Throughout this book, I serve up plenty of inspiration and essential information for making impressive layer cakes at home.

WHY LAYER CAKES?

Layer cakes are composed of cake, filling, and frosting to create well-balanced, delectable desserts. The multiple components of a layer cake provide the opportunity to add a variety of textures within a single cake and to blend different complementary flavors together to create something both simple and complex—something artisanal. Ranging from textured buttercream to pure, rustic finishes, and even those covered in sprinkles, layer cakes are the perfect canvases for an array of decorations and a chance to add a bit of drama to one's dessert. With all the different kinds of cakes, buttercreams, ganaches, and garnishes, just think of the countless combinations you can make!

Beyond being sweet and delicious, layer cakes are a symbol of celebration. It is a layer cake with swooping frosting on which children blow out candles on their birthdays, that happy couples slice into on their wedding day, and that one parades into a dinner party with, turning heads with each step. Velvety layers of yellow butter cake smothered in fluffy fudge frosting bring back memories of youth, and a slice of decadent, almost sinful chocolate cake shared with a loved one keeps romance alive.

And let's face it—everyone loves a layer cake. Eating it, baking it, admiring sky-high layers of it elegantly frosted in buttercream. I'm talking two-, three-, and even up to six-layer confections adorned with edible decorations and candied garnishes—the sugar-clad flights of fancy that are wrongly assumed to be out of reach for the home baker. *Layered* empowers you to create awe-worthy cakes in your own kitchen. It covers classic to contemporary baking techniques, industry tips and tricks, and new, innovative flavors that make you wish your birthday came more than once a year. It's time to toss the cake mix and canned frosting and reach the height of your cake-baking potential!

HOW TO USE THIS BOOK

Layered is intended to inspire and challenge experienced bakers as well as guide eager amateurs toward making their own bakery-style cakes. The cake and frosting recipes have been strategically paired to create exquisite flavor combinations, but I strongly encourage each reader to make the recipes his or her own. (See page 279 for more pairing inspiration.) While there is still some science necessary for baking the perfect cake, feel free to play with flavors and experiment with different textures. Mix and match the decorating techniques and edible garnishes to create custom cakes to celebrate any occasion.

Throughout the book, you will find a variety of tips and tricks from my years spent as a pastry chef and cake-maker. Baker's notes, shortcuts, decoration ideas, and suggested uses for extra ingredients are sprinkled over the pages to enhance the baking experience.

In the end, baking should be fun! Confidence is key, but with the right knowledge and a little bit of practice, the possibilities are truly endless. This book is not just pretty pictures and delicious flavors, but also the stories they tell. It is about selecting just the right recipe with a special recipient or occasion in mind, hand-picking the finest ingredients and sharing your hard work with people you care about. It is not about spreading the frosting flawlessly on the first try, but about turning an ordinary day into a celebration. Making cakes is more than putting sweets in our bellies; it's what the process says when you present someone with a homemade, decorated cake. In this way, a thoughtfully prepared layer cake speaks its own language. When other words or actions cannot express how much you care, say it with a layer cake!

After my husband (who has become well versed in all things baking over the years) glanced over the first draft of recipes for this book, he looked at me quizzically and asked, "How did you come up with all of these?" This opened a can of worms, as I launched into memories about each and every recipe. The following pages are full of those stories and the tips and techniques you need to make the cakes your own.

A Well-Layered Pantry

INGREDIENTS

To make layer cakes with excellent flavor, it is important to pay close attention to your ingredients and the ways they should be used within a recipe. Using the wrong flour or using cold butter when it is supposed to be softened can result in vastly different textures and can quickly compromise the structure of your cake. Here, you can find an overview of many of the ingredients used throughout the book. Most of them are probably already in your pantry, but I've noted how each should be treated for baking, when you should splurge on high-quality items like premium chocolate and real vanilla beans, and why I find it important to keep a spare jar of instant espresso powder and a few lemons in my kitchen at all times.

BUTTER

Unless otherwise specified, butter for baking should always be unsalted. It is easier to control the salt content of a recipe when it is added separately, plus a salty buttercream is not always appetizing. Most recipes call for softened, room-temperature butter. It should be malleable but not separated. Depending on the temperature of your kitchen, remove butter from the refrigerator thirty to sixty minutes prior to use to soften it.

CHOCOLATE

If you are looking to splurge, go for the good chocolate. I am not talking a bag of chocolate chips off the grocery store shelf, although sometimes that can be sufficient. If you decide to use a premium chocolate, then I recommend purchasing chocolate disks in bulk or large blocks of milk, semisweet, or bittersweet chocolate. I prefer Callebaut brand for my personal baking needs.

For a deeper, fudgier taste in frostings or glazes, look for unsweetened Dutch-processed or alkalized cocoa powder—meaning it has been treated to neutralize the cocoa's natural acidity. Unless otherwise specified, use Dutch-process cocoa powder for baking.

For white chocolate, I recommend a premium brand, especially in recipes for white chocolate ganache, like my Mango Ganache and Matcha Ganache (pages 166 and 93).

CREAM CHEESE

As with butter, cream cheese should also be used at room temperature, although it typically requires less time out of the refrigerator to become soft, just ten to fifteen minutes. Cream cheese should be of the full-fat variety, unless otherwise specified.

EGGS

The quantities for eggs in these recipes are based on large eggs. I always recommend organic or free-range eggs, when available.

Many of the recipes call for just the egg yolk or just the egg white, so store whichever is not being used for later use. In order to keep the structure of whipped egg whites from being compromised, remember to keep the egg whites pure and to not let any drips of yolk fall back in.

Eggs, like the rest of the ingredients, should be room temperature when used in a cake recipe.

FLAVORINGS

Unless otherwise specified, always use pure extracts and fresh citrus juices. Many recipes call for vanilla, almond, and peppermint extracts, and their imitation counterparts do not carry the same flavor profiles. A high-end vanilla extract can go a long way, as can fresh-squeezed lemon juice.

Citrus zests can add a flavorful punch to any recipe. When mixed with sugar, the rubbing action helps release their natural oils and flavors. Be sure to only zest the thin outer layer of the fruit and leave the bitter white pith behind. When specified in a recipe, vanilla bean paste is highly recommended over vanilla extract. The paste contains real vanilla bean seeds and is one of my favorite ingredients to use. It's one of those ingredients that can really step up your yellow cake or buttercream game. You may substitute pure vanilla extract if the paste is unavailable to you.

I always keep a jar of instant espresso powder on hand. Coffee and espresso help enhance the flavor of chocolate in most recipes, and you'll find yourself reaching for the jar more often than you think. If you do not have instant espresso powder available to you, you may substitute instant coffee, but it is not as rich in flavor, so you many need to increase the amount by as much as 25 to 50 percent.

FLOUR

Not all flours are created equal, so be sure to note what type a recipe calls for. For the most part, different types of flour cannot be substituted for one another.

All-purpose flour is more common in sturdier cakes. It contains more protein than cake flour and is used in more-forgiving cakes such as chocolate, carrot, and other oil-based batters. Cake flour is required for more tender, delicate cakes. It is in nearly all the butter-based cakes in this book and cannot be substituted unless otherwise specified.

A few of the recipes in this book call for specialty flours like almond, whole wheat, and spelt. Luckily, these can now be found fairly easily at regular grocery stores. They add an extra element of flavor and/or texture, but can usually be substituted.

To measure flour, use the scoop-and-sweep method. First, aerate the flour in its container by briefly mixing the contents with a whisk. Then scoop flour into the measuring cup until it is slightly overflowing. Level off the flour with a knife by swiping the blade across the top edge of the cup.

LEAVENING AGENTS

We are trying to bake sky-high cakes here, so pay close attention to the ingredients that are going to make your cakes rise.

Baking powder and baking soda are not interchangeable. Baking soda is usually called for in recipes with chocolate, buttermilk, or citrus to react with and balance the acidic elements of these ingredients.

LIQUIDS

Liquids can provide fat used to lubricate gluten in dry ingredients and are necessary for structure and texture development. When a recipe calls for milk, use whole milk.

Buttermilk is often used; be careful when substituting since the other ingredients may depend on its acidity to develop properly. Using sour cream provides the perfect balance of fat and acidity for some recipes. Milk, buttermilk, and sour cream should all be at room temperature before being added to a cake batter.

Heavy cream is often used to create frostings and fillings. For whipped cream, be sure that the heavy cream contains at least 35 percent milk fat. For best results, heavy cream should be chilled before being whipped.

OILS

Instead of butter, oils are sometimes used to coat flour proteins to create supermoist cakes. The recipes in this book call for grapeseed oil, but other neutral oils like vegetable, canola, or safflower may be used instead. Unless otherwise called for, do not substitute olive oil or it will change the flavor of the cake.

SALT AND SPICES

Although you may think salt does not belong with sweets, it helps enhance other flavors. Use fine grain (kosher or sea) salt in cake recipes and flake or fleur de sel as a garnish.

Most spices are used ground, unless otherwise specified. Whole or freshly grated spices typically provide a more intense flavor. Ground spices have a long shelf life, but you might want to splurge for a new jar if a spice has been sitting in your cupboard for the past couple of years or so.

SUGAR

Cakes are sweet, so of course you can expect to find sugar in most recipes. Most call for granulated white sugar. Confectioners' sugar, or powdered sugar, is used in many frostings and should always be sifted after being measured using the scoop-and-sweep method (see "Flour"). I love the addition of brown sugar in different recipes, from spice, chocolate, and buttermilk cakes to even buttercream. Muscovado sugar is an unrefined cane sugar and should only be used in recipes that call for it, due to its high moisture level and stronger molasses flavor. Be sure to firmly pack brown sugars when measuring.

SWEETENERS

In addition to sugar, many recipes call for sweeteners like molasses, honey, light corn syrup, maple syrup, and brown rice syrup. Not only do these ingredients provide sweetness but also they add different layers of flavor to a recipe.

TOOLS OF THE TRADE

In addition to basic baking and cake-making equipment like utensils, mixing bowls, and an oven, there are some more specific tools that will help you create the cakes in this book. Not all of them are completely necessary, but they will make achieving your cake goals easier.

BALLOON WHISK

This all-purpose whisk is the best choice for whipping cream, beating eggs, making pastry cream, and most of your other whisking needs.

CAKE BOARDS

Cake boards are essential for stability when building tiered cakes. You can usually find them at your local craft or hobby store. Keeping a variety of different-size cake boards on hand may make transporting cakes much easier. They are available in different finishes, plain and greaseproof.

CAKE PANS

The cakes in this book have been baked in 6-inch (15-cm), 8-inch (20-cm), and 10-inch (25-cm) round cake pans, with sides that are 2 inches (5 cm) tall. Square pans of the same size are larger in volume and should not be used as a substitution for round pans. A few cakes have been baked in a rectangular cake pan measuring 10 by 15 inches (25 by 38 cm). A 9 by 13-inch (23 by 33-cm) pan will suffice, but may require a slightly longer baking time. Rectangular cake pans should have sides that are at least 2 inches (5 cm) tall, as opposed to 1-inch (2.5-cm) sides that are typically found on standard sheet and jelly-roll pans.

CAKE RING

A cake ring is similar to a cake pan, but without a bottom. Several recipes call for a 6-inch (15-cm) cake ring to cut out rounds of cake or to help build layers.

CANDY THERMOMETER

A candy thermometer is necessary in several recipes, especially when boiling sugar or heating egg mixtures. A trained eye and experience may get you fairly far, but a candy thermometer is essential when noted.

ELECTRIC STAND MIXER

Nearly all the methods and instructions in this book that require mixing are based on using a stand mixer. A hand mixer may be used, but mixing times and speeds may vary. Plus, a stand mixer frees up both hands, which is helpful when you're making things like meringue that require pouring one ingredient into another while mixing.

FINE-MESH SIEVE

A fine-mesh sieve is often used as a strainer in a variety of recipes, including flavored simple syrups, curds, and purees. A large fine-mesh sieve is my preferred tool for sifting dry ingredients.

GEL FOOD COLORING

Gel varieties are typically more concentrated than liquid food coloring. They yield more vibrant results while using less quantity. When tinting cake batter or frosting, I recommend gel coloring to minimize the amount of liquid added.

ICING COMB

An icing comb is used for creating different textures and buttercream finishes. It comes in metal or plastic and can be found in the cake decorating section of your local craft or hobby store.

ICING SMOOTHER OR METAL BENCH SCRAPER

To create smooth frosting finishes and crisp buttercream edges, a metal bench scraper or metal icing smoother is essential. Many icing combs have a flat side, so if you find one in that style, it can do double duty for both smooth and combed finishes.

KITCHEN SCALE

For more accurate measurements, use a kitchen scale and the listed metric quantities, especially in recipes with chocolate.

MEASURING CUPS

A full set of flat-rimmed metal or plastic dry measuring cups is important to have in any working kitchen. Be sure to measure liquid ingredients in a liquid measuring cup—usually glass or clear plastic, with the measurements marked on the side and a spout for pouring.

MEASURING SPOONS

Like measuring cups, a full set of measuring spoons is also important. Baking requires very exact measurements, and the difference between even ½ and ¾ teaspoon could make or break a recipe.

METAL SPATULAS

Metal spatulas come in a variety of shapes and sizes. Straight spatulas can be handy for applying frosting to the outside of cakes and a multitude of other tasks. I personally prefer offset spatulas of all sizes. A small offset spatula is great for creating even layers of filling within a cake or for frosting smaller cakes. A medium offset spatula is great for frosting larger cakes. Either a medium or large offset spatula may be used to lift and transport cakes from a turntable or cake board to a serving dish.

OVEN THERMOMETER

It is essential to know if your oven is calibrated to the correct temperature. It is definitely worth investing in a small oven thermometer to know what temperature your oven actually bakes at, if there are hot or cool spots within the oven, or if it loses heat easily once the door opens. Knowledge is power in this situation, so you can adjust the temperature or bake times accordingly.

PARCHMENT PAPER AND/OR PARCHMENT ROUNDS

Parchment paper is handy in almost any kitchen. You may find yourself using it to dry garnishes on, create piping bags with, and to line cake pans.

PASTRY BAGS

There are advantages to both disposable plastic pastry bags and canvas ones. I typically use smaller disposable bags for messy or small tasks like piping borders and keep a variety of canvas pastry bags for larger jobs like filling a cake or creating particular buttercream finishes. That way, I am not constantly needing to refill the bag and keep air bubbles to a minimum.

PASTRY BRUSH

A pastry brush is great for brushing syrups and sauces onto cake layers for extra flavor and moisture. One with plastic, silicone, or natural bristles will be sufficient.

PIPING TIPS

These small tools can add big drama to your cake designs. Piping tips come in a huge range of shapes and sizes. Smaller varieties are typically used for piping borders, while large piping tips can be used to fill cakes and create particular buttercream finishes. The designs throughout this book use round, star, and petal tips in various sizes.

RUBBER SPATULAS

I find myself constantly reaching for rubber spatulas for an array of tasks. They are great for scraping down bowls, folding batters, and pretty much all mixing. The heat-resistant silicone ones are great for work being done on the stovetop.

SERRATED KNIFE

A long serrated knife is helpful for "torting" cakes, that is, splitting a cake into multiple layers. I also use a serrated knife when chopping chocolate off a large block for ganache and glazes.

SIFTER

Dry ingredients and confectioners' sugar need to be sifted before heading into a recipe. While I prefer to use a fine-mesh sieve, a sifter certainly also does the trick.

TURNTABLE

If you plan on making and frosting several layer cakes, then a turntable is definitely a good investment. A turntable will help you achieve a variety of frosting finishes, especially super-smooth sides and swirls.

VEGETABLE PEELER

A vegetable peeler is not only good for peeling carrots but also for creating chocolate curls.

ZESTER

A good citrus zester is great for collecting all the essential flavors of a fruit while leaving the bitter pith behind. I personally love my Microplane and use it for both sweet and savory dishes daily.

Cake Making and Decorating 101

While there are endless lessons to be learned in regard to baking and pastry, here are some of the methods I find most important for creating a perfect cake. Many of the following will appear throughout the book, and I recommend understanding these terms and processes before getting started. This chapter also covers how to stack and frost a layer cake—the building blocks to creating any of these showstoppers. Additionally, I will explain how to create many of the textured finishes showcased in the photos throughout the book.

BAKING AND PASTRY TECHNIQUES

———

Creaming

IN MY HUMBLE OPINION, creaming the butter and sugar in a recipe just might be the most important step. If you are looking for a soft, tender texture in your velvety butter cakes, then listen up. Creaming is the process in which softened butter and sugar are mixed together to perfection.

First, everything (including the mixing bowl and paddle attachment) needs to be room temperature before getting started. For many of the cake recipes throughout this book, you start by beating the butter in the bowl of a stand mixer fitted with the paddle attachment on medium speed until smooth, about 2 minutes. Add the sugar and increase the speed to medium-high. Continue to mix for 3 to 5 minutes, until the mixture has lightened and is pale in color.

During this process, the sugar granules cut into the butter to incorporate small pockets of air. The friction helps the sugar start dissolving and the butter to soften even more. Creamed butter and sugar distribute throughout the batter more evenly. Do not skip this important step. Once you start adding more ingredients, you can't go back.

Folding

FOLDING IS A PARTICULAR TYPE OF MIXING that is generally used to combine two mixtures or ingredients that are vastly different in weight and density. It is often used to incorporate lighter mixtures, like whipped egg whites, without deflating them.

To fold, use a large rubber spatula. For whipped egg whites, place them on top of the cake batter. Push the spatula down the side of the mixing bowl until you hit the bottom. Fold the batter from the bottom of the bowl up and over to the top of the bowl. Rotate the bowl 90 degrees and repeat. Continue to gently but deliberately fold the ingredients together until the mixture is homogenous. Use this method when folding whipped cream as well.

The folding method may also be seen as the final step of mixing a particular cake when adding items like nuts or chocolate chips to prevent overmixing the batter.

Whipping Egg Whites

EGG WHITES SHOULD BE WHIPPED with a completely clean whisk. Be sure the egg whites are free from fat or any drips of egg yolk and the equipment is grease-free, or the whites may not hold air as well. Whip egg whites until stiff peaks just begin to form, but before they start to clump and separate. They will collapse over time, so be sure to whip them up fresh just before use.

Whipping Cream

AS MENTIONED IN THE "INGREDIENTS" SECTION (PAGE 17), be sure to use chilled heavy cream that is at least 35 percent milk fat. Depending on what the recipe calls for, whip the cream in the bowl of a stand mixer fitted with the whisk attachment to either soft or medium-stiff peaks. Overwhipped cream will begin to separate, appear granulated, and start to turn into butter.

For best results where whipped cream is used as a filling or frosting, whip the cream just before serving. Alternatively, whipped cream may be stored separately in an airtight container in the refrigerator before assembly. Gently rewhip it by hand before use. Assembled cakes with whipped cream will need to stay refrigerated until 30 minutes before serving to prevent spoilage, so be sure to plan accordingly.

Using a Double Boiler

A DOUBLE BOILER is a double-decker pan/pot system that is used to warm ingredients over simmering water, which acts as indirect heat. It can be purchased as a specific set or easily made with a medium saucepan under a heatproof mixing bowl: Fill the bottom pan with a few inches of water and place the mixing bowl on top. The bowl should sit snugly in the pan but never touch the water. Place it on the stove over medium heat and bring the water to a simmer. Most of the recipes that call for a double boiler are for melting chocolate. This method may also be used for heating other delicate mixtures, like those with eggs, to keep them from scrambling.

Reverse or "Two-Step" Cake Method

YIELDING SIMILAR RESULTS to the creaming method, this technique is used for creating a cake that is light in texture with a fine crumb. In the reverse method, the dry ingredients and butter are combined first, with the fat coating the flour particles. Then the egg whites are incorporated into the batter. Since there is quite a bit of liquid involved, as in the Neapolitan Cake (page 48), slowly adding in the egg whites and milk makes a more even mixture with a stable structure.

This method can be a bit less forgiving, so be careful not to overmix the final batter. Instead, add the liquids very slowly.

Tempering

THIS TECHNIQUE IS USED to incorporate two mixtures that are different temperatures. Most of the recipes that call for tempering involve mixing together hot cream and room-temperature eggs. To prevent the eggs from cooking too quickly or scrambling, a small amount of the hot liquid is whisked into the eggs to slowly raise the temperature of the eggs before combining all the contents.

Checking for Doneness

THE BAKE TIMES FOR THE CAKES in this book are given as a range to account for variations in actual oven temperatures, the placement of cake pans within the oven, humidity, etc. To make sure a cake is done baking, here are a few easy testing methods:

BY TOOTHPICK: Insert a toothpick into the center of the cake, then remove it. If the toothpick comes out clean or with few crumbs, then the cake is done baking.

BY SIGHT: The edges of a cake should just barely start to pull away from the cake pan when done baking. For lighter-colored cakes like yellow butter or buttermilk, the tops of the cakes should start to turn golden.

BY TOUCH: For sponge or chiffon cakes, when the surface of the cake is touched with a fingertip, the cake should bounce back.

Sifting

ALL DRY INGREDIENTS AND CONFECTIONERS' SUGAR should be sifted, preferably with a fine-mesh sieve (see page 20), to aerate and eliminate any lumps before use. Sift after measuring. When recipes call for the dry ingredients to be sifted, this includes flours, salt, spices, leavening agents, and cocoa powder—unless otherwise specified. This typically does not include granulated or brown sugars.

Tinting Buttercream

TO TINT VANILLA SWISS MERINGUE BUTTERCREAM (page 41), add a few drops of gel food coloring (see page 20) to the finished buttercream. Mix thoroughly, adding more food coloring until your desired shade is achieved. Tinting buttercream is always optional and can be done with any cake calling for vanilla buttercream.

Preparing Cake Pans

TO PREVENT CAKES from getting stuck in their cake pans, first grease the inside of the cake pan with butter or nonstick spray. Sprinkle with flour and shake the pan around until the inside is covered in a thin layer of flour. Flip the pan over and tap out the excess.

Mise en Place

FOR BETTER BAKING, practice *mise en place*, or "putting in place." This refers to having all of your ingredients prepped and measured before getting started. It may seem a bit excessive, but it will make things easier in the long run. Often, time is of the essence, like when making caramel, and you wouldn't want your sugar to burn while you measure the rest of your ingredients. This will also ensure that you have all of the ingredients that the recipe calls for so you don't get halfway into a recipe before realizing you don't have enough eggs.

For me, this also means reading and understanding the instructions from start to finish and making sure my ingredients are the correct temperature. Unless otherwise specified, butter, eggs, and dairy products should be room temperature before starting a recipe. Butter must be softened, but not melted, for creaming with sugar and when being added to meringue to make buttercream. Having all of your ingredients the same temperature makes for a more homogenous, smooth batter.

Cutting the Cake

BEFORE SLICING STRAIGHT into your beautiful cake, score the cake perfectly in half with your knife. From there, score one of the halves into quarters or thirds, depending on the size of your cake. Continue to divide each section in half to create even pieces of cake. If necessary, remove or rearrange garnishes before slicing. Most cakes should be cut with a large chef's knife. For those cakes with fresh fruit filling or a crunchy element, use a long, serrated knife and a gentle sawing motion. Remember to let the cake stand at room temperature (if applicable) to make cutting smoother. Once cut, gently remove each piece from underneath with an offset spatula. If you are finding it difficult to cut through chilled buttercream or ganache frosting, run the blade of your knife under hot water to slightly warm the metal. The warm blade will help melt and soften the frosting, making it easier to cut through. Wipe your knife with a clean kitchen or paper towel between slices.

Cake Storage

IN GENERAL, cakes may be made in advance and stored separately from their fillings and frostings until ready to assemble. Cake layers may be stored for up five days in the refrigerator and up to one month in the freezer, individually wrapped in a double layer of plastic wrap. Let frozen cakes thaw in the refrigerator still wrapped in plastic.

Assembled cakes that need to be stored in the refrigerator should be lightly covered in plastic wrap or in a cake box, away from foods with strong odors. For cakes with unfrosted sides, leave ungarnished and without glaze. Wrap the sides with the plastic wrap to prevent them from drying out. When storing leftover cake that has been cut into, press a piece of plastic or parchment directly onto the surface of the cut side of the cake to prevent it from drying out. Cakes are typically best eaten within 48 hours of assembly, but will keep for a number of days after that (see each recipe for specific times). In general, a refrigerated cake should be brought to room temperature before serving by letting it stand for 30 to 90 minutes. Many cakes may be frozen (and when possible this is specified in the recipe), but note that their frostings and appearances may be altered during storage and thawing. To freeze leftovers, chill in the freezer until set (20 to 30 minutes), then tightly wrap the cake in a double layer of plastic and store in the freezer for up to 2 months, unless otherwise specified.

HOW TO FROST A CAKE

Frosting a cake with perfectly smooth sides and a crisp top edge is not a skill reserved for just professionals. Using a few tools and simple tricks, anyone can make a beautifully frosted cake.

WHAT YOU'LL NEED

1 baked and cooled cake recipe of choice

Frosting of choice

Filling of choice

Large pastry bag

Round piping tip; ½ to ¾ inch (12 mm to 2 cm) in diameter

Turntable

Cake board

Long serrated knife

Large and small offset spatulas

Rubber spatula

Icing smoother or metal bench scraper

Preparing the Cake

To create a level, stable cake, you must start from the bottom. Not only do you need a delicious, well-structured cake, but the cake layers should also be equal in shape and size. Most cakes are not 100 percent ready to go straight from the cake pan. You will need to "torte" the cakes, or cut them so the layers are flat and the correct height.

Before cutting or frosting a cake, be sure the cake layers are completely cool. After they are removed from their pans, it is best to wrap the cakes in plastic wrap and chill them in the refrigerator for a couple of hours. A chilled cake means fewer crumbs when it is cut or handled.

Next, any domes created during baking must be removed. Start by placing the cake on a clean turntable or cake board. Use a long serrated knife held parallel to your work surface to score the top of the cake where the dome starts. As you spin the turntable, begin cutting into and across the cake. Keep the knife as level and parallel to your work surface as possible and cut in toward the center of the cake until the dome detaches from the body of the cake. If the cakes do not have domes on top, use the same technique to make sure all the layers are the same height.

Many recipes call for the cakes to be split into multiple layers. For two even layers, measure the height of the cake, and divide that amount in half. Score the cake halfway up with a serrated knife or mark with toothpicks. While spinning the turntable, carefully cut the cake in half horizontally with a long serrated knife. For even layers, keep the knife as level as possible and only cut a little a time.

Before assembling a cake, decide how you will layer it. When there are multiple layers to choose from, select the most stable one for the bottom layer. Sometimes cakes break and crumble a bit, but you will want to use the sturdiest layer as the base of your cake. Use the imperfect layer(s), if any, as the middle and save the second-best layer for the very top. If possible, the top layer should be placed cut-side down for minimal crumbs when frosting.

Filling the Cake

The most beautifully frosted cakes start from the inside out. Depending on the cake recipe and filling(s) involved, filling a cake may be a bit tricky. All the cakes in this book have different instructions for assembly, but for cakes with softer fillings, follow these guidelines.

Place a cake board in the center of the turntable and place the bottom cake layer on top. Prepare a pastry bag with a round piping tip and fill it one-half to three-quarters full with buttercream or your frosting of choice. Pipe a ring of buttercream ½ to ¾ inch (12 mm to 2 cm) high around the top edge of the cake layer. Fill the ring or "frosting dam" with the filling of your choice. Even out the filling with a small offset spatula, if necessary. Top with the next layer of cake and repeat. Once all the layers are filled and stacked, make sure that the cake is sitting up straight and is as level as possible. If the cake is leaning at all, use clean hands to push and manipulate the cake layers slightly so that everything is even.

Applying the Crumb Coat

The first coat of frosting is called the crumb coat. This thin layer helps hold in all the crumbs and prevents bits of cake from getting into the final coat. Start by placing a medium dollop of frosting on top of the cake. Using an offset spatula, begin to spread it out. Continue coating by applying frosting to the sides of the cake. The crumb coat should be even and completely cover the cake, but does not need to be perfectly smooth. Refrigerate the cake uncovered for 10 to 15 minutes to set it before adding the final coat.

Finishing the Cake Smooth

Vanilla Swiss Meringue Buttercream (page 41) makes for the smoothest finish, but the same techniques should be used with whatever frosting you choose. Even cakes with a rustic finish (see page 31) should start with this process.

Starting with the top of the cake, place a generous amount of frosting on top of the crumb coat. Use an offset spatula to begin spreading out and flattening the mound of frosting on top. Spin the turntable simultaneously to create an even layer of icing. Push any excess frosting to the edges so that it creates an overhang off the top edge of the cake. The frosting here does not have to be perfect, as we will be smoothing out the top again later on.

Using an offset or straight metal spatula, attach the frosting that may be overhanging from the top of the cake to the sides of the cake. Working on only the top half of the cake, begin applying frosting to the sides of the cake. The frosting does not need to be smooth, but should be applied in an even layer. Continue on to the bottom half of the cake.

Once there is an even layer of frosting on all sides of the cake, begin smoothing the frosting out. While spinning the turntable, use an offset spatula to smooth out the final layer, removing any excess frosting and adding more, when necessary.

After this first round of smoothing, it's time to put our tools to work. Place the icing smoother parallel to the side of the cake. The long, smooth edge should be touching the cake and the bottom edge should sit directly on top of the turntable or cake board. Keeping the icing smoother still, slowly begin to spin the turntable. The icing smoother should pick up any excess frosting to create a smooth finish. After a couple of spins, stop and step back. Fill in any gaps with frosting using a small offset spatula and check to make sure the sides of the cake are straight. Continue to use the icing smoother until you are satisfied.

As the sides of the cake are smoothed out, frosting will be pushed up toward the top of the cake. To remove this lip of frosting and to smooth out the top, carefully take the edge of an offset spatula to pull the lip of frosting toward the center of the cake. Keep the spatula as level as possible and try not to interfere with the frosting on the sides of the cake. Continue around the entire top edge. Finally, lightly place the edge of the icing smoother on the top of the cake. Give the turntable one final spin to even out the top.

TIPS AND TROUBLESHOOTING

- When crumb-coating the cake, do not return any frosting that contains crumbs to the original bowl of clean frosting.

- Always clean off the spatula and icing smoother between frosting applications.

- When working with an offset spatula, focus on using the center of the spatula as opposed to the tip of the spatula for more control.

- Work with a small amount of icing at a time for better control and cleanliness, especially when just learning how to frost a cake.

- Use the turntable to your advantage. Let the spinning action work for you when leveling out the top and smoothing out the sides.

- If you do not have a turntable, try placing the cake and cake board on top of an inverted mixing bowl and carefully rotate the cake board as you go.

- Apply a thick enough layer of frosting to the sides of the cake so the cake layers do not show through. Essentially, you will be applying more frosting than needed in the end, since some of it will be removed when smoothing.

- If the cake or frosting ever seems soft or runny, chill the cake in the refrigerator for 15 to 20 minutes.

- If the buttercream appears to have air bubbles or is too thick, try remixing the frosting until silky smooth.

- For an even smoother finish, heat a metal spatula or icing smoother by running it under hot water. Dry and continue the smoothing process. The warmed metal will help by slightly melting the frosting. Try this technique on a chilled cake.

- You will need about 3 cups (720 ml) buttercream to frost a three-layer 6-inch (15-cm) round cake. You will need about 4½ cups (1 L) buttercream to frost a three-layer 8-inch (20-cm) round cake.

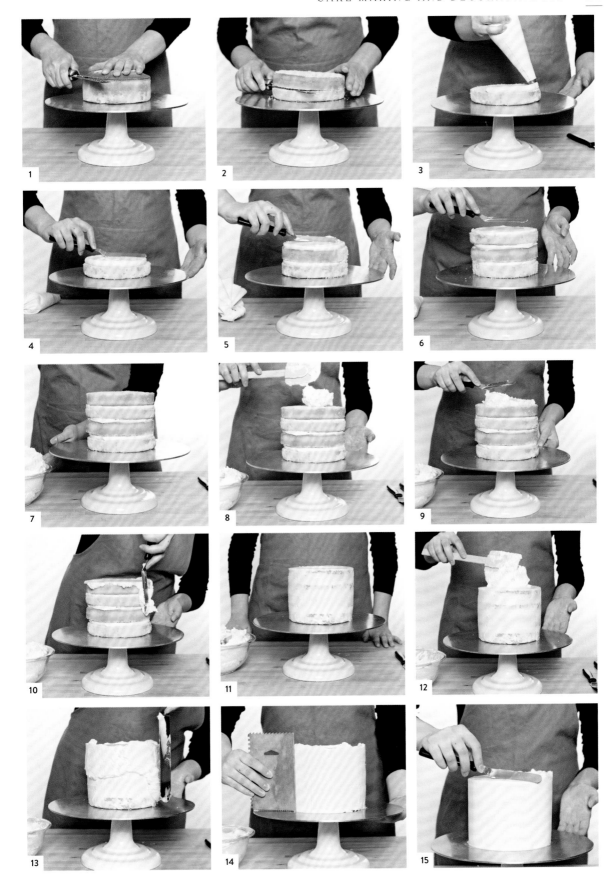

MORE SIMPLE FINISHES

In addition to smooth frosting, there are endless finishes that are equally gorgeous to choose from. Using just your trusty offset spatula or an icing comb, you can instantly change up the texture and overall look of a frosted cake. Use these techniques just after the frosting has been applied and not yet chilled.

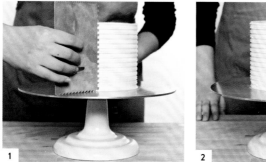

Striped Finish

To create a simple horizontal stripe around a cake, use an icing comb. Start with a smoothly frosted cake sitting on top of a turntable. Keeping it completely parallel to the side of the cake, gently press the edge of the icing comb into the side. Leave the comb still and rotate the cake by spinning the turntable an entire 360 degrees until the ends of the stripes meet. For best results, use buttercream.

  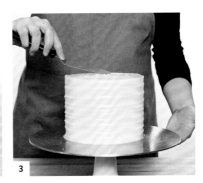

Swirl Finish

To create a simple swirl finish, start with a smoothly frosted cake. Place the cake on top of a turn-table. Take the tip of an offset spatula and, holding it almost completely parallel to the sides of the cake, gently place it on the bottom of the cake. Pressing slightly into the cake, begin spinning the turntable. As the cake rotates, pull the tip of the spatula straight up the side of the cake until it reaches the top. To finish the top of the cake, place the tip of the spatula toward the edge of the cake. Pressing slightly into the cake, begin spinning the turntable again, moving the spatula toward the center of the cake to create a swirl. This technique may be used with a variety of frostings including buttercream, fudge, and cream cheese.

Rustic Finish

A rustic finish looks effortless, but there is still some skill involved. You do not need to start with a perfectly smooth cake, but there should be an even layer of frosting applied to all sides. Start by filling and crumb-coating the cake as normal. Apply an even layer of frosting to all sides, then make swooping motions with an offset spatula. Try creating free-form swirls, diagonals, or a design of your choice. This technique may be used with a variety of frostings, including buttercream, whipped cream, cream cheese, and more!

PIPING BAG FINISHES

Piping frosting is not just reserved for borders and details. I love using medium and large piping tips to decorate the entire surface of the cake. Simply swapping out different piping tips can dramatically switch up the entire design, creating everything from delicate ruffles to intricate textures.

  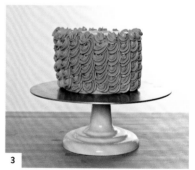

Spiral Finish

This is one of my favorite ways to decorate a cake. Start with a thicker crumb coat or thin final coat of frosting. Frost the top of the cake as normal before working on the sides. Place the cake on a cake board or serving dish on top of a turntable. To help make the pattern even, score the coat of frosting underneath with the edge of a metal spatula or paring knife to make evenly spaced vertical lines. Fill a pastry bag fitted with a medium-large open star tip with frosting. Hold the piping bag at a 45-degree angle to the cake. Creating vertical rows, start by piping frosting spirals from the bottom of the cake up to the top. The coils should slightly overlap to ensure the cake is completely covered. Count the number of spirals, and try to use the same amount per column around the cake. Continue to pipe more spirals around the cake until it's completely covered. For best results, use buttercream.

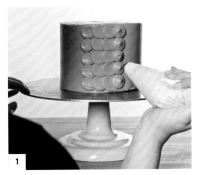
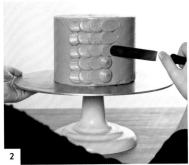
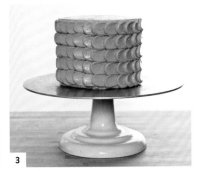

Petal Finish

Use just a round piping tip and a small spatula or spoon to create this simple petal or scalloped frosting finish. Start with a crumb coat that is slightly thicker than normal or a thin final coat of frosting. This inner layer does not need to completely hide the cake layers, but should still be smooth and even. Frost the top of the cake as normal before working on the sides.

Place the frosting in a pastry bag fitted with a ½- to ¾-inch (12-mm to 2-cm) round tip. Pipe large dots or "bulbs" of frosting following a straight, vertical column down the side of the cake. The bulbs should be touching but not overlapping, so adjust their size accordingly. Place the tip of a small spatula or spoon on the center of the first, top-most frosting bulb. Gently pull the frosting straight across to the right to create a petal shape. Working down the row, continue to pull and create petals with the frosting bulbs down the side of the cake. Once one column is complete, pipe a new set of bulbs, slightly overlapping the tails of the petals. Continue around the cake until complete. For best results, use buttercream or fudge frosting.

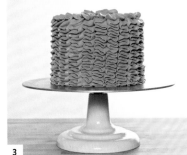

Ruffle Finish

This technique is extremely impressive and surprisingly simple to create. Place the cake on a cake board or serving dish. Like for the petal finish (see above), start with a thicker crumb coat or thin final coat of frosting. To help make the pattern even, score the coat of frosting underneath with the edge of a metal spatula or paring knife. Fill a pastry bag fitted with a petal tip with frosting. With the narrow point of the petal tip facing out, hold the piping bag perpendicular to your cake board or serving plate. Starting from the bottom, pipe about 1-inch-wide (2.5-cm) columns, zigzagging back and forth until you reach the top of the cake. Count the number of zigzags, and try to use the same amount per column around the cake. Keeping even pressure, continue until the cake is completely covered. To pipe ruffles on top of the cake, keep the narrow point facing out and pipe ruffle swags (see page 36) around the top edge of the cake. Continue piping concentric rings of ruffles, overlapping slightly, until you reach the center of the cake. For best results, use buttercream. See opposite page for an example of a finished cake decorated with this technique.

Smooth Ombré Finish

To start, give your cake a good crumb coat. Divide a recipe of buttercream among three to five bowls. Using gel food coloring, tint the buttercream different colors of your choice (or keep one white, if desired). Decide in which order you would like the colors to go. Place a dollop of the last color of buttercream on the top of the cake. Begin spreading out the top layer of frosting with an offset spatula as you would in the first step of frosting a smooth cake.

Fit a pastry bag with a round, ½- to ¾-inch-wide (12-mm to 2-cm) piping tip. Fill the pastry bag with the first color of buttercream. Starting at the bottom of the cake, pipe a ring around the sides of the cake. Continue to pipe rings going up the sides of the cake, adding more buttercream in the different colors to the pastry bag as you go. Essentially, the buttercream rings will change in color as you progress up the cake. Depending on how tall the cake is and how many colors you are using, there should be two to three rings of each color.

Once the buttercream has been piped around the cake, begin smoothing. Start by using an offset spatula held parallel against the cake to remove any excess frosting. Once the buttercream starts to smooth and even out, use an icing smoother to finish off the smoothing process. The colors should blend together as you go. Fill in any gaps in the buttercream with the coordinating color. Finish off the top edge of the cake as you would in the final stages for frosting a smooth cake. For best results, use buttercream. See page 177 for a photo of the finished cake.

Watercolor Ombré Finish

For a more rustic or watercolor look, apply the different colors of buttercream with an offset spatula instead of a piping bag. After crumb-coating, place a dollop of frosting on the top of the cake and smooth it out. Starting at the bottom of the cake, add different colors of buttercream to the sides of the cake with an offset spatula. Work with one color at a time until the cake is completely covered. Smooth out with an offest spatula until desired look is achieved. (See pages 170–72 for more on the cake pictured above and opposite.)

PIPING TECHNIQUES

PETAL

ROUND

SMALL STAR

LARGE STAR

The variety of shapes and designs you can make using simple tools like a piping bag and piping tip always amazes me. Piping tips come in a vast array of sizes and shapes. If you use different pressure and movements, the decorating possibilities are endless.

Petal Tip

RUFFLE BORDER: Hold the piping bag at a 45-degree angle to the cake surface. Point the narrow end of the tip away from the cake. While keeping even pressure, pipe frosting ruffles by moving the tip up and down while going around the cake.

RUFFLE SWAGS: Hold the piping bag at a 45-degree angle to the cake surface. Always pointing the narrow end out, increase the pressure while moving the tip slightly out and away from the starting point and then back in while decreasing pressure. This pressure change will create the curved edge of the swag. Pipe swags on the sides of a cake or create a border around the bottom of the cake.

ROUNDED RUFFLE SWAGS: To cover the top of a cake, use the same technique as the ruffle swags (see above), but slightly pivot the angle of the tip between ruffles. Follow the curvature around the top edge of the cake and fill in the center with concentric circles of ruffles.

BAKER'S NOTE: *I recommend Wilton brand tips #104 and #125 for ruffles.*

Round Tip

LINES, STRIPES, AND WRITING: Hold the piping bag at a 45-degree angle to the cake surface. Keeping the tip slightly hovered over the surface, pipe with continuous, even pressure until your desired design is achieved. Release the pressure before pulling up on the piping bag.

DOTS: Keeping the tip perpendicular to the cake, hover it slightly above your cake surface. Apply even pressure to the piping bag until the frosting forms the dot of your desired size. Release the pressure before pulling up on the piping bag. If a small peak forms at the end, use a clean paintbrush or fingertip dampened with water to gently flatten.

PEARL BORDER: Hold the piping bag at a 45-degree angle to the cake surface. Apply pressure to create a small bulb of frosting, and then decrease the pressure while dragging the tip away from the bulb to form a tail. Begin the next pearl slightly overlapping the tail of the previous bulb.

BRAIDED BORDER: Use the same technique as for the pearl border, but alternate the angle of each pearl's tail inward to create overlapping Vs.

BAKER'S NOTES: *I recommend Wilton brand tips #3, #5, and #8 for writing and borders. For bulbs (large dots) or kisses and frosting dams (page 27), I recommend Ateco brand tip #808.*

Small Star Tip

STARS: Use the same technique as for dots (see above), but with a small star tip.

SHELL BORDER: Use the same technique as for a pearl border, but with a small star tip.

REVERSE SHELL BORDER: Hold the piping bag at a 45-degree angle to the cake surface. Begin applying even pressure while forming a tight spiral, and then decrease the pressure while dragging the tip away to form a tail. Begin the next shell by slightly overlapping the tail of the previous shell and reverse the rotation of the spiral. Continue around the cake.

BAKER'S NOTE: *I recommend Wilton brand tips #18 and #21 for stars and 1M for borders.*

Large Star Tip

SPIRAL: Hold the piping bag at a 45-degree angle to the cake surface. Using even pressure, begin piping a spiral motion, letting the frosting fall back on itself. Use a tight spiral motion for complete coverage or move the piping bag in the direction of the spiral as you go for a looser design.

ROSETTE: Keeping the tip perpendicular to the cake surface, pipe frosting in a tight circle while using even pressure. Release the pressure just as you complete the spiral to create a tail that tapers off. Be sure the pressure is completely released before pulling the tip away.

BAKER'S NOTE: *I recommend Ateco brand tip #824 for spirals and rosettes.*

TIPS AND TROUBLESHOOTING

- Try writing out words on a piece of parchment paper, then tracing over them with frosting.

- Never let the tip touch the surface of the cake or there will be nowhere for the frosting to go.

- To fill a piping or pastry bag, fit the bag with your desired tip first. Hold the center of the bag with one hand and fold over the top end of the bag to open it up. Use a spoon or rubber spatula to scoop frosting into the bag, scraping it against the crook of the hand that is holding the bag (between your thumb and index finger). Once it is partially full, grasp the bag where the top of the frosting is and unfold the top of the bag. Twist the top of the bag one time around and gently squeeze the frosting toward the tip of the bag to release any trapped air. It is best to only fill the bag one-half to three-quarters full to prevent frosting from overflowing out of the top of the bag.

- To pipe with a piping or pastry bag, hold the bag with your dominant hand. Place the bag in the crook of your hand and gently wrap your fingers around the twisted area. Carefully squeeze the bag until the frosting begins to flow. Use your other hand to guide the piping tip, not to try to squeeze out more frosting. Once you can no longer squeeze out any more frosting, stop and relax your hand. Move your hand down the bag toward where the remaining icing is, twist once and repeat.

THE FINAL TOUCHES

Now that we've filled and stacked our cakes, then frosted them with an array of finishes, let's talk presentation! From candied nuts sprinkled on top, down to the tablecloth that the cake will be sitting on, there are plenty of details to consider to really make your cake shine. Feel free to mix up your garnishes and decorations in order to match each occasion.

Edible Garnishes

From simple chopped nuts to candied citrus, adding edible garnishes is an easy way to decorate cakes without any fancy tools or additional equipment. Garnishes add texture and drama to cakes and can even hint at flavors found within the cake. There are many recipes throughout the book for edible garnishes, such as chocolate curls, homemade sprinkles, candied nuts, spun sugar, and more, but feel free to add your own embellishments when inspired to do so.

Many recipes call for a particular ingredient, like shredded coconut, sprinkles, or sanding sugar to cover the entire surface of the cake. Start by placing a baking sheet on your work surface and the garnish ingredient in a mixing bowl. Place a frosted cake on a cake board or serving dish and hold it with one hand. Use the other hand to generously scoop up whatever ingredient is being applied and press it to the top and sides of the cake. Work over the baking sheet so that any bits that do not stick to the cake fall back on the baking sheet and can be reused. It is best to add the garnish while the frosting is still fresh. To prevent the cake from sliding around while you work, dab a bit of frosting between the cake board and the bottom layer of cake.

Fresh Flowers

Adding fresh flowers is an easy way to add color and elegance to a finished cake. Before placing fresh flowers on anything edible, be sure that the type of flower is nontoxic and unsprayed. Some common flowers that are available in edible and/or nontoxic versions include roses, orchids, hibiscus, marigolds, carnations, violets, lavender, lilacs, and sunflowers. Do not stick the stem of a flower directly into the cake. Instead, wrap the stems in floral tape or place only the blossoms on the top or side of the cake. Herbs like fresh mint, thyme, and rosemary can help give a design a fresh, rustic look too.

Decoration and Display

A big part of what makes a cake awe-worthy is the presentation. Beyond frosting, glazes, and edible garnishes, there are plenty of other ways to decorate a cake. Tying on ribbon or using cake flags and bunting can add a whimsical, playful touch. Try even something as classic as candles to finish the look. Also, keep in mind how you'd like to serve and showcase the cake: Will you use a fancy serving plate or will the cake be displayed on your favorite cake pedestal? Consider coordinating the table linens, sprinkling the cake table with confetti, or stringing up a banner or backdrop behind the cake. See Sources (page 282) for a list of some of my favorite places to buy decorations.

Sweet Staples

These recipes are used multiple times throughout the book in one form or another. Many cakes call for different variations and amounts of these recipes, but the base recipes and methods can be found here.

vanilla swiss meringue buttercream

——

I LOVE SWISS MERINGUE BUTTERCREAM for its smooth, silky qualities and the fact that it is not overly sweet. It can be easily flavored and pairs perfectly with a variety of cakes without overpowering them. I find it to be the easiest frosting to ice cakes with, too! My favorite varieties include passion fruit, peppermint, and Earl Grey—just to name a few—and we will explore these and many others in the pages to come.

SMALL RECIPE

Makes about 3¼ cups (780 ml); enough to frost a three-layer 6-inch (15-cm) round cake

½	cup (120 ml) large egg whites
1	cup (200 g) granulated sugar
1½	cups (3 sticks / 340 g) unsalted butter, at room temperature, cubed
1½	teaspoons pure vanilla extract

MEDIUM RECIPE

Makes about 4½ cups (1 L); enough to frost a three-layer 8-inch (20-cm) round cake or fill and frost a three-layer 6-inch (15-cm) round cake

½	cup plus 2 tablespoons (150 ml) large egg whites
1¼	cups (250 g) granulated sugar
2	cups (4 sticks / 450 g) unsalted butter, at room temperature, cubed
2	teaspoons pure vanilla extract

LARGE RECIPE

Makes about 6½ cups (1.5 L); enough to fill and frost a three-layer 8-inch (20-cm) round cake

1	cup (240 ml) large egg whites
2	cups (400 g) granulated sugar
3	cups (6 sticks / 675 g) unsalted butter, at room temperature, cubed
1	tablespoon pure vanilla extract

1. Place the egg whites and sugar in the bowl of a stand mixer. Whisk them together by hand to combine. Fill a medium saucepan with a few inches of water and place it over medium-high heat. Place the mixer bowl on top of the saucepan to create a double boiler. The bottom of the bowl should not touch the water.

2. Whisking intermittently, heat the egg mixture until it registers 160°F (70°C) on a candy thermometer or is hot to the touch. Once hot, carefully fit the mixer bowl onto the stand mixer.

3. With the whisk attachment, beat the egg white mixture on high speed for 8 to 10 minutes, until it holds medium-stiff peaks. When done, the outside of the mixer bowl should return to room temperature and no residual heat should be escaping the meringue out of the top of the bowl. Stop the mixer and swap out the whisk attachment for the paddle.

4. With the mixer on low speed, add the butter, a few tablespoons at a time, then the vanilla. Once incorporated, turn up the mixer speed to medium-high and beat until the buttercream is silky smooth, 3 to 5 minutes.

STORAGE

Buttercream may be stored in an airtight container in the refrigerator for up to 10 days or in the freezer for up to 2 months. Thaw frozen buttercream in the refrigerator. Bring it to room temperature before remixing.

TIPS AND TROUBLESHOOTING

- The mixer bowl should be clean and completely dry before use. Be sure there are no traces of grease and that the egg whites are free of any bits of yolk.

- Be sure to stir together the sugar and egg whites before heating, because the egg whites may start to cook on their own.

- Adjust the temperature of the stove so that the water in the double boiler stays at a simmer.

- When testing the temperature of the outside of the bowl after mixing, use your inner wrist. It is more accurate than the palm of your hand.

- If the buttercream begins to look curdled or separated in the final stages, then the butter was probably too cold when it was added to the meringue. Try mixing longer, as it may just require a bit more time to incorporate the cold butter. If this does not work, try removing a small portion of the buttercream and heating it in the microwave until melted but not hot. With the mixer on, slowly pour in the melted buttercream to help even out the overall temperature.

- If the buttercream appears almost soupy but not separated, try placing the mixer bowl with its contents in the refrigerator for 5 to 10 minutes before mixing again.

- For frosting a cake, the buttercream should be as silky and smooth as possible. If necessary, let the mixer run on low speed for a few minutes to remove any air bubbles.

salted caramel sauce

—

MAKES ABOUT 1 CUP (240 ML)

THE IDEA OF BOILING SUGAR can seem a bit daunting at first, but a jar of homemade caramel sauce will outshine anything you might find on a grocery store shelf. Once you make this and see how easy it can be, there is no turning back. I love adding salt to caramel sauce, but you may adjust the amount according to your taste. Many of the recipes that call for this salted caramel sauce do not require the full yield, but the leftovers can be easily stored in the refrigerator and used in your next cake creation, simply stirred into a coffee drink, or poured over ice cream.

¾ cup (150 g) granulated sugar

2 tablespoons light corn syrup

½ cup (120 ml) heavy cream, at room temperature

2 tablespoons unsalted butter, diced

¾ teaspoon sea salt

1 teaspoon pure vanilla extract

1. Place the sugar, corn syrup, and 2 tablespoons water in a heavy-bottomed small or medium saucepan. Stir to combine.

2. Heat over high heat, occasionally swirling the pan, until it turns a medium golden amber color, 8 to 10 minutes. The sugar mixture will begin to rapidly boil before slowing down and darkening in color. Remove the saucepan from the heat once the correct color is reached and the bubbles start to subside.

3. Slowly and carefully whisk in the cream.

4. The mixture will foam up and sputter, so stand clear and keep stirring.

5. Add the butter and continue to stir until melted. Add the salt and vanilla and stir to combine. Pour the caramel into a heat-safe container and let it cool until it reaches the desired consistency or refrigerate it until ready to use. It will thicken as it cools.

STORAGE

Caramel may be stored in an airtight glass jar in the refrigerator for up to 10 days.

TIPS AND TROUBLESHOOTING

- When determining the correct color of amber, note that it may be lighter in the middle and darker toward the outside of the pan. Swirl the pan, but do not stir, to combine.

- Note that the darker and longer the sugar cooks, the deeper the caramel flavor.

- The cream should be room temperature or it may seize up when added to the hot sugar and create lumps in the caramel.

- Make sure all your ingredients are measured and ready to go. Once the sugar is removed from the heat, everything else should be added rather quickly.

- When used to pour over the top of a cake, the caramel should be at room temperature and still in a thick, liquid state. Caramel stored in the refrigerator will become too thick to pour, but may be reheated in the microwave.

- For even heat distribution, use a saucepan that is the same size as your burner.

SALTED CARAMEL SAUCE

DARK CHOCOLATE GANACHE

dark chocolate ganache

MAKES ABOUT 1 CUP (240 ML)

GANACHE IS THE MOST LUSCIOUS and decadent of all fillings and frostings. It sounds super fancy, but is made with only two ingredients. If you can manage, try not to skimp on the chocolate here. The better the quality, the tastier the ganache will be. You can easily double this recipe if you want to make more to use as frosting or for a new creation.

1   cup (6 ounces / 170 g) chopped dark chocolate (60 to 85% cacao)

½   cup (120 ml) heavy cream

1.   Place the chocolate in a heat-safe bowl and set aside.

2.   Pour the cream into a saucepan and slowly bring it to a simmer over medium-low heat. Once the cream begins to simmer, remove it from the heat and pour it over the chopped chocolate.

3.-4.   Let stand for about 30 seconds, then whisk until smooth.

5.   Depending on the purpose of the ganache (glaze, filling, or frosting), let it cool until it reaches the desired consistency. For glazes, ganache should be in a liquid state but not hot. For fillings and frostings, ganache should be cooled and thickened, but not solid. It should be spreadable but not runny.

STORAGE

Ganache may be stored in an airtight container in the refrigerator for up to 1 week. Reheat in the microwave in short intervals (usually no more than 20 seconds at a time, depending on the microwave), stirring in between, until it reaches the desired consistency. Alternatively, ganache may be gently reheated in the top portion of a double boiler.

TIPS AND TROUBLESHOOTING

- If using chocolate from a large block or bar, chop off the chocolate with a long serrated knife.

- Be careful not to scorch or burn the cream, especially when working in small quantities. Instead, heat the cream slowly at a lower heat.

- Chocolate hates water, so be sure not to drip in any other liquids or get any moisture into the bowl of chocolate—especially when reheating using a double boiler.

- If the chocolate does not completely melt during the final step, try heating the ganache in the top portion of a double boiler or in short intervals in the microwave.

- If the chocolate begins to split or separate, try to emulsify the mixture with an immersion blender. If that does not work, try heating up a small amount of cream (about half what the original recipes called for) and slowly stirring it into the mixture until smooth and shiny.

- This method is for dark chocolate, or anything between 60 and 85 percent cacao. Milk and white chocolates have different amounts of fat and should not be used in the ratios in this recipe.

- Ganache may be placed in the refrigerator to speed up the cooling process, but be sure to stir it intermittently to keep an even consistency.

CLASSIC CAKES

Some occasions call for nothing more than a tried-and-true classic cake. They are the first flavors that come to mind when someone says "layer cake." These cakes veer more toward the traditional, but with a contemporary touch. From the retro Brooklyn Blackout Cake to the century-old French Opera Cake, this collection explores cherished diner desserts and patisserie favorites. While this book delves into more unique ingredients and lavish flavors later on, it would not be complete without these reinvented classics.

neapolitan cake

—

MAKES ONE FOUR-LAYER 8-INCH (20-CM) CAKE; SERVES 12 TO 15

AS MOST RECIPES OF MINE DO, this cake started out as a vision. I imagined gorgeous drips of chocolate glaze and equally stunning chocolate-covered strawberries. I wanted to incorporate the simple flavors of classic Neapolitan desserts—chocolate, vanilla, and strawberry—but in a dramatic way.

Instead of vanilla and strawberry cake layers, I opted for a velvety white chocolate cake and a simple strawberry jam. The contrast between the alternating layers of white chocolate and dark chocolate cakes makes for a striking presentation when sliced, and the strawberry jam keeps everything nice and moist while adding a touch of sweetness. Iced in silky, smooth vanilla buttercream, this cake is the perfect blank canvas to adorn with the chocolate glaze and dipped strawberries.

For the
WHITE CHOCOLATE CAKE

	Butter or nonstick cooking spray, for the pans
5	large egg whites
¾	cup (180 ml) whole milk
2¾	cups (360 g) cake flour, plus more for the pans
1¼	cups (250 g) granulated sugar
1	tablespoon plus ½ teaspoon baking powder
½	teaspoon salt
¾	cup (1½ sticks / 170 g) unsalted butter, at room temperature
1½	teaspoons pure vanilla extract
6	ounces (170 g) white chocolate, melted and cooled

For the
CLASSIC CHOCOLATE CAKE

	Butter or nonstick cooking spray, for the pans
2½	cups (315 g) all-purpose flour, plus more for the pans
1	cup (95 g) unsweetened cocoa powder
2½	teaspoons baking powder
1	teaspoon salt
¾	teaspoon baking soda
½	cup plus 2 tablespoons (150 ml) grapeseed oil
2	cups (400 g) granulated sugar
2	large eggs
1	large egg yolk
2	teaspoons pure vanilla extract
½	teaspoon pure almond extract
1½	cups (360 ml) whole milk
1	cup (240 ml) hot strong-brewed coffee

For the
CHOCOLATE-DIPPED STRAWBERRIES

1⅓	cups (8 ounces / 225 g) chopped semisweet chocolate
12	medium strawberries, washed and completely dry

For the
ASSEMBLY

1	cup (240 ml) strawberry preserves
1	medium recipe Vanilla Swiss Meringue Buttercream (page 41)

For the
CHOCOLATE GLAZE

⅔	cup (4 ounces / 115 g) chopped semisweet chocolate
½	cup (120 ml) heavy cream
¼	cup (60 ml) light corn syrup
1	teaspoon pure vanilla extract
⅛	teaspoon salt

Make the
WHITE CHOCOLATE CAKE

1. Preheat the oven to 350°F (175°C). Grease and flour two 8-inch (20-cm) cake pans and set aside.

2. Stir together the egg whites and ¼ cup (60 ml) of the milk in a small bowl and set aside.

3. Sift the flour, sugar, baking powder, and salt into the bowl of a stand mixer fitted with the paddle attachment. Mix on low until combined. With the mixer on low, add the butter, vanilla, and the remaining ½ cup (120 ml) milk until the dry ingredients are moistened. Turn the mixer to medium-high and mix for about 1 minute until combined. Stop the mixer and scrape down the bowl.

4. Turn the mixer to medium. Add the egg white mixture in three parts, mixing for about 20 seconds after each before adding the next. Stop the mixer and scrape down the bowl. Add the white chocolate and mix until just combined.

5. Evenly divide the batter between the prepared pans. Bake for 25 to 28 minutes, or until a toothpick inserted into the center of the cakes comes out clean. Let them cool on a wire rack for 10 to 15 minutes before removing the cakes from their pans.

Make the
CLASSIC CHOCOLATE
CAKE

6. While the white chocolate cakes bake, grease and flour two 8-inch (20-cm) cake pans and set aside.

7. Sift together the flour, cocoa powder, baking powder, salt, and baking soda and set aside.

8. In the bowl of a stand mixer fitted with the paddle attachment, beat together the oil and sugar on medium for 2 minutes. Add the eggs, egg yolk, vanilla, and almond extract. Stop the mixer and scrape down the bowl.

9. Turn the mixer to low and add the flour mixture in three batches, alternating with the milk, beginning and ending with the flour mixture. Stop the mixer and scrape down the bowl. With the mixer on low, stream in the coffee. Mix on medium-low for no more than 30 seconds, or until combined.

10. Evenly divide the batter between the prepared pans. Bake for 25 to 28 minutes, or until a toothpick inserted into the center of the cakes comes out clean. Let them cool on a wire rack for 10 to 15 minutes before removing the cakes from their pans.

Make the
CHOCOLATE-DIPPED
STRAWBERRIES

11. Melt the chocolate in the top portion of a double boiler. Meanwhile, line a baking sheet with parchment paper. Remove the chocolate from the heat. Carefully dip each strawberry into the chocolate, one at a time, and set it on the parchment paper to dry and harden completely.

ASSEMBLE THE CAKE

12. Once the cakes have completely cooled, level them and choose which layer will be at the bottom. Place it on a cake plate or serving dish. Spread on about ⅓ cup (80 ml) of the strawberry preserves. Place the second layer of cake on top, alternating between the white and dark chocolate cakes, and repeat. Smoothly frost the cake with the buttercream and refrigerate it, uncovered, until firm, 15 to 20 minutes.

Make the
CHOCOLATE GLAZE

13. Place the chocolate, cream, and corn syrup in a small saucepan. Heat over medium-low until the cream begins to steam and the chocolate starts to melt. Remove from the heat and stir in the vanilla and salt until combined. Let the mixture cool to room temperature, until it is syrup-like, about 10 minutes.

14. Starting with about ½ cup (120 ml) at a time, carefully pour the chocolate glaze into the center of the frosted cake and use an offset spatula to spread it around the top, allowing it to drip over the edges. Add more glaze until the desired look is achieved. Decorate with any remaining buttercream and chocolate-dipped strawberries.

DECORATE IT

Fill a pastry bag fitted with a star tip with any remaining buttercream. After the glaze has set, pipe rosettes (see page 37) around the top edge of the cake. Once the chocolate-dipped strawberries have dried, place them on the rosettes or simply place one on a plate with a slice of cake when serving.

BAKER'S NOTES

Not sure if your chocolate glaze is the correct temperature? Try a few practice drips on the side of the cake that will be turned to the back. Once refrigerated, chocolate glaze may lose its sheen. The cake will keep in the fridge for up to 4 days; it may also be frozen (see page 25). Store the chocolate-dipped strawberries separately.

GOT LEFTOVERS?

Pour the chocolate glaze over ice cream to make a decadent sundae.

IMAGINE AN HEIRLOOM TIN FULL OF RECIPE CARDS that have been passed down from generation to generation. Filed under "Desserts," there is a batter-splattered card that is well worn and loved. This card has been used for dozens of birthdays and simple celebrations, although the recipe itself is probably already committed to memory. I personally don't have such a recipe box, but this would be the start of my own collection. If you don't already have a go-to yellow cake recipe, this is it. Memorize it and pass it along. Your future grandchildren will thank you.

For the **YELLOW BUTTER CAKE**	
	Butter or nonstick cooking spray, for the pans
3¼	cups (425 g) cake flour, plus more for the pans
1	tablespoon baking powder
¾	teaspoon salt
1	cup (2 sticks / 225 g) unsalted butter, at room temperature
2	cups (400 g) granulated sugar
2	teaspoons vanilla bean paste
6	large egg yolks
1½	cups (360 ml) whole milk

For the **FUDGE FROSTING**	
1½	cups (3 sticks / 340 g) unsalted butter, at room temperature
5½	cups (690 g) confectioners' sugar, sifted
½	cup (50 g) unsweetened cocoa powder
1½	teaspoons pure vanilla extract
⅛	teaspoon salt
¼	cup (60 ml) heavy cream or whole milk
8	ounces (225 g) semisweet chocolate, melted and cooled

the birthday cake

MAKES ONE FOUR-LAYER 8-INCH (20-CM) CAKE; SERVES 12 TO 15

Make the
YELLOW BUTTER CAKE

1. Preheat the oven to 350°F (175°C). Grease and flour two 8-inch (20-cm) cake pans and set aside.

2. Sift together the flour, baking powder, and salt and set aside.

3. In the bowl of a stand mixer fitted with the paddle attachment, beat the butter on medium speed until smooth. Add the sugar and mix on medium-high until the butter is light and fluffy, 3 to 5 minutes. Stop the mixer and scrape down the bowl.

4. Turn the mixer to medium-low and add the vanilla and egg yolks, one at a time. Stop the mixer and scrape down the bowl.

5. Turn the mixer to low and add the flour mixture in three batches, alternating with the milk, beginning and ending with the flour mixture. Mix on medium for no more than 30 seconds after the last streaks of the dry ingredients are combined.

6. Evenly divide the batter between the prepared pans. Bake for 25 to 28 minutes, or until a toothpick inserted into the center of the cakes comes out clean. Let them cool on a wire rack for 10 to 15 minutes before removing the cakes from their pans.

Make the
FUDGE FROSTING

7. In the bowl of a stand mixer fitted with the paddle attachment, beat the butter until smooth and creamy. With the mixer on low, gradually add the confectioners' sugar, cocoa powder, vanilla, and salt. Pour in the cream and mix until incorporated. Turn the mixer to high and mix until the frosting is light and fluffy. Stop the mixer and scrape down the bowl. Add the chocolate and mix until smooth.

ASSEMBLE THE CAKE

8. Once the cakes have completely cooled, carefully halve them horizontally to create four even layers of cake (see Baker's Notes). Level the cakes and choose which layer will be at the bottom. Place it on a plate or serving dish. Spread on ¾ cup (180 ml) of the fudge frosting with an offset spatula. Place the next layer of cake on top and repeat. Frost with the remaining fudge frosting.

DECORATE IT

Toss on some colorful sprinkles or add a handful of candles for an extra-festive element.

BAKER'S NOTES

If you would prefer a two-layer cake, keep the two cakes whole. Adjust the filling amount accordingly, using 1 to 1½ cups (240 to 360 ml) of the fudge frosting between the two layers. The cake will keep in the fridge for up to 4 days; it may also be frozen (see page 25).

strawberry shortcake

―――

MAKES ONE FOUR-LAYER 8-INCH (20-CM) CAKE; SERVES 10 TO 12

THE VERY FIRST LAYER CAKE I EVER MADE from scratch turned into a sliced-strawberries-and-cream disaster. It was my senior year of college, and I wanted to make a cake—the special kind, where the major components did not come from a box or can—for my room-mate's birthday. I went with a simple sponge cake, fresh strawberries, and homemade buttercream. Food blogs were just starting back then, and I did not own a single baking cookbook. I went online to look for a frosting recipe and just could not believe that one batch of buttercream required so much sugar. I figured there must be a mistake and decided to just go for it on my own. The buttercream was a runny mess, and the berry slices kept slipping and sliding out from between the cake layers. Needless to say, the cake did not last until her birthday party. However, we did all have a good laugh, and only a few years later, I made the same friend's wedding cake.

This strawberry shortcake has a perfectly light sponge cake and basil whipped cream. The basil is subtle, but pairs exquisitely with sun-ripened strawberries and summer-time picnics. Make this cake when celebrating friends, or on any sunny afternoon.

For the **CHIFFON CAKE**		*For the* **BASIL WHIPPED CREAM**		*For the* **ASSEMBLY**	
	Butter or nonstick cooking spray, for the pans	2½	cups (600 ml) heavy cream, plus more if needed	1	quart (580 g) fresh strawberries
2	cups (260 g) cake flour	1	to 1½ cups (40 to 60 g) lightly packed fresh basil leaves, chopped		
2	teaspoons baking powder	2	tablespoons granulated sugar		
½	teaspoon salt	½	teaspoon pure vanilla extract		
½	cup (120 ml) grapeseed oil				
1¼	cups plus 2 tablespoons (275 g) granulated sugar				
2	teaspoons pure vanilla extract				
6	large egg yolks				
½	cup (120 ml) whole milk				
8	large egg whites				
¾	teaspoon cream of tartar				

Make the CHIFFON CAKE

1. Preheat the oven to 350°F (175°C). Grease and line the bottoms of two 8-inch (20-cm) cake pans with parchment paper and set aside.

2. Sift together the flour, baking powder, and salt and set aside.

3. In the bowl of a stand mixer fitted with the paddle attachment, beat together the oil and 1¼ cups (250 g) of the sugar on medium speed for 1 minute. Add the vanilla and egg yolks, one at a time, and mix for about 3 minutes. The mixture will increase in volume and be pale in color. Stop the mixer and scrape down the bowl.

4. Turn the mixer to low and add the flour mixture in three batches, alternating with the milk, beginning and ending with the flour mixture. Mix on medium for no more than 30 seconds after the last streaks of the dry ingredients are combined. Pour the batter into a large bowl and set it aside.

5. Clean the mixer bowl thoroughly and dry it well. In the clean bowl of the stand mixer fitted with the whisk attachment, whisk the egg whites on medium-low speed until foamy. Add the remaining 2 tablespoons sugar and the cream of tartar and whisk on high until stiff peaks form.

6. Stop the mixer and carefully but deliberately fold the egg whites into the cake batter. Evenly divide the batter between the prepared pans. Bake for 25 to 28 minutes, or until a toothpick inserted into the center of the cakes comes out clean. Let them rest on a wire rack until cool before running a paring knife or metal spatula around the edges of the cakes and removing them from their pans.

Make the BASIL WHIPPED CREAM

7. Slowly heat 2 cups (480 ml) of the cream in a medium saucepan over medium-low heat until it begins to simmer.

8. Meanwhile, gently muddle the basil leaves with a mortar and pestle.

9. Once the cream begins to steam and simmer, remove the pan from the heat. Add the basil leaves, cover, and let them steep for 30 minutes. Transfer the mixture to a container and refrigerate until cold.

10. Strain out the basil leaves. Remeasure the cream and top it off with more cream, if necessary, so you have a total of 2 cups (480 ml).

11. In the bowl of a stand mixer fitted with the whisk attachment, whisk the cream on medium speed until it begins to thicken. Add the sugar and vanilla and whisk on high until it forms medium peaks. For best results, store the whipped cream in the refrigerator and assemble the cake just before serving.

ASSEMBLE THE CAKE

12. Hull and slice the fresh strawberries ¼ inch (6 mm) thick until you have about 4 cups (660 g) of sliced berries. Reserve a few whole strawberries for decoration, if you'd like.

13. Once the cakes have completely cooled, carefully halve them horizontally to create four even layers. Level the cakes and choose which layer will be at the bottom. Place it on a cake plate or serving dish and spread on one-quarter of the basil whipped cream (¾ to 1 cup / 180 to 240 ml) and 1 cup (165 g) of the sliced berries. Top with the next layer of cake and repeat. Place the reserved strawberries, either whole or sliced in half, on top of the last layer of cream to decorate, if desired.

BAKER'S NOTES

The whipped cream may be made up to 8 hours ahead of time and stored separately and tightly covered in the refrigerator. Once assembled, eat the cake immediately or keep refrigerated, for up to 2 days, until 30 minutes before serving (see page 25).

---

red velvet cake

—

MAKES ONE SIX-LAYER 6-INCH (15-CM) CAKE; SERVES 10 TO 12

ALTHOUGH WIDELY CONSIDERED A SOUTHERN DESSERT, red velvet cake was actually first served at the Waldorf-Astoria Hotel in New York City. While many of the recipes today pair the cake with cream cheese frosting, red velvet cake was originally frosted with ermine or "heritage" icing. Made from cooked flour and boiled milk, this not-so-sweet icing is much softer and fluffier than cream cheese frosting.

To be completely honest, it took me a long time to appreciate red velvet cake. Most versions I had tasted seemed to be just plain cake with a gallon of red food dye, smothered in sickeningly sweet cream cheese frosting. After countless requests for red velvet cake at my bakery, though, I finally gave in. If I could create a recipe that I personally enjoyed, then it could be an acceptable item on the menu. Finally, I developed this recipe about six years ago and have been making it ever since. It is supermoist, and the hint of cocoa gives this luscious, "velvety" cake a subtle chocolate flavor.

For the
RED VELVET CAKE

	Butter or nonstick cooking spray, for the pans
1¾	cups plus 2 tablespoons (235 g) all-purpose flour, plus more for the pans
3	tablespoons natural unsweetened cocoa powder
¾	teaspoon baking powder
½	teaspoon salt
¾	cup (180 ml) grapeseed oil
1½	cups (300 g) granulated sugar
2	large eggs
2	teaspoons pure vanilla extract
1	to 2 tablespoons red gel food coloring (see Baker's Notes, page 60)
1	cup (240 ml) buttermilk
1	teaspoon baking soda
1	teaspoon distilled white vinegar

For the
HERITAGE FROSTING

1	cup (240 ml) milk
¼	cup (30 g) all-purpose flour
⅛	teaspoon salt
1	cup (2 sticks / 225 g) unsalted butter, at room temperature
1	cup (200 g) granulated sugar
1	teaspoon pure vanilla extract

For the
WHITE CHOCOLATE CURLS

1	(6- to 10-ounce / 170- to 280-g) block white chocolate

Make the
RED VELVET CAKE

1. Preheat the oven to 350°F (175°C). Grease and flour three 6-inch (15-cm) cake pans and set aside.

2. Sift together the flour, cocoa powder, baking powder, and salt and set aside.

3. In the bowl of a stand mixer fitted with the paddle attachment, beat together the oil and sugar on medium speed until combined. With the mixer on medium-low, gradually add the eggs one at a time, the vanilla, and the food coloring. Mix on medium until combined. Stop the mixer and scrape down the bowl.

4. Turn the mixer to low and add the flour mixture in three batches, alternating with the buttermilk, beginning and ending with the flour mixture. Stop the mixer just as the last streaks of flour disappear and scrape down the bowl.

5. In a small bowl, whisk together the baking soda and vinegar. With the mixer on medium-low, add the baking soda mixture. Mix for an additional 30 seconds to combine.

6. Evenly divide the batter among the prepared pans. Bake for 23 to 25 minutes, or until a toothpick inserted into the center of the cakes comes out clean. Let them cool on a wire rack for 10 to 15 minutes before removing the cakes from their pans.

Make the
HERITAGE FROSTING

7. In a small saucepan, whisk together the milk, flour, and salt to remove any lumps. While stirring with a wooden spoon, cook the flour mixture over medium heat until it is thick and pasty. Remove it from the heat and transfer the mixture to a bowl. Cover and refrigerate until it is cool.

8. After the flour mixture has chilled, in the bowl of a stand mixer fitted with the paddle attachment, cream together the butter and sugar on medium-high for 2 to 4 minutes. Turn the mixer to medium-low speed and add the flour mixture and the vanilla. Beat on medium-high until the frosting is light, fluffy, and pale in color.

Make the
WHITE CHOCOLATE CURLS

9. Microwave the block of chocolate at medium power until it is ever so slightly softened. Try first heating it for 20 seconds, then in 5- to 10-second intervals until the desired softness is reached. Depending on the microwave, it should take a total of about 35 seconds. Test the softness by scraping a vegetable peeler against a smooth, long side of the chocolate block. If the chocolate curls without the curl shattering or breaking, it is warm enough. Do not overheat the chocolate, or it will not curl. Continue to make 1 to 2 cups (55 to 110 g) of chocolate curls with the peeler, letting them fall over a piece of parchment paper, reheating the block if necessary (see Baker's Notes).

ASSEMBLE THE CAKE

10. Once the cakes have completely cooled, halve them horizontally to create six even layers. Level the cakes and choose which layer will be at the bottom. Place it on a cake plate or serving dish. Spread on ⅓ cup (80 ml) of the frosting with an offset spatula. Top with another layer of cake and repeat. Finish the cake with the remaining frosting using a smooth (see page 28) or rustic finish (see page 31). Before the frosting sets, very carefully place on the white chocolate curls. Gently snuggle them into the fresh frosting if they do not stick on their own. Place the curls two-thirds of the way up the cake, as pictured, or create your own design.

BAKER'S NOTES

Hold the block of chocolate with a piece of parchment paper so that the heat from your hand does not transfer to the chocolate and melt it. Once a curl is created, you may quickly manipulate it to create your desired shape before it sets. Once set, try to avoid touching the curls as much as possible. You may use red liquid food coloring in the cake recipe instead of gel, if desired. The cake will keep in the fridge for up to 3 days (see page 25).

WHILE THE FIRST BOSTON CREAM PIE RECIPE GOES all the way back to 1856 at the Parker House Hotel in Boston, Massachusetts, I've always known it as my uncle's favorite dessert. Growing up, my mom and her siblings each had their own special cake. For their birthdays, my grandmother would bake up their favorites from scratch—angel food with sprinkles for my mom, whipped cream with loads of maraschino cherries for my aunt, and Boston cream pie for my uncle. Personally, I love anything with pastry cream, so this cake is a dream. Velvety buttermilk cake, rich vanilla pastry cream, and silky chocolate icing make this classic cake impossible to resist.

For the VANILLA PASTRY CREAM

- 1 vanilla bean, split lengthwise
- 2 cups (480 ml) whole milk
- ⅔ cup (135 g) granulated sugar
- 5 large egg yolks
- 6 tablespoons (45 g) cornstarch
- 2 tablespoons unsalted butter, diced

For the BUTTERMILK CAKE

- Butter or nonstick cooking spray, for the pans
- 3 cups (390 g) cake flour, plus more for the pans
- 2 teaspoons baking powder
- ½ teaspoon baking soda
- ½ teaspoon salt
- 1 cup (2 sticks / 225 g) unsalted butter, at room temperature
- 2 cups (400 g) granulated sugar
- 1½ teaspoons vanilla bean paste
- 3 large eggs
- 2 large egg yolks
- 1¼ cups (300 ml) buttermilk

For the SILKY CHOCOLATE ICING

- ½ cup (120 ml) heavy cream
- 1 tablespoon light corn syrup
- 1 cup (6 ounces / 170 g) chopped semisweet chocolate
- ⅛ teaspoon salt
- ½ teaspoon pure vanilla extract
- 1½ cups (190 g) confectioners' sugar, sifted

boston cream pie

MAKES ONE TWO-LAYER 8-INCH (20-CM) CAKE; SERVES 10 TO 12

Make the
VANILLA PASTRY CREAM

1. In a medium saucepan, heat the vanilla bean pod and seeds and milk together over medium-low heat. Bring slowly to a simmer, being careful not to burn the milk. Remove from the heat and discard the vanilla bean pod.

2. Meanwhile, whisk together the sugar, egg yolks, and cornstarch in a bowl with a balloon whisk.

3. Temper the milk into the egg mixture by whisking a small amount of milk into the egg mixture to slowly raise the temperature of the eggs before transferring everything back to the saucepan. Place the saucepan back on the stove and cook over low heat. Whisk the mixture until it thickens and starts to bubble. Remove it from the heat and stir in the butter until smooth.

4. Transfer to a bowl and cover by pressing plastic wrap directly against the top of it to prevent a skin from forming. Refrigerate until it is cool and thick, at least 2 hours or overnight.

Make the
BUTTERMILK CAKE

5. Preheat the oven to 350°F (175°C). Grease and flour two 8-inch (20-cm) cake pans and set aside.

6. Sift together the flour, baking powder, baking soda, and salt and set aside.

7. In the bowl of a stand mixer fitted with the paddle attachment, beat the butter on medium speed for 2 minutes. Add the sugar and mix on medium-high until the butter is light and fluffy, 3 to 5 minutes. Stop the mixer and scrape down the bowl.

8. Turn the mixer to medium-low and add the vanilla, eggs, and egg yolks, one at a time. Stop the mixer and scrape down the bowl.

9. Turn the mixer to low and add the flour mixture in three batches, alternating with the buttermilk, beginning and ending with the flour mixture. Mix on medium for no more than 30 seconds after the last streaks of the dry ingredients are combined.

10. Evenly divide the batter between the prepared pans. Bake for 25 to 28 minutes, or until a toothpick inserted into the center of the cakes comes out clean. Let them cool on a wire rack for 10 to 15 minutes before removing the cakes from their pans.

ASSEMBLE THE CAKE

11. Once the pastry cream has cooled and thickened, whisk to loosen it, if necessary. Transfer the pastry cream to a pastry bag fitted with a large round piping tip.

12. Once the cakes have completely cooled, level them and choose which layer will be at the bottom. Place it on a cake plate or serving dish. Pipe the pastry cream on top, starting with an outer ring and working in toward the center. Invert the second cake layer and place it top-side down on top of the pastry cream.

Make the
SILKY CHOCOLATE ICING

13. Place the heavy cream, corn syrup, and chocolate in a saucepan and heat over medium-low heat until the cream starts to steam and the chocolate begins to melt. Remove it from the heat and stir until the chocolate is completely melted. Stir in the salt and vanilla. Whisk in the confectioners' sugar until combined. Frost just the top of the assembled cake immediately or wait until the icing has cooled slightly.

BAKER'S NOTES

The pastry cream may be prepared up to 3 days ahead of time and stored separately and tightly covered in the refrigerator. The cake is best eaten within 30 minutes of assembly. Leftovers will keep in the fridge for up to 3 days from when the pastry cream was made (see page 25). Note that the Silky Chocolate Icing may lose its sheen after being in the refrigerator.

lemon supreme cake

MY GRANDMOTHER HAS A MILD OBSESSION WITH any and all things lemon-dessert related. Some of my earliest memories are of my mom rushing around to pick up a lemon meringue pie whenever my grandmother came to visit. I did not understand why she liked lemon desserts so much when my only experience was with sweet, artificial lemon pie filling topped with commercialized, spongy meringue. I don't blame my mom for the store-bought stuff, especially since the memories inspired me to create something using fresh ingredients and real lemons.

When I first started making cakes back in 2006, I made Grandma one of my first lemon cake creations from scratch. I frosted the cake as smooth as I could and cut tiny pink cherry blossoms out of sugar paste to decorate it with. Since then, the recipe has improved a bit, but it is still bright and fresh and will satisfy the craving for all things lemony. The curd is ultracreamy and luscious yet lively, especially with the fresh lemon juice—a superb match to the light lemon buttermilk cake.

For the
LEMON CURD

5	tablespoons (70 g) unsalted butter, diced
¾	cup (150 g) granulated sugar
5	tablespoons (75 ml) fresh lemon juice
2	large egg yolks
1	large egg

For the
LIGHT LEMON CAKE

	Butter or nonstick cooking spray, for the pans
2¼	cups (295 g) cake flour, plus more for the pans
1½	teaspoons baking powder
¾	teaspoon baking soda
¼	teaspoon salt
1½	cups (300 g) granulated sugar
1	tablespoon finely grated lemon zest
¾	cup (1½ sticks / 170 g) unsalted butter, at room temperature
2	tablespoons fresh lemon juice
1	teaspoon pure vanilla extract
3	large eggs
2	egg whites
1	cup (240 ml) buttermilk

For the
LEMON SIMPLE SYRUP

¼	cup (50 g) granulated sugar
2	tablespoons fresh lemon juice
2	teaspoons finely grated lemon zest

For the
ASSEMBLY

1	small recipe Vanilla Swiss Meringue Buttercream (page 41)
	Gel food coloring (*optional*)
	Sugar pearls (*optional*)

Make the
LEMON CURD

1. Place the butter in a heat-safe bowl and set it aside.

2. Whisk together the sugar, lemon juice, egg yolks, and egg in a medium saucepan. Cook over medium heat, stirring continuously to prevent the eggs from curdling. Cook until the mixture is thick enough to coat the back of a spoon, 6 to 8 minutes, or registers 160°F (70°C) on a candy thermometer.

3. Remove the curd from the heat and strain it through a fine-mesh sieve over the bowl containing the butter. Stir to combine. Cover with plastic wrap, pressing it directly against the surface of the curd to prevent a skin from forming, and refrigerate until set, at least 4 hours or overnight.

Make the
LIGHT LEMON CAKE

4. Preheat the oven to 350°F (175°C). Grease and flour three 6-inch (15-cm) cake pans and set aside.

5. Sift together the flour, baking powder, baking soda, and salt and set aside.

6. Place the sugar and lemon zest in a small bowl. Rub them together between your fingertips until fragrant.

7. In the bowl of a stand mixer fitted with the paddle attachment, beat the butter on medium speed for 2 minutes. Add the sugar mixture and mix on medium-high until light and fluffy, 3 to 5 minutes. Stop the mixer and scrape down the bowl.

8. Turn the mixer to medium-low and add the lemon juice, vanilla, eggs, and egg whites, one at a time. Stop the mixer and scrape down the bowl.

9. Turn the mixer to low and add the flour mixture in three batches, alternating with the buttermilk, beginning and ending with the flour mixture. Mix on medium for no more than 30 seconds after the last streaks of the dry ingredients are combined.

10. Evenly divide the batter among the prepared pans. Bake for 22 to 24 minutes, or until a toothpick inserted into the center of the cakes comes out clean. Let them cool on a wire rack for 10 to 15 minutes before removing the cakes from their pans.

Make the
LEMON SIMPLE SYRUP

11. Stir together the sugar, lemon juice, and zest in a saucepan with ¼ cup (60 ml) water. Bring the mixture to a boil over medium-high heat. Reduce the heat to low and simmer for 10 minutes, or until the mixture thickens to a syrup. Remove from the heat to cool.

ASSEMBLE THE CAKE

12. Tint the buttercream with the food coloring of your choice, if using. Fill a pastry bag fitted with a large round tip with about 1 cup (240 ml) buttercream.

13. Once the cakes have completely cooled, level them and choose which layer will be at the bottom. Using a pastry brush, generously brush the tops of each cake with the lemon simple syrup. Place the bottom layer on a cake plate or serving dish. Pipe a buttercream dam around the top edge of the cake (see page 27). Fill in with half the lemon curd. Place the next cake on top and repeat the buttercream and lemon curd. Add any buttercream left in the piping bag to the remaining buttercream and mix together. Crumb coat and frost the cake with the buttercream and decorate with sugar pearls, if using.

BAKER'S NOTES

If the butter does not melt into the lemon curd, place all of the contents in the top of a double boiler. Stir until the butter is completely incorporated. The lemon curd may be made in advance and will keep up to 1 month stored in an airtight container in the refrigerator. The cake will keep in the fridge for up to 3 days (see page 25).

SHORTCUT

Use 1¼ cups (300 ml) store-bought lemon curd.

DECORATE IT

Smoothly frost the cake with buttercream and randomly scatter sugar pearls around the base of the cake, gently pressing a small handful at a time into the fresh buttercream if they do not stick on their own. Alternatively, place the pearls on the top edge of the cake and let them trickle down the sides to create a graduated effect.

french opera cake

MAKES ONE THREE-LAYER 6-INCH (15-CM) CAKE; SERVES 8 TO 10

SOMETIMES I WONDER HOW I FELL INTO THE WORLD of pastry. If you took a peek at my messy baking notebooks, or the desk that I am typing this book on, for that matter, then you too would question how I could ever work in an industry that requires such organization, patience, and attention to detail. However, if I really think about it, I can attribute my hard work and discipline to my nearly twenty years of ballet training. After spending years of my childhood trying to perfect pirouettes, I can muster up the precision required to make an opera cake.

This cake is famous for its elaborate form of layering coffee-soaked sponge cake with ganache and buttercream. Most likely dating back to early twentieth-century Paris, it was typically made in sheets and then cut into neat, individual servings. While it has a reputation for being difficult to make with its meticulous layers and precise portions, my opera cake is assembled as a round layer cake and is a bit more user-friendly. There are still plenty of steps and layers, but it makes for an impressive presentation, and when all of the flavors come together, you won't begrudge any of the time and patience required.

For the
COFFEE ALMOND SPONGE CAKE

	Butter or nonstick cooking spray, for the pan
⅔	cup (85 g) confectioners' sugar, sifted
4	large eggs
1	teaspoon pure vanilla extract
1	cup (115 g) almond flour
½	cup (65 g) all-purpose flour
2	tablespoons instant espresso powder
1	teaspoon baking powder
⅛	teaspoon salt
2	tablespoons unsalted butter, melted
4	large egg whites
¼	cup (50 g) granulated sugar
1	teaspoon cream of tartar

For the
COFFEE SOAK

¼	cup (50 g) granulated sugar
2	teaspoons instant espresso powder
2	tablespoons coffee liqueur

For the
COFFEE FRENCH BUTTERCREAM

1	cup (200 g) granulated sugar
6	large egg yolks
2	teaspoons instant espresso powder
3	tablespoons hot water
2	teaspoons pure vanilla extract
1¼	cups (2½ sticks / 280 g) unsalted butter, at room temperature, cut into tablespoons

For the
ASSEMBLY

1	recipe Dark Chocolate Ganache (page 45)

Make the COFFEE ALMOND SPONGE CAKE

1. Preheat the oven to 375°F (190°C). Grease a 10 by 15-inch (25 by 38-cm) rectangular cake pan (see Baker's Notes) and line it with parchment paper, letting the parchment paper overhang the edges by a couple of inches.

2. In a large bowl, whisk together the confectioners' sugar, eggs, and vanilla until pale ribbons form. Sift in the flours, espresso powder, baking powder, and salt and mix until combined. Stir in the butter.

3. In the clean bowl of a stand mixer fitted with the whisk attachment, begin whipping the egg whites on medium-low speed until they start to foam. Add the granulated sugar and cream of tartar and turn the mixer to high. Whisk until stiff peaks form.

4. Carefully but deliberately fold the egg whites into the cake batter.

5. Pour the batter into the prepared pan and evenly spread it out with an offset spatula. Bake for 5 to 10 minutes, or until the cake springs back when lightly pressed. Let the cake cool on a wire rack for 5 to 10 minutes before removing from the pan.

Make the COFFEE SOAK

6. Combine the sugar, espresso powder, and ¼ cup (60 ml) water in a saucepan. Bring them to a boil over medium-high, then reduce the heat to low and simmer for about 5 minutes. Remove from the heat and stir in the coffee liqueur. Let the mixture cool slightly before use, about 5 minutes.

Make the COFFEE FRENCH BUTTERCREAM

7. Place the sugar and ¼ cup (60 ml) water in a medium saucepan. Stir to combine. Heat over high heat until the mixture reaches 238°F (114°C) on a candy thermometer.

8. Meanwhile, in the clean bowl of a stand mixer fitted with the whisk attachment, whisk the egg yolks on high until pale in color and at least doubled in volume.

9. Once the sugar mixture reaches 238°F (114°C), remove the pan from the heat. With the mixer running on low, carefully stream the sugar syrup down the side of the bowl into the egg yolks. Once the sugar has been added, increase the speed to high and continue mixing until the outside of the bowl cools to room temperature.

10. Meanwhile, in a small bowl, mix the espresso powder with the hot water to make a thick, strong shot of espresso.

11. Stop the mixer and swap out the whisk for the paddle attachment. With the mixer on low, add the vanilla and butter, a couple of tablespoons at a time. Pour in the shot of espresso and turn the mixer to medium-high. Mix for about 20 seconds, or until the frosting is smooth and creamy.

ASSEMBLE THE CAKE

12. Once the cake has completely cooled, carefully lift it out of the cake pan using the edges of the parchment paper. Invert the cake onto a large cutting board or clean work surface and peel off the parchment paper. Using a 6-inch (15-cm) cake ring, cut out three rounds of cake. Flip them right-side up and use a pastry brush to brush each round with the coffee soak.

13. On top of one cake round, spread ⅓ cup (80 ml) of the ganache with an offset spatula. Repeat with a second round. Refrigerate them for 5 to 10 minutes, or until the ganache sets. Once set, spread ½ cup (120 ml) of the buttercream on top of the ganache on each round.

14. Place one of the cake rounds with filling on a cake plate or serving dish. Place the second cake round with filling on top. Place the last layer of cake on top.

15. Use the remaining ganache to carefully frost only the top of the cake. Refrigerate it to set, if necessary. Frost the sides of the cake with the coffee buttercream and decorate the cake with any remaining buttercream.

IN TERMS OF CUISINE, I'VE ALWAYS KNOWN GERMANY to have great schnitzel, bratwurst, and apple strudel. One of my best food memories is sharing a giant pork knuckle and a couple of pints at the Hofbräuhaus in Munich with my old roommate and hundreds of other locals, tourists, and beer maidens. I am half German on my father's side, although his ancestors moved to the United States generations ago. The only real connection I make with my German heritage is through the food. Even today, I look forward to the annual German Christmas Festival held here in Vancouver, just for the snacks.

Only recently, I found out that Black Forest cake is a German dessert—and that made this chocolate and cherry combination taste even sweeter. The Black Forest region in Germany is known for producing a cherry liqueur that was used to help flavor the first Black Forest cake back in 1915. While today's Black Forest cakes are typically covered in whipped cream, I prefer the creamy, smooth milk chocolate frosting and silky yet fluffy vanilla heritage frosting used as filling in this recipe. Feel free to use preserved sour cherries if fresh cherries are not in season.

For the
SOUR CREAM
CHOCOLATE CAKE

Butter or nonstick cooking spray, for the pans

1¾ cups (220 g) all-purpose flour, plus more for the pans

½ cup plus 2 tablespoons (60 g) unsweetened cocoa powder

1¼ teaspoons baking powder

½ teaspoon baking soda

½ teaspoon salt

6 tablespoons (90 ml) grapeseed oil

½ cup (100 g) granulated sugar

½ cup (110 g) firmly packed brown sugar

1 large egg

1 large egg yolk

1 teaspoon pure vanilla extract

½ teaspoon pure almond extract

½ cup (120 ml) sour cream

¾ cup (180 ml) hot coffee

For the
CHERRY GANACHE

1 cup (6 ounces / 170 g) chopped bittersweet chocolate

½ cup (120 ml) heavy cream

¾ cup (125 g) chopped pitted fresh cherries, rinsed and dried

For the
MILK CHOCOLATE
BUTTERCREAM

1 small recipe Vanilla Swiss Meringue Buttercream (page 41)

2½ ounces (70 g) milk chocolate, melted and cooled

For the
CHOCOLATE CURLS

1 (2- to 4-ounce / 55- to 115-g) block semisweet or bittersweet chocolate

For the
ASSEMBLY

½ recipe Heritage Frosting (page 58)

6 to 8 fresh cherries (*optional*)

black forest cake

MAKES ONE FOUR-LAYER 6-INCH (15-CM) CAKE; SERVES 6 TO 8

Make the
SOUR CREAM CHOCOLATE CAKE

1. Preheat the oven to 350°F (175°C). Grease and flour two 6-inch (15-cm) cake pans and set aside.

2. Sift together the flour, cocoa powder, baking powder, baking soda, and salt and set aside.

3. In the bowl of a stand mixer fitted with the paddle attachment, beat the oil and sugars on medium speed for 2 minutes. With the mixer on, add the egg, egg yolk, vanilla, and almond extract. Stop the mixer and scrape down the bowl.

4. Turn the mixer to low and add the flour mixture in three batches, alternating with the sour cream, beginning and ending with the flour mixture. Stop the mixer and scrape down the bowl. With the mixer on low, stream in the coffee. Mix on medium-low for no more than 30 seconds, or until combined.

5. Evenly divide the batter between the prepared cake pans. Bake for 24 to 26 minutes, or until a toothpick inserted into the center of the cakes comes out clean. Let them cool on a wire rack for 10 to 15 minutes before removing the cakes from their pans.

Make the
CHERRY GANACHE

6. Place the chocolate in a heat-safe bowl and set aside. Pour the cream in a small saucepan and slowly bring it to a simmer over medium heat. Once the cream begins to simmer, remove it from the heat and pour it over the chopped chocolate.

Let stand for about 30 seconds, then whisk until smooth. Stir in the cherries and let stand until cool and spreadable, about 20 minutes.

Make the
MILK CHOCOLATE BUTTERCREAM

7. In a stand mixer fitted with the paddle attachment, mix the buttercream until silky smooth. Add the cooled chocolate and mix until combined.

Make the
CHOCOLATE CURLS

8. Scrape a sharp paring knife or vegetable peeler against the edge of the block of chocolate. Let the curls fall onto a piece of parchment paper and limit handling when placing on the cake. Create enough curls to decorate the sides and/or top of the cake, according to your final vision of the cake.

ASSEMBLE THE CAKE

9. Once the cakes have completely cooled, halve them horizontally to create four even layers. Level the cakes and choose which layer will be at the bottom. Place it on a serving dish. Spread on ¾ cup (180 ml) of the heritage frosting with an offset spatula. Slightly hollow out the frosting in the center with the back of a large spoon to create a "bowl" of frosting. Fill that with ⅓ cup (80 ml) of the cherry ganache. Top with the next layer of cake and repeat.

10. Crumb coat the cake and frost it with the milk chocolate buttercream. Garnish with chocolate shavings, remaining buttercream, and fresh cherries, if using.

DECORATE IT

Fill a pastry bag fitted with a medium star tip with any remaining buttercream. Pipe frosting rosettes (see page 37) around the top of the cake and place fresh cherries on the top of the rosettes. Garnish the bottom portion of the cake with chocolate curls. Working over a baking sheet, carefully scoop up a small amount of curls and very gently press them into the frosting, making sure not to crush the curls. Alternatively, sprinkle them over the top of the buttercream rosettes before placing on the cherries.

BAKER'S NOTES

If cherries are out of season, preserved sour cherries may be used. Be sure they are drained and dried. If you are having trouble creating the chocolate curls, try microwaving the block of chocolate at medium power to slightly soften— no more than 10 seconds at a time. The cake will keep in the fridge for up to 3 days (see page 25).

brooklyn blackout cake

MAKES ONE THREE-LAYER 8-INCH (20-CM) CAKE; SERVES 12 TO 15

IF YOU LIVED IN BROOKLYN PRIOR TO THE 1970S, you probably had the privilege of eating a slice or two of this decadent chocolate cake. And we are all jealous. Named after World War II blackout drills, this masterpiece was developed by Ebinger's Bakery. The Brooklyn Blackout Cake became a staple of the borough for decades, until sadly the bakery went bankrupt in 1972.

It was the end of an era. Many have tried to replicate the chocolate-on-chocolate creation, but nothing can be compared to the original. Hopefully my version, which combines devil's food cake and chocolate custard, can satisfy this generation. Although the filling can be a bit finicky and difficult to work with at times, it does an excellent job of moistening the cake layers, making each bite more decadent than the last. I've provided a few variations and tips for overcoming some common pitfalls, but no matter which method you choose, it's going to taste amazing. And how can you say no to at least attempting a double chocolate cake covered in more cake crumbs? It is a historical treasure, after all.

For the
DEVIL'S FOOD CAKE

	Butter or nonstick cooking spray, for the pans
¾	cup (70 g) unsweetened cocoa powder
½	cup (120 ml) hot water
1	cup (240 ml) sour cream
3	cups (390 g) cake flour, plus more for the pans
1	teaspoon baking soda
¾	teaspoon baking powder
½	teaspoon salt
1	cup (2 sticks / 225 g) unsalted butter, at room temperature
½	cup (120 ml) grapeseed oil
1½	cups (300 g) granulated sugar
½	cup (110 g) firmly packed brown sugar
2	teaspoons pure vanilla extract
4	large eggs

For the
CHOCOLATE CUSTARD

2½	cups (500 g) granulated sugar
1¼	cups (120 g) unsweetened cocoa powder
1	tablespoon light corn syrup
¼	teaspoon salt
½	cup (120 ml) warm water
⅔	cup (60 g) cornstarch
4	tablespoons (½ stick / 55 g) unsalted butter
1	teaspoon pure vanilla extract

Make the
DEVIL'S FOOD CAKE

1. Preheat the oven to 350°F (175°C). Grease and flour three 8-inch (20-cm) cake pans and set aside.

2. In a bowl, whisk together the cocoa powder and hot water until combined. Stir in the sour cream and set aside.

3. In a separate bowl, sift together the flour, baking soda, baking powder, and salt and set aside.

4. In the bowl of a stand mixer fitted with the paddle attachment, cream together the butter, oil, and sugars on medium speed, 3 to 5 minutes. With the mixer on medium-low, add the vanilla and eggs, one at a time. Stop the mixer and scrape down the bowl.

5. Turn the mixer to low and add the flour mixture in three batches, alternating with the cocoa mixture, beginning and ending with the flour mixture. Mix on medium for no more than 30 seconds after the last streaks of the dry ingredients are combined.

6. Evenly divide the batter among the prepared pans. Bake for 25 to 28 minutes, or until a toothpick inserted into the center of the cakes comes out clean. Let them cool on a wire rack for 10 to 15 minutes before removing the cakes from their pans.

Make the
CHOCOLATE CUSTARD

7. Place the sugar, cocoa powder, corn syrup, salt, and 2 cups (480 ml) water in a medium saucepan. Bring them to a boil over medium-high heat, stirring intermittently.

8. Meanwhile, combine the warm water and cornstarch in a small bowl. With an immersion blender or electric hand whisk, mix until it is pasty and completely free of lumps.

9. Remove the cocoa mixture from the heat and stir in the cornstarch slurry. Return the pan to the heat. While stirring continuously, bring it back to a boil and cook over medium heat until the custard has thickened, 5 to 8 minutes.

10. Remove the pan from the heat and stir in the butter and vanilla until smooth. Pour the custard into a shallow heat-safe container and cover it with plastic wrap, pressing it directly against the surface of the custard to prevent a skin from forming. Refrigerate the custard until completely cool and thick, about 2 hours or overnight.

ASSEMBLE THE CAKE

11. Once the cakes have completely cooled, level off any domes that may have developed on top. Even if no domes are present, remove a good ¼ inch (6 mm) of cake from the top of each cake. Place the cake scraps in the bowl of a food processor and process them into a medium-fine crumb. Alternatively, break up the cake pieces by hand in a large bowl. Set aside.

12. Choose which layer will be the bottom cake layer and place it on a cake plate or serving dish. Spoon on about ¾ cup (180 ml) of the custard, as evenly as possible. Gently top it with the next cake and repeat with the custard. Frost the top and sides of the cake with the remaining custard using an offset spatula. The custard may be difficult to frost with, but do the best you can. Cover the entire cake with the cake crumbs by pressing them against the surface of the custard while stabilizing the cake at the same time. Refrigerate loosely covered with plastic wrap for 1 hour before serving.

BAKER'S NOTES

The truth about the Brooklyn Blackout Cake is that it can be messy and super stressful to make, but it's so delicious and totally worth it. The traditional custard "frosting" can be runny and give you quite a headache, however. If you'd like to save your sanity, try mixing 1 cup (240 ml) Chocolate Custard into 1 small recipe of Vanilla Swiss Meringue Buttercream (page 41) and pipe a buttercream dam (see page 27) on each layer to contain the filling. Spread on the filling, then frost the outside of the cake with the Chocolate Custard Buttercream and finish with the cake crumbs. Alternatively, frost the cake with Dark Chocolate Ganache (page 45). If you'd prefer the more traditional route, it is possible to get the job done if you forge on through the messy parts and keep filling in any gaps with the cake crumbs. The cake will keep in the fridge for up to 3 days (see page 25).

CHOCOLATE CAKES

A perfectly moist and rich chocolate cake is possibly the most indulgent dessert. When done right, the combination of a decadent chocolate cake with creamy fudge frosting cannot be beat. Chocolate is very versatile and pairs brilliantly with a variety of spices, nuts, teas, and even beer—like in the London Fog Cake and Peanut Porter Cake. In this chapter, there is a smorgasbord of ways to get your chocolate fix. Cheers to all you chocoholics out there—these are for you!

ultimate candy bar cake

—

MAKES ONE TWO-LAYER 8-INCH (20-CM) CAKE; SERVES 12 TO 15

I ENJOY COMBINING DESSERT CONCEPTS and giving old classics a modern twist. This extra-indulgent cake combines my love for cake (obviously) and chocolate candy bars. Moist chocolate cake paired with a fluffy caramel marshmallow filling is covered in dark chocolate ganache—it's like a party in every slice! My favorite part is the soft, nougat-like filling. I encourage everyone who makes this cake to add his or her own twist. I've stuffed mine with wafer cookies, but feel free to add chopped-up candy bars, your favorite nuts, mini peanut butter cups, or whatever you like! This cake is your playground.

For the
CLASSIC CHOCOLATE CAKE

	Butter or nonstick cooking spray, for the pans
2½	cups (315 g) all-purpose flour, plus more for the pans
1	cup (95 g) unsweetened cocoa powder
2½	teaspoons baking powder
¾	teaspoon baking soda
1	teaspoon salt
½	cup plus 2 tablespoons (150 ml) grapeseed oil
2	cups (400 g) granulated sugar
2	large eggs
1	large egg yolk
2	teaspoons pure vanilla extract
½	teaspoon pure almond extract
1½	cups (360 ml) whole milk
1	cup (240 ml) hot strong-brewed coffee

For the
CARAMEL-MARSHMALLOW FILLING

2	cups (480 ml) Vanilla Swiss Meringue Buttercream (page 41)
¾	cup (180 ml) marshmallow cream
2	tablespoons Salted Caramel Sauce (page 43), or to taste

For the
CHOCOLATE GANACHE FROSTING

	Scant 2¼ cups (13 ounces / 370 g) chopped bittersweet chocolate
1	cup (240 ml) heavy cream

For the
ASSEMBLY

1	cup filling of choice (such as wafer cookies, chopped-up candy bars, or nuts)
	Chocolate-covered cereal balls such as Callebut Crispearls for decoration (*optional*)
	Salted Caramel Sauce (page 43), for serving (*optional*)

Make the
CLASSIC CHOCOLATE CAKE

1. Preheat the oven to 350°F (175°C). Grease and flour two 8-inch (20-cm) cake pans and set aside.

2. Sift together the flour, cocoa powder, baking powder, baking soda, and salt and set aside.

3. In the bowl of a stand mixer fitted with the paddle attachment, beat together the oil and sugar on medium speed for 2 minutes. With the mixer on, add the eggs, egg yolk, vanilla, and almond extract. Stop the mixer and scrape down the bowl.

4. Turn the mixer to low and add the flour mixture in three batches, alternating with the milk, beginning and ending with the flour mixture. Stop the mixer and scrape down the bowl. With the mixer on low, stream in the coffee. Mix on medium-low for no more than 30 seconds, or until combined.

5. Evenly divide the batter between the prepared pans. Bake for 25 to 28 minutes, or until a toothpick inserted into the center of the cakes comes out clean. Let them cool on a wire rack for 10 to 15 minutes before removing the cakes from their pans.

Make the
CARAMEL-MARSHMALLOW FILLING

6. In the bowl of a stand mixer fitted with the paddle attachment, mix the buttercream until silky smooth. Add the marshmallow cream and caramel sauce and mix until combined.

Make the
CHOCOLATE GANACHE FROSTING

7. Place the chocolate in a heat-safe bowl and set it aside. In a saucepan, slowly bring the cream to a simmer. Remove it from the heat and pour it over the chocolate. Let stand for 30 seconds, then whisk until smooth. Stirring intermittently, let the ganache cool until it reaches a thick but spreadable consistency.

ASSEMBLE THE CAKE

8. Once the cakes have completely cooled, level them and choose which layer will be at the bottom. Place it on a cake plate or serving dish. Spread on half the caramel-marshmallow filling with an offset spatula. Top with about 1 cup of your favorite candy or filling of choice. Spread the remaining caramel-marshmallow filling on top. Top with the second layer of cake. Frost the top and sides with the cooled yet spreadable ganache frosting and decorate with candies, if using. Serve with extra caramel sauce, if desired.

DECORATE IT

Arrange chocolate-covered cereal crisps or other candies in straight rows around the sides of the cake. To create an even grid, place one candy near the top edge and the next at the bottom. Evenly space the next two candies and place them in between the first two. Using the same distance in between the first set of candies, begin the next column and repeat.

BAKER'S NOTES

If the ganache frosting sets before the cake is completely frosted, gently reheat it in the top of a double boiler or briefly in the microwave. The cake will keep in the fridge for up to 4 days; it may also be frozen (see page 25).

mocha spice cake

—

MAKES ONE FOUR-LAYER 6-INCH (15-CM) CAKE; SERVES 10 TO 12

WITH SO MANY INTRIGUING AND DYNAMIC SPICES out there, it would be a shame to limit ourselves to just a few during the chillier times of year. We all know about, and love, anything of the pumpkin-spice variety (and the Pumpkin Pie Cake on page 253 is actually one of my favorites), but warm spices pair beautifully with chocolate cake as well.

This cake not only combines deep chocolate flavors with vibrant spices, but is also soaked and frosted with cardamom coffee. Coffee brewed with cracked cardamom pods is a common warm beverage in the Middle East and is becoming increasingly popular internationally. Albeit stronger than other spices, cardamom works wonderfully in both savory and sweet dishes. It is highly aromatic, with hints of spice and herbal and citrus flavors, and even brings out a slight smokiness in the coffee. Brew a fresh pot with cardamom, or any of your other favorite spices, and serve it with a slice of this cake.

For the
MOCHA SPICE CAKE

Butter or nonstick cooking spray, for the pans

2 cups (250 g) all-purpose flour, plus more for the pans

1 tablespoon ground cinnamon

1½ teaspoons baking soda

1 teaspoon baking powder

1 teaspoon ground ginger

¾ teaspoon salt

½ teaspoon freshly grated nutmeg

¼ teaspoon ground cloves

1 cup (240 ml) strong-brewed coffee

¾ cup (1½ sticks / 170 g) unsalted butter

⅔ cup (160 ml) sour cream

2 large eggs

2 teaspoons pure vanilla extract

¾ cup (70 g) unsweetened cocoa powder

¾ cup (150 g) granulated sugar

1 cup (220 g) firmly packed dark brown sugar

For the
CARDAMOM
COFFEE SYRUP

½ cup (100 g) granulated sugar

½ cup (120 ml) strong-brewed coffee

1 tablespoon whole green cardamom pods, cracked (about 40 pods)

For the
CARDAMOM COFFEE
BUTTERCREAM

1 large recipe Vanilla Swiss Meringue Buttercream (page 41)

3 tablespoons brewed espresso, cooled

1½ teaspoons ground cardamom

Make the
MOCHA SPICE CAKE

1. Preheat the oven to 350°F (175°C). Grease and flour four 6-inch (15-cm) cake pans and set aside.

2. Sift together the flour, cinnamon, baking soda, baking powder, ginger, salt, nutmeg, and cloves and set aside.

3. Combine the coffee and butter in a medium-large saucepan. Heat them over medium heat until the butter has melted.

4. Meanwhile, whisk together the sour cream, eggs, and vanilla in a separate bowl.

5. Over medium heat, whisk the cocoa powder and sugars into the coffee mixture until combined. Remove from the heat and stir in the sour cream mixture. Whisk in the dry ingredients until smooth.

6. Evenly divide the batter among the prepared pans. Bake for 22 to 24 minutes, or until a toothpick inserted into the center of the cakes comes out clean. Let them cool on a wire rack for 10 to 15 minutes before removing the cakes from their pans.

Make the
CARDAMOM
COFFEE SYRUP

7. Place the sugar, coffee, and cracked cardamom pods in a saucepan and bring to a boil over medium-high heat. Reduce the heat to low and simmer for 5 to 10 minutes, until the mixture becomes syrupy. Remove from the heat and discard the cardamom pods.

Make the
CARDAMOM COFFEE
BUTTERCREAM

8. In a stand mixer fitted with the paddle attachment, mix the buttercream until silky smooth. Add the espresso and cardamom and mix until combined.

ASSEMBLE THE CAKE

9. Once the cakes have completely cooled, level them and choose which layer will be at the bottom. Generously brush the cakes with the cardamom coffee syrup. Place the bottom layer on a cake board or serving dish. Spread on ⅓ cup (80 ml) of the buttercream with an offset spatula. Top with the next layer of cake and repeat with the buttercream. Frost the cake with the remaining buttercream.

DECORATE IT

Use a pastry bag fitted with a medium-small open star tip to create a spiral finish (see page 32) on the sides. Finish the top of the cake with a swirl (see page 31). For a simpler finish, a half recipe of the cardamom coffee buttercream will do.

BAKER'S NOTES

The cake will keep in the fridge for up to 4 days; it may also be frozen (see page 25).

GOT LEFTOVERS?

Use the cardamom coffee syrup to sweeten coffee drinks. It can be stored in the fridge for up to 2 weeks.

peanut porter cake

—

MAKES ONE THREE-LAYER 6-INCH (15-CM) CAKE; SERVES 8 TO 10

WHAT DO YOU BAKE YOUR BIG BRO for a special birthday celebration? Something extra indulgent, of course! This grown-up cake has it all: booze, beer, and espresso. No fluffy pink frosting, artificial dyes, or sprinkles in sight. I typically make my brother his favorite, Lemony Carrot Cake (page 246) with cream cheese frosting, but the year I decided to create this decadent chocolate cake, I aimed for something bold and flavorful. Let's face it: Adults love cake on their birthdays, too, especially when said cake is smothered in a whiskey-coffee glaze. Paired with a peanut butter cream cheese filling, this boozy chocolate porter cake is sure to deliver. Top it all off with some crunchy peanut brittle bits or serve with a side of beer nuts.

For the
PORTER
CHOCOLATE CAKE

Butter or nonstick cooking spray, for the pans

1½ cups (190 g) all-purpose flour, plus more for the pans

1 teaspoon baking soda

¾ teaspoon baking powder

½ teaspoon salt

¾ cup (180 ml) porter or stout beer

½ cup (1 stick / 115 g) unsalted butter

½ cup (120 ml) sour cream

1 large egg

1 large egg yolk

1½ teaspoons pure vanilla extract

½ cup (50 g) unsweetened cocoa powder

1½ cups (300 g) granulated sugar

For the
PEANUT BUTTER CREAM
CHEESE FROSTING

4 ounces (115 g) cream cheese, softened

4 tablespoons (½ stick / 55 g) unsalted butter, at room temperature

3 tablespoons smooth peanut butter

2 cups (250 g) confectioners' sugar, sifted

⅛ teaspoon salt

½ teaspoon pure vanilla extract

1 to 2 tablespoons whole milk or heavy cream

For the
MAPLE
PEANUT BRITTLE

4 tablespoons (½ stick / 55 g) unsalted butter

½ cup (110 g) firmly packed brown sugar

¼ cup (60 ml) maple syrup

¼ cup (60 ml) light corn syrup

¼ teaspoon baking soda

½ teaspoon salt

1 cup (150 g) unsalted peanuts

For the
WHISKEY
ESPRESSO GLAZE

3 tablespoons heavy cream

2 tablespoons corn syrup

2 tablespoons unsweetened cocoa powder

1½ teaspoons instant espresso powder

⅓ cup (2 ounces / 55 g) chopped bittersweet chocolate

2 tablespoons whiskey

½ teaspoon pure vanilla extract

⅛ teaspoon salt

Make the
PORTER CHOCOLATE CAKE

1. Preheat the oven to 350°F (175°C). Grease and flour three 6-inch (15-cm) cake pans and set aside.

2. Sift together the flour, baking soda, baking powder, and salt and set aside.

3. Combine the porter and butter in a medium-large saucepan and heat over medium until the butter has melted.

4. Meanwhile, whisk together the sour cream, egg, egg yolk, and vanilla in a separate bowl.

5. Over medium heat, whisk the cocoa powder and sugar into the porter mixture until combined. Remove from the heat and stir in the sour cream mixture. Whisk in the dry ingredients until smooth.

6. Evenly divide the batter among the prepared pans. Bake for 22 to 24 minutes, or until a toothpick inserted into the center of the cakes comes out clean. Let them cool on a wire rack for 10 to 15 minutes before removing the cakes from their pans.

Make the
PEANUT BUTTER CREAM CHEESE FROSTING

7. In the bowl of a stand mixer fitted with the paddle attachment, beat together the cream cheese, butter, and peanut butter until creamy. With the mixer on low, gradually add the confectioners' sugar, salt, vanilla, and milk until incorporated. Mix on medium-high until smooth.

Make the
MAPLE PEANUT BRITTLE

8. Line a baking sheet with a piece of parchment paper.

9. Place the butter, brown sugar, maple syrup, and corn syrup in a medium saucepan. Gently stirring intermittently, heat over medium-high for about 8 minutes, or until the mixture reaches 298°F (149°C) on a candy thermometer. Remove from the heat and carefully stir in the baking soda and salt. Fold in the peanuts and spread the mixture out evenly on the prepared baking sheet while it is still warm. Let the brittle cool, then break it into pieces by hand. Crush about ½ cup (60 g) with a rolling pin or kitchen mallet into small but not crumbly pieces to use for the topping.

ASSEMBLE THE CAKE

10. Once the cakes have completely cooled, level them and choose which layer will be at the bottom. Place it on a cake plate or serving dish. Fill a pastry bag fitted with a medium, round piping tip with the peanut butter cream cheese frosting. Pipe a frosting dam (see page 27), about ½ inch (12 mm) high, around the top edge of the cake. Fill in the ring with about ½ cup (120 ml) of the frosting. Top with the second layer of cake and repeat. Carefully pipe on a third ring of frosting on the very top of the cake and fill in the middle with the remaining frosting. Even out the top with an offset spatula, creating nice, crisp edges for the glaze to drip from. Refrigerate until set, 15 to 20 minutes.

Make the
WHISKEY ESPRESSO GLAZE

11. Place the cream, corn syrup, cocoa powder, and espresso powder in a small saucepan. Heat over medium-low until the mixture begins to steam and the cocoa powder begins to dissolve. Stir to combine.

12. Remove from the heat and add the chocolate. Let it stand for 30 seconds, then whisk to combine. Add the whiskey, vanilla, and salt and mix until smooth. Let the glaze cool for about 10 minutes, or until it is room temperature and has thickened slightly (you can test using the method in the Baker's Notes on page 51).

13. Pour the cooled glaze onto the center of the top of the cake and smooth it around with an offset spatula. Let the glaze drip over the edges. Garnish the cake with the crushed peanut brittle.

BAKER'S NOTES

If making in advance, cover the cake in plastic wrap in the fridge and make the glaze just before serving. Leftovers will keep in the fridge for up to 3 days (see page 25). Store the glaze and peanut brittle separately.

GOT LEFTOVERS?

Stir the whiskey-espresso glaze into coffee to make an adult after-dinner drink, or pour it over ice cream. Maple Peanut Brittle may be made in advance. Store in a cool, dry place layered between pieces of parchment paper in an air-tight container for up to 2 months.

chocolate matcha cake

—

I WENT TO TOKYO RIGHT AROUND THE TIME I seriously got into pastry as a full-time profession. I was continuously on the lookout for inspiration and new recipe ideas. Japanese desserts are in a category of their own, and I was excited to incorporate some of the concepts I saw into my own baking. Up until that point, I was fairly familiar with green tea. But matcha—that was new. Even though I could not make out one single bit of the instructions, I bought a tin of matcha powder to take home and experiment with. A couple of years later, I created this Chocolate Matcha Cake and the most delicious, creamy Matcha Ganache.

For the
CLASSIC CHOCOLATE CAKE

	Butter or nonstick cooking spray, for the pans
2½	cups (315 g) all-purpose flour, plus more for the pans
1	cup (95 g) unsweetened cocoa powder
2½	teaspoons baking powder
¾	teaspoon baking soda
1	teaspoon salt
½	cup plus 2 tablespoons (150 ml) grapeseed oil
2	cups (400 g) granulated sugar
2	large eggs
1	large egg yolk
2	teaspoons pure vanilla extract
½	teaspoon pure almond extract
1½	cups (360 ml) whole milk
1	cup (240 ml) hot strong-brewed coffee

For the
MATCHA CAKE

	Butter or nonstick cooking spray, for the pans
2¾	cups (360 g) cake flour, plus more for the pans
2½	teaspoons baking powder
¼	teaspoon salt
2	tablespoons matcha tea powder (see Baker's Notes, page 94)
14	tablespoons (1¾ sticks / 195 g) unsalted butter, at room temperature
1½	cups (300 g) granulated sugar
1	teaspoon vanilla bean paste
½	teaspoon pure almond extract
2	large eggs
2	large egg yolks
1	cup (240 ml) whole milk

For the
MATCHA GANACHE

2	cups (12 ounces / 340 g) chopped white chocolate
1	teaspoon matcha tea powder (see Baker's Notes, page 94)
½	cup (120 ml) heavy cream

For the
ASSEMBLY

1	large recipe Vanilla Swiss Meringue Buttercream (page 41)
	Gel food coloring (*optional*)

Make the
CLASSIC CHOCOLATE CAKE

1. Preheat the oven to 350°F (175°C). Grease and flour two 8-inch (20-cm) cake pans.

2. Sift together the flour, cocoa powder, baking powder, baking soda, and salt and set aside.

3. In the bowl of a stand mixer fitted with the paddle attachment, beat together the oil and sugar on medium for 2 minutes. Add the eggs, egg yolk, vanilla, and almond extract. Stop the mixer and scrape down the bowl.

4. Turn the mixer to low and add the flour mixture in three batches, alternating with the milk, beginning and ending with the flour mixture. Stop the mixer and scrape down the bowl. With the mixer on low, stream in the coffee. Mix on medium-low for no more than 30 seconds, or until combined.

5. Evenly divide the batter between the prepared pans. Bake for 25 to 28 minutes, or until a toothpick inserted into the center of the cakes comes out clean. Let cool on a wire rack for 10 to 15 minutes before removing the cakes from their pans.

Make the
MATCHA CAKE

6. While the chocolate cakes bake, grease and flour two 8-inch (20-cm) cake pans.

7. Sift together the flour, baking powder, salt, and matcha powder and set aside.

8. In the bowl of a stand mixer fitted with the paddle attachment, beat the butter on medium speed for 2 minutes. Add the sugar and mix on medium-high until light and fluffy, 3 to 5 minutes. Stop the mixer and scrape down the bowl.

9. Turn the mixer to medium-low and add the vanilla and almond extract, then add the eggs and egg yolks one at a time. Stop the mixer and scrape down the bowl.

10. Turn the mixer to low and add the flour mixture in three batches, alternating with the milk, beginning and ending with the flour mixture. Mix on medium for no more than 30 seconds after the last streaks of the dry ingredients are combined.

11. Evenly divide the batter between the prepared pans. Bake for 24 to 26 minutes, or until a toothpick inserted into the center of the cakes comes out clean. Let cool on a wire rack for 10 to 15 minutes before removing the cakes from their pans.

Make the
MATCHA GANACHE

12. Place the chocolate in a heat-safe bowl and sift the matcha powder over the top. Set aside.

13. In a saucepan, bring the cream to a simmer over medium-low heat. Remove from the heat and pour the cream over the chocolate. Let sit for 30 seconds, then whisk until smooth. Cover and chill until the ganache has a spreadable consistency.

ASSEMBLE THE CAKE

14. Tint the buttercream with the food coloring of your choice, if using.

15. Once the cakes have completely cooled, level them and choose which chocolate layer will be at the bottom. Place it on a cake plate or serving dish. Spread on one-third of the ganache with an offset spatula. Top with a layer of matcha cake and repeat, being sure to alternate the layers of cake. Frost the cake with the buttercream.

DECORATE IT

Crumb coat the cake with buttercream. Fill a piping bag fitted with a medium star tip with buttercream. Starting at the top edge of the cake, pipe straight vertical rows of stars (see page 37) down the side of the cake. Repeat around the entire cake until it is covered in buttercream. Pipe concentric rings of stars around the top of the cake until it is completely covered. Make sure to pipe the stars as uniformly as possible to create even rows. The stars may interlock slightly for more complete coverage.

BAKER'S NOTES

To frost the cake in a simpler style than the star pattern, you need only the medium recipe of Vanilla Swiss Meringue Buttercream (page 41). Different brands of matcha tea may yield a different color of cake than the one pictured. Typically, the brighter green the matcha is, the better the quality. Matcha can be quite pricey, so feel free to use a less-expensive culinary grade, as opposed to the premium grade used for drinking. Zen Organics Matcha is a good, moderate choice; DoMatcha is another. Try finding matcha at Whole Foods, specialty groceries, and Asian foods stores. The cake will keep in the fridge for up to 4 days; it may also be frozen (see page 25).

chocolate hazelnut praline crunch cake

MAKES ONE THREE-LAYER 6-INCH (15-CM) CAKE; SERVES 8 TO 10

I'LL ADMIT IT: I'VE BEEN KNOWN to eat a spoonful—or two—of chocolate-hazelnut spread right out of the jar, and I bet you have on occasion, too. Let's try to be grown-ups for just a minute. Let's put down the spoon and screw the lid back on. For just this once, let's turn those fabulous flavors into an even more extraordinary cake! And if you feel the urge to add some kid-like flair back into your life, serve a slice with a tall glass of milk and a playful printed straw.

For the
SMALL CLASSIC CHOCOLATE CAKE

Butter or nonstick cooking spray, for the pans

1¾ cups plus 2 tablespoons (235 g) all-purpose flour, plus more for the pans

¾ cup (70 g) unsweetened cocoa powder

1½ teaspoons baking powder

1 teaspoon baking soda

¾ teaspoon salt

½ cup (120 ml) grapeseed oil

1½ cups (300 g) granulated sugar

2 large eggs

1 teaspoon pure vanilla extract

½ teaspoon pure almond extract

¾ cup (180 ml) whole milk

1 cup (240 ml) hot strong-brewed coffee

For the
HAZELNUT PRALINE BUTTERCREAM

2 cups (480 ml) Vanilla Swiss Meringue Buttercream (page 41)

⅓ cup (80 ml) hazelnut praline paste, stirred

For the
CHOCOLATE HAZELNUT FUDGE FROSTING

¾ cup (1½ sticks / 170 g) unsalted butter, at room temperature

½ cup (120 ml) chocolate-hazelnut spread, such as Nutella

3½ to 4 cups (440 to 500 g) confectioners' sugar, sifted

2 tablespoons unsweetened cocoa powder

⅛ teaspoon salt

1 teaspoon pure vanilla extract

2 to 3 tablespoons heavy cream or whole milk

6 ounces (170 g) semisweet chocolate, melted and cooled

For the
ASSEMBLY

½ cup (70 g) hazelnuts, toasted and chopped, plus 6 to 8 whole

Make the
SMALL CLASSIC CHOCOLATE CAKE

1. Preheat the oven to 350°F (175°C). Grease and flour three 6-inch (15-cm) cake pans and set aside.

2. Sift together the flour, cocoa powder, baking powder, baking soda, and salt and set aside.

3. In the bowl of a stand mixer fitted with the paddle attachment, beat the oil and sugar on medium speed for 2 minutes. With the mixer on, add the eggs, vanilla, and almond extract. Stop the mixer and scrape down the bowl.

4. Turn the mixer to low and add the flour mixture in three batches, alternating with the milk, beginning and ending with the flour mixture. Stop and scrape down the bowl. With the mixer on low, stream in the coffee. Mix on medium-low for no more than 30 seconds, or until combined.

5. Evenly divide the batter among the prepared pans. Bake for 25 to 28 minutes, or until a toothpick inserted into the center of the cakes comes out clean. Let them cool on a wire rack for 10 to 15 minutes before removing the cakes from their pans.

Make the
HAZELNUT PRALINE BUTTERCREAM

6. In the bowl of a stand mixer fitted with the paddle attachment, mix the buttercream until silky smooth. Add the praline paste and mix until combined.

Make the
CHOCOLATE HAZELNUT FUDGE FROSTING

7. In the bowl of a stand mixer fitted with the paddle attachment, beat the butter and chocolate-hazelnut spread on medium-low until smooth and creamy. With the mixer on low, gradually add the confectioners' sugar, cocoa powder, salt, and vanilla. Pour in the cream and mix until everything starts to incorporate. Turn the mixer to medium-high and mix until light and fluffy. Stop the mixer and scrape down the bowl. Add the cooled melted chocolate and mix until smooth.

ASSEMBLE THE CAKE

8. Once the cakes have completely cooled, level them and choose which layer will be at the bottom. Place it on a cake plate or serving dish. Spread on ¾ cup (180 ml) of the praline buttercream with an offset spatula. Place the next layer of cake on top and repeat. Frost the top and sides of the cake with the fudge frosting and decorate with the chopped hazelnuts, whole hazelnuts, and any remaining buttercream.

DECORATE IT

Working with a small handful at a time, press the chopped hazelnuts onto the bottom third of the frosted cake. Fill a pastry bag fitted with a medium star tip with the remaining buttercream and pipe rosettes (see page 37) around the top of the cake. For even placement, pipe the first rosette at 12 o'clock on the top of the cake. Pipe the next rosette directly across at 6 o'clock, and then pipe rosettes at 3 and 9 o'clock. Pipe the remaining rosettes evenly spaced in between. Place a whole hazelnut on top of each rosette.

BAKER'S NOTES

The cake will keep in the fridge for up to 4 days; it may also be frozen (see page 25).

peanut butter lover's chocolate bombe

——

MAKES ONE TWO-LAYER 6-INCH (15-CM) CAKE; SERVES 6 TO 8

MY HUSBAND AND I KNEW WE WERE MEANT for each other when we discovered our mutual love for all things sweet. We met just after I decided to turn baking into my full-time career, and he has been one of my biggest supporters ever since. He encouraged me to open my bakery, provided reassurance that everything would work out when we decided to pick up and move to another country, and has washed more dishes and taste-tested more cakes for this book than I can count. Naturally, I had to develop a cake just for him. He has an affinity for salted caramel sauce, gravitates toward anything with peanut butter, and firmly believes that there is no such thing as "too rich." So, Brett, this one is for you!

For the
PEANUT BUTTER MOUSSE

4	ounces (115 g) cream cheese, softened
½	cup (120 ml) smooth peanut butter
1	cup (125 g) confectioners' sugar, sifted
2	teaspoons whole milk
1	teaspoon pure vanilla extract
⅛	teaspoon salt
1¼	cups (300 ml) cold heavy cream

For the
CLASSIC CHOCOLATE CAKE

	Butter or nonstick cooking spray, for the pans
1¼	cups (155 g) all-purpose flour, plus more for the pans
½	cup (50 g) unsweetened cocoa powder
1¼	teaspoons baking powder
½	teaspoon baking soda
½	teaspoon salt

5	tablespoons (75 ml) grapeseed oil
1	cup (200 g) granulated sugar
1	large egg
1	large egg yolk
1	teaspoon pure vanilla extract
½	teaspoon pure almond extract
¾	cup (180 ml) whole milk
½	cup (120 ml) hot strong-brewed coffee

For the
PEANUT CARAMEL SAUCE

¼	cup (60 ml) Salted Caramel Sauce (page 43)
3	tablespoons unsalted peanuts

For the
PEANUT BUTTER CHOCOLATE GLAZE

2	tablespoons unsalted butter
2	tablespoons smooth peanut butter
2	tablespoons light corn syrup
⅛	teaspoon salt
1	cup (6 ounces / 170 g) chopped semisweet chocolate
½	teaspoon pure vanilla extract
¼	cup (30 g) confectioners' sugar, sifted

For the
ASSEMBLY

½	recipe Milk Chocolate Buttercream (page 72)
	Peanuts, for garnishing

Make the
PEANUT BUTTER MOUSSE

1. In the bowl of a stand mixer fitted with the paddle attachment, beat the cream cheese and peanut butter together on medium speed until creamy. With the mixer on low, gradually add the confectioners' sugar, milk, vanilla, and salt until incorporated. Turn the mixer up to medium and mix until smooth. Place the mixture in a large bowl and set aside.

2. Clean the mixer bowl thoroughly and dry it well. In the clean bowl of the stand mixer fitted with the whisk attachment, whip the cream on medium until it starts to thicken. Turn the mixer up to high and whisk until medium peaks form.

3. Gently fold the whipped cream into the peanut butter mixture.

4. Line a 6-inch-diameter (15-cm) bowl with plastic wrap. Gently spoon the mousse into the bowl, up to the rim. Cover the top with plastic wrap and freeze until it is set, at least 4 hours or overnight.

Make the
CLASSIC CHOCOLATE CAKE

5. Preheat the oven to 350°F (175°C). Grease and flour two 6-inch (15-cm) cake pans and set aside.

6. Sift together the flour, cocoa powder, baking powder, baking soda, and salt and set aside.

7. In the bowl of a stand mixer fitted with the paddle attachment, beat together the oil and sugar on medium for 2 minutes. Add the egg, egg yolk, vanilla, and almond extract. Stop the mixer and scrape down the bowl.

8. Turn the mixer on low and add the flour mixture in three batches, alternating with the milk, beginning and ending with the flour mixture. Stop the mixer and scrape down the bowl. With the mixer on low, stream in the coffee. Mix on medium-low for no more than 30 seconds, or until combined.

9. Evenly divide the batter between the prepared pans. Bake for 25 to 28 minutes, or until a toothpick inserted into the center of the cakes comes out clean. Let them cool on a wire rack for 10 to 15 minutes before removing the cakes from their pans.

Make the
PEANUT CARAMEL SAUCE

10. Heat the caramel sauce until malleable, then stir in the peanuts and set aside.

Make the
PEANUT BUTTER CHOCOLATE GLAZE

11. Combine the butter, peanut butter, corn syrup, salt, and chocolate in a heat-safe bowl or the top portion of a double boiler. Heat over simmering water until the chocolate starts to melt. Remove from the heat and stir in the vanilla until smooth. Stir in the confectioners' sugar until combined. Let the glaze cool to room temperature. It should be thick yet syrupy when assembling the cake.

ASSEMBLE THE CAKE

12. Once the cakes have completely cooled, level them and choose which layer will be at the bottom. Place it on a cake plate or serving dish. Fill a pastry bag fitted with a medium round piping tip with buttercream. Pipe a buttercream dam (see page 27) about ½ inch (12 mm) tall around the top edge of the cake. Fill it in with buttercream. Pipe a second dam about ½ inch (12 mm) tall on top of the buttercream and fill it with the peanut caramel sauce. Top with the second layer of cake.

13. Remove the peanut butter mousse from the freezer. Using the edges of the plastic wrap, gently unmold the mousse from the bowl. Flip the dome over and place the flat edge of the mousse on top of the cake. Peel off the plastic wrap. Drizzle the glaze over the top and garnish with peanuts.

BAKER'S NOTES

If the mousse is difficult to remove from the bowl, let it soften for a few minutes and try again. See Baker's Notes, page 51, for a way to test the temperature of the glaze, which can be cooled or reheated as neccesary. Warm the blade of a chef's knife by running it under hot water, then dry before slicing. If making in advance, store the cake and mousse separately, keeping the cake wrapped in plastic in the fridge and mousse in the freezer until ready to assemble. The cake is best eaten 30 to 45 minutes after assembly. Leftovers will keep in the fridge for up to 2 days (see page 25). Store the mousse separately in the freezer.

red currant chocolate cake

—

MAKES ONE THREE-LAYER 6-INCH (15-CM) CAKE; SERVES 8 TO 10

RED CURRANTS ARE THE JEWELS of British Columbia summer markets. Or at least that's what they look like to me. I can't help but purchase a basket whenever they come into season, and then come up with a recipe or two after the fact.

These tart, yet sweet, little berries literally burst with flavor. They can usually be found in jams, jellies, or even kept whole. Not only do they make for a gorgeous garnish for this Red Currant Chocolate Cake, but also their juices make a vibrant curd. In addition, crème de cassis (currant liqueur) adds great depth to the rich chocolate cake.

For the
RED CURRANT RASPBERRY CURD

½	cup (75 g) red currants (with stems)
½	cup (60 g) fresh raspberries
5	tablespoons (70 g) unsalted butter, diced
1	large egg
2	large egg yolks
¾	cup (150 g) granulated sugar

For the
CHOCOLATE CASSIS CAKE

	Butter or nonstick cooking spray, for the pans
1½	cups (190 g) all-purpose flour, plus more for the pans
1	teaspoon baking soda
¾	teaspoon baking powder
½	teaspoon salt
¼	cup (60 ml) strong-brewed coffee
½	cup (120 ml) crème de cassis (see Baker's Notes, page 104)
½	cup (1 stick / 115 g) unsalted butter
½	cup (120 ml) sour cream
1	large egg
1	large egg yolk
2	teaspoons pure vanilla extract
½	cup (50 g) unsweetened cocoa powder
1½	cups (300 g) granulated sugar

For the
RED CURRANT BUTTERCREAM

1½	cups (360 ml) Vanilla Swiss Meringue Buttercream (page 41)

For the
ASSEMBLY

½	recipe Dark Chocolate Ganache (page 45)
	Whole red currants, for decorating (*optional*)

Make the
RED CURRANT RASPBERRY CURD

1. Place the currants and raspberries in a saucepan over medium-high heat. Heat until the raspberries start to break down and the currants can be crushed with a potato masher or the back of a wooden spoon, about 10 minutes. Remove from the heat.

2. Strain the juice through a fine-mesh sieve into a bowl, pressing the fruit solids against the sieve with a spoon or rubber spatula to extract as much liquid as possible. Discard the stems and solids.

3. Place the butter in a heat-safe bowl and set aside.

4. Place ¼ cup plus 1 tablespoon (75 ml) of the currant-raspberry juice, the egg, egg yolks, and sugar in a medium saucepan. Whisk to combine. Cook over medium heat, stirring continuously to prevent the eggs from curdling, until the mixture is thick enough to coat the back of a spoon or registers 160°F (70°C) on a candy thermometer, 6 to 8 minutes.

5. Remove from the heat and strain the egg mixture through a fine-mesh sieve over the bowl containing the butter (see Baker's Notes). Stir to combine. Cover with plastic wrap, pressing it directly against the surface of the curd to prevent a skin from forming. Refrigerate until set, at least 4 hours, or overnight.

Make the
CHOCOLATE CASSIS CAKE

6. Preheat the oven to 350°F (175°C). Grease and flour three 6-inch (15-cm) cake pans and set aside.

7. Sift together the flour, baking soda, baking powder, and salt and set aside.

8. Combine the coffee, crème de cassis, and butter in a medium-large saucepan. Heat over medium heat until the butter has melted.

9. Meanwhile, combine the sour cream, egg, egg yolk, and vanilla in a separate bowl.

10. Over medium heat, whisk the cocoa powder and sugar into the cassis mixture until combined. Remove the saucepan from the heat and stir in the sour cream mixture. Whisk in the dry ingredients until smooth.

11. Evenly divide the batter among the prepared pans. Bake for 23 to 25 minutes, or until a toothpick inserted into the center of the cakes comes out clean. Let them cool on a wire rack for 10 to 15 minutes before removing the cakes from their pans.

Make the
RED CURRANT BUTTERCREAM

12. In the bowl of a stand mixer fitted with the paddle attachment, mix the buttercream until silky smooth. Add 3 tablespoons of the red currant raspberry curd and mix until combined.

ASSEMBLE THE CAKE

13. Once the cakes have completely cooled, level them and choose which layer will be at the bottom. Place it on a cake plate or serving dish. Spread on ¾ cup (180 ml) of the buttercream with an offset spatula. Hollow out the frosting slightly in the center with the back of a large spoon to create a "bowl" of frosting. Fill it with about ½ cup (120 ml) of the red currant–raspberry curd. Top with the next layer of cake and repeat with the buttercream and curd, ending with the third layer. Frost the top of the cake with the ganache and garnish with whole currants, if desired.

BAKER'S NOTES

You may substitute pomegranate juice or red currant juice for the crème de cassis. If the butter does not melt into the curd, place all of the contents in the top of a double boiler. Stir until the butter is completely incorporated. The red currant raspberry curd may be made in advance and stored in a glass jar in the refrigerator for up to 1 month. The cake will keep in the fridge for up to 3 days (see page 25). For a smoother finish, pipe on the buttercream instead of spreading it and use a buttercream dam (see page 27) to contain the curd.

DECORATE IT

Artfully arrange whole red currants around the base of the cake, letting a few stems fall over the edge of the serving platter before slicing. Fill a pastry bag fitted with a round tip with any remaining ganache. Pipe ganache kisses around the edge of the top of the cake in a crescent shape. Make them by building pressure to create the mound and then stopping pressure before pulling up to release. Scatter the top and plate with any remaining whole currants.

cookies and cream cake

—

MAKES ONE THREE-LAYER 6-INCH (15-CM) CAKE; SERVES 10 TO 12

COOKIES IN ICE CREAM? SURE. It was my favorite ice cream as a kid. But cookies in a cake? Get outta here!! This Cookies and Cream Cake is what dreams are made of. With moist chocolate cake layers, white chocolate filling, and cookie frosting, this cake taps into your inner child in the most delicious way.

For the
**SMALL CLASSIC
CHOCOLATE CAKE**

	Butter or nonstick cooking spray, for the pans
1¾	cups plus 2 tablespoons (235 g) all-purpose flour, plus more for the pans
¾	cup (70 g) unsweetened cocoa powder
1½	teaspoons baking powder
1	teaspoon baking soda
¾	teaspoon salt
½	cup (120 ml) grapeseed oil
1½	cups (300 g) granulated sugar
2	large eggs
1	teaspoon pure vanilla extract
½	teaspoon pure almond extract
¾	cup (180 ml) whole milk
1	cup (240 ml) hot strong-brewed coffee

For the
**WHITE CHOCOLATE-
CREAM CHEESE FROSTING**

1	cup (2 sticks / 225 g) unsalted butter, at room temperature
6	ounces (170 g) cream cheese, softened
5½	cups (690 g) confectioners' sugar, sifted
6	ounces (170 g) white chocolate, melted and cooled
2	teaspoons pure vanilla extract

For the
ASSEMBLY

10	chocolate sandwich cookies, crushed

Make the
SMALL CLASSIC CHOCOLATE CAKE

1. Preheat the oven to 350°F (175°C). Grease and flour three 6-inch (15-cm) cake pans and set aside.

2. Sift together the flour, cocoa powder, baking powder, baking soda, and salt and set aside.

3. In the bowl of a stand mixer fitted with the paddle attachment, beat the oil and sugar on medium speed for 2 minutes. With the mixer on, add the eggs, vanilla, and almond extract. Stop the mixer and scrape down the bowl.

4. Turn the mixer to low and add the flour mixture in three batches, alternating with the milk, beginning and ending with the flour mixture. Stop and scrape down the bowl. With the mixer on low, stream in the coffee. Mix on medium-low for no more than 30 seconds, or until combined.

5. Evenly divide the batter among the prepared pans. Bake for 25 to 28 minutes, or until a toothpick inserted into the center of the cakes comes out clean. Let them cool on a wire rack for 10 to 15 minutes before removing the cakes from their pans.

Make the
WHITE CHOCOLATE-CREAM CHEESE FROSTING

6. In the bowl of a stand mixer fitted with the paddle attachment, beat the butter and cream cheese on medium-low for 2 minutes. With the mixer on low, gradually add the confectioners' sugar, white chocolate, and vanilla until combined. Turn the mixer up to medium-high and mix until it is light and fluffy.

ASSEMBLE THE CAKE

7. Once the cakes have completely cooled, level them and choose which layer will be at the bottom. Place it on a cake plate or serving dish. Spread on ½ cup (120 ml) of the cream cheese frosting with an offset spatula. Top with the next layer of cake and repeat, finishing with the third layer of cake.

8. Transfer the remaining cream cheese filling to a bowl and fold in the crushed cookies until combined. Frost the cake with the cookies and cream frosting.

BAKER'S NOTES

The cake will keep in the fridge for up to 4 days; it may also be frozen (see page 25).

DECORATE IT

Use an icing smoother to create a smooth finish on the sides of the cake and an offset spatula to create a swirl (see page 31) on the top. Alternatively, create a rustic finish (see page 31), especially if the cookie frosting is making it difficult to achieve a smooth finish.

london fog cake

MAKES ONE THREE-LAYER 8-INCH (20-CM) CAKE; SERVES 12 TO 15

I AM VERY PASSIONATE ABOUT TEA. More accurately, I love to hoard (ahem, collect) it. I first started after drinking Earl Grey and English breakfast teas in London and bringing home the best almond black tea I have ever tasted. I've been sipping and collecting ever since—with Earl Grey always being a top favorite.

This robust black tea has a distinct yet subtle citrus flavor from the oils of the bergamot orange. Some drink it black or with a simple slice of lemon, but I can't ever pass up an Earl Grey tea latte, called a "London Fog." Contrary to the name, the London Fog first originated here in Vancouver, British Columbia. Perhaps that is why I like them so much. Steamed milk, flavorful tea, and sweet vanilla syrup; if you have yet to try one, you must! After one sip, you'll immediately want to make this chocolate cake smothered in tea-flecked buttercream and drizzled with salted caramel sauce.

For the CLASSIC CHOCOLATE CAKE		*For the* EARL GREY BUTTERCREAM		*For the* ASSEMBLY	
	Butter or nonstick cooking spray, for the pans	2	cups (4 sticks / 450 g) unsalted butter, at room temperature	1	recipe Salted Caramel Sauce (page 43)
2½	cups (315 g) all-purpose flour, plus more for the pans	¼	cup (12 g) loose Earl Grey tea		
1	cup (95 g) unsweetened cocoa powder	½	cup plus 2 tablespoons (150 ml) large egg whites		
2½	teaspoons baking powder	1¼	cups (250 g) granulated sugar		
¾	teaspoon baking soda	1½	teaspoons vanilla bean paste		
1	teaspoon salt				
½	cup plus 2 tablespoons (150 ml) grapeseed oil				
2	cups (400 g) granulated sugar				
2	large eggs				
1	large egg yolk				
2	teaspoons pure vanilla extract				
½	teaspoon pure almond extract				
1½	cups (360 ml) whole milk				
1	cup (240 ml) hot strong-brewed coffee				

Make the
CLASSIC
CHOCOLATE CAKE

1. Preheat the oven to 350°F (175°C). Grease and flour three 8-inch (20-cm) cake pans and set aside.

2. Sift together the flour, cocoa powder, baking powder, baking soda, and salt and set aside.

3. In the bowl of a stand mixer fitted with the paddle attachment, beat together the oil and sugar on medium speed for 2 minutes. With the mixer on, add the eggs, egg yolk, vanilla, and almond extract. Stop the mixer and scrape down the bowl.

4. Turn the mixer to low and add the flour mixture in three batches, alternating with the milk, beginning and ending with the flour mixture. Stop the mixer and scrape down the bowl. With the mixer on low, stream in the coffee. Mix on medium-low for no more than 30 seconds, or until combined.

5. Evenly divide the batter among the prepared pans. Bake for 23 to 25 minutes, or until a toothpick inserted into the center of the cakes comes out clean. Let them cool on a wire rack for 10 to 15 minutes before removing the cakes from their pans.

Make the
EARL GREY
BUTTERCREAM

6. Place 1 cup (225 g) of the butter in a saucepan with the loose tea. Heat over medium heat until the butter melts, then reduce the heat to low and simmer for 5 minutes. Remove from the heat and let the tea steep for 5 minutes more. Strain the butter through a fine-mesh sieve set over a bowl and refrigerate it until it reaches the same consistency as softened butter, 20 to 30 minutes. Small bits of tea may remain in the butter.

7. Place the egg whites and sugar in the bowl of a stand mixer. Whisk them together by hand to combine. Fill a medium saucepan with a few inches of water and place it over medium-high heat. Place the mixer bowl on top of the saucepan to create a double boiler. The bottom of the bowl should not touch the water. Whisking intermittently, heat the egg mixture until it registers 160°F (70°C) on a candy thermometer or is hot to the touch. Carefully fit the mixer bowl onto the stand mixer.

8. With the whisk attachment, beat the egg white mixture on high speed for 8 to 10 minutes, until it holds medium-stiff peaks. When done, the outside of the mixer bowl should return to room temperature and no residual heat should be escaping from the meringue out of the top of the bowl. Stop the mixer and swap out the whisk attachment for the paddle.

9. With the mixer on low speed, add the vanilla, tea-infused butter, and remaining 1 cup (225 g) butter, a couple tablespoons at a time. Once incorporated, turn the mixer to medium-high and beat until the buttercream is silky smooth, 3 to 5 minutes.

ASSEMBLE THE CAKE

10. Once the cakes have completely cooled, level them and choose which layer will be at the bottom. Place it on a cake plate or serving dish. Spread on ½ cup (120 ml) of the buttercream with an offset spatula. Top with the next layer of cake and repeat, ending with the third layer. Frost the cake with the remaining buttercream and refrigerate it until set, 15 to 20 minutes.

11. Pour caramel sauce onto the top of the cake, letting it drip over the edges. Begin by adding ½ cup (120 ml) of caramel to the center of the cake and then smooth it out with an offset spatula. Add more caramel as necessary until desired look is achieved.

BAKER'S NOTES

The cake will keep in the fridge for up to 4 days; it may also be frozen (see page 25). Store the caramel sauce separately in the fridge for up to 2 weeks.

GOT LEFTOVERS?

Pour unused caramel sauce over ice cream or stir it into coffee!

DECORATE IT

Use an icing comb to create a striped finish (see page 30) before adding the caramel sauce over the top of the cake.

chocolate coconut cake

MAKES ONE FOUR-LAYER 6-INCH (15-CM) CAKE; SERVES 10 TO 12

AS YOU CAN TELL BY THE RECIPES SO FAR, I don't have any dietary restrictions, nor do I keep Kosher, practice vegetarianism, or follow any gluten-free, sugar-free, and/or nut-free diets. However, on occasion, I do find myself enjoying a meat-free meal or accidentally coming up with a vegan recipe. So while this chocolate cake can be eggless and dairy-free, you know it is in this book because it just happens to taste great that way. Try substituting vegan butter sticks and vegan cream cheese in the frosting to make this treat completely dairy-free!

For the
EGGLESS CHOCOLATE CAKE

	Butter, nonstick cooking spray, or coconut oil for the pans
2¼	cups (280 g) all-purpose flour, plus more for the pans
1½	cups (300 g) granulated sugar
6	tablespoons (35 g) natural unsweetened cocoa powder
1½	teaspoons baking soda
½	teaspoon ground cinnamon
¾	teaspoon salt
½	cup (120 ml) melted coconut oil
1½	tablespoons distilled white vinegar
1½	teaspoons pure vanilla extract
1½	cups (360 ml) hot strong-brewed coffee

For the
COCONUT CREAM CHEESE FROSTING

1	cup (2 sticks / 225 g) unsalted butter, at room temperature (see Baker's Notes, page 116)
4	ounces (115 g) cream cheese, softened (see Baker's Notes, page 116)
3	to 4 tablespoons coconut cream (see Baker's Notes, page 116)
3½	cups (440 g) confectioners' sugar, sifted

For the
COCONUT CARAMEL GLAZE

¾	cup (150 g) granulated sugar
1	tablespoon agave nectar
½	cup (120 ml) coconut cream or full-fat coconut milk
½	teaspoon vanilla bean paste

For the
ASSEMBLY

2	to 3 cups (170 to 255 g) unsweetened coconut flakes

Make the
EGGLESS
CHOCOLATE CAKE

1. Preheat the oven to 350°F (175°C). Grease and flour four 6-inch (15-cm) cake pans and set aside.

2. In a large bowl, sift together the flour, sugar, cocoa powder, baking soda, cinnamon, and salt. Create a well in the center of the dry mixture and pour in the coconut oil, vinegar, and vanilla. Stir to combine.

3. While whisking, carefully stream in the coffee. Mix until fully combined, making sure to scrape the bottom of the bowl to incorporate any dry ingredients that may have gotten left behind.

4. Evenly divide the batter among the prepared pans. Bake for 24 to 26 minutes, or until a toothpick inserted into the center of the cakes comes out clean. Let them cool on a wire rack for 10 to 15 minutes before removing the cakes from their pans.

Make the
COCONUT CREAM CHEESE
FROSTING

5. In the bowl of a stand mixer fitted with the paddle attachment, beat the butter and cream cheese together on medium until smooth. With the mixer on low, gradually add the coconut cream and confectioners' sugar until incorporated. Turn the mixer up to medium-high and mix until it is combined and creamy.

Make the
COCONUT CARAMEL
GLAZE

6. Combine the sugar, agave, and 2 tablespoons water in a saucepan. Stir until combined. Heat over high heat until the mixture becomes a medium amber color and the rate of boiling slows (about 305°F / 152°C on a candy thermometer). Remove from the heat and carefully whisk in the coconut cream. Add the vanilla and stir until combined. Transfer to a heat-safe container and let it cool.

ASSEMBLE THE CAKE

7. Once the cakes have completely cooled, level them and choose which layer will be at the bottom. Place it on a cake plate or serving dish. Spread on ⅓ cup (80 ml) of the cream cheese frosting with an offset spatula. Top with the next layer of cake and repeat twice, ending with the fourth layer. Frost the cake with the remaining cream cheese frosting and cover it with the coconut flakes. Serve slices of the cake with the coconut caramel glaze alongside.

BAKER'S NOTES

To make this nondairy, substitute vegan butter sticks and vegan cream cheese in the Coconut Cream Cheese Frosting. I recommend Earth Balance and Daiya brands. If the coconut cream is unavailable, you may substitute 3 tablespoons coconut milk. If canned coconut milk separates, use ¼ cup (60 ml) of the coconut solids that rise to the top of the can. This recipe for cream cheese frosting tends to be a bit on the runnier side. It may be more difficult to frost the cake, but just keep trying and cover with the coconut flakes to help with stability. Refrigerate it along the way to set the frosting, if necessary. The cake will keep in the fridge for up to 3 days (see page 25). Store any leftover caramel in a glass jar in the fridge for up to 1 week.

CASUAL CAKES

For a simple Sunday brunch, afternoon tea, or indulgent week-day treat, these cakes can be enjoyed any time. Without needing extra frosting or too much pizzazz, these more informal yet thoughtfully paired combinations allow the flavors to shine and speak for themselves. Savor a slice of Espresso Walnut Cake with a cup of coffee or share a Honey Fig Cake on a sunny picnic. Their simplicity goes hand-in-hand with crisp mornings, easy weekends, and good conversation.

honey apple cake

MAKES ONE FOUR-LAYER 8-INCH (20-CM) CAKE; SERVES 10 TO 12

EARLY FALL REMINDS ME OF CRISPY, JUICY APPLES—before all the leaves fall off the trees and the rainy season starts. It reminds me of chilly yet sunny mornings, vibrant colors, and lots of cozy flannel.

Not all apple cakes have to be chock-full of cinnamon and dripping with caramel (although I have an amazing recipe for that, too, on page 250). This cake is a fresh and bright version of an apple spice cake. With hints of citrus, honey, and cardamom, this is just the thing to bake after a day of apple picking or to serve as a treat after the first day back at school.

For the FRESH APPLE CAKE

	Butter or nonstick cooking spray, for the pans
2½	cups (315 g) all-purpose flour, plus more for the pans
2	teaspoons baking powder
½	teaspoon baking soda
½	teaspoon salt
½	teaspoon ground cinnamon
¼	teaspoon ground cardamom
½	cup plus 2 tablespoons (150 ml) grapeseed oil
1¼	cups (250 g) granulated sugar
2	teaspoons finely grated lemon zest
2	large eggs
1	large egg yolk
½	cup (120 ml) buttermilk
1¾	cups (280 g) finely diced peeled apples, such as Granny Smith, Honeycrisp, or Pink Lady

For the HONEY SOUR CREAM BUTTERCREAM

2½	cups (600 ml) Vanilla Swiss Meringue Buttercream (page 41)
⅔	cup (160 ml) sour cream
2	tablespoons honey
¼	teaspoon ground cardamom

For the SKILLET OAT CRUMBLE

1	cup (85 g) quick-cooking oats
⅓	cup (40 g) chopped walnuts (*optional*)
2	tablespoons honey
1	tablespoon unsalted butter
¼	teaspoon freshly grated nutmeg
⅛	teaspoon salt

For the ASSEMBLY

	Honey or Honey Caramel (see page 139), for drizzling (*optional*)

Make the FRESH APPLE CAKE

1. Preheat the oven to 350°F (175°C). Grease and flour two 8-inch (20-cm) cake pans and set aside.

2. Sift together the flour, baking powder, baking soda, salt, cinnamon, and cardamom and set aside.

3. In the bowl of a stand mixer fitted with the paddle attachment, beat the oil, sugar, and lemon zest on medium speed for 2 minutes. Turn the mixer to medium-low and add the eggs and egg yolk one at a time. Stop the mixer and scrape down the bowl.

4. Turn the mixer to low and add the flour mixture in three batches, alternating with the buttermilk, beginning and ending with the flour mixture. Mix on medium for no more than 30 seconds after the last streaks of the dry ingredients are combined. Fold in the apples.

5. Evenly divide the batter between the prepared pans. Bake for 24 to 26 minutes, or until a toothpick inserted into the center of the cakes comes out clean. Let them cool on a wire rack for 10 to 15 minutes before removing the cakes from their pans.

Make the HONEY SOUR CREAM BUTTERCREAM

6. In the bowl of a stand mixer fitted with the paddle attachment, mix the buttercream until silky smooth. Add the sour cream, honey, and cardamom and mix until combined.

Make the SKILLET OAT CRUMBLE

7. Heat a heavy-bottomed skillet over medium heat. Stirring intermittently with a wooden spoon, dry roast the oats and walnuts, if using, until fragrant and slightly browned, 5 to 8 minutes. Add the honey, butter, nutmeg, and salt and stir to evenly coat the oats. Cook, while stirring, for 3 to 5 minutes more. Remove from the heat, spread out the mixture on a piece of parchment paper, and let it cool.

ASSEMBLE THE CAKE

8. Once the cakes have completely cooled, halve them horizontally to create four even layers (see page 27). Level the cakes and choose which layer will be at the bottom. Place it on a cake plate or serving dish. Spread on one-quarter of the buttercream with an offset spatula. Top with the next layer of cake and repeat two times more with the buttercream, ending with the fourth layer. Frost the top of the cake with the remaining buttercream. Garnish the top with a generous handful of the skillet oat crumble. Drizzle with honey or honey caramel, if using.

BAKER'S NOTES

The cake will keep in the fridge for up to 3 days (see page 25). Store the oat crumble separately.

GOT LEFTOVERS?

Sprinkle the Skillet Oat Crumble over yogurt.

SHORTCUT

Use store-bought granola in place of the Skillet Oat Crumble.

JUST AFTER I GRADUATED FROM COLLEGE, my big brother let me live at his house in a spacious attic bedroom. In return, I helped take care of his little pug and did a majority of the cooking. One of the first baked goods I learned how to make from scratch was zucchini bread. It was supermoist, full of canola oil, and topped with a mound of cream cheese frosting. My twenty-year-old self was in love with the bread, and big bro was happy to have me as an extra-long houseguest, as long as I kept making that treat. This version may not be that much healthier, but with the addition of lemon and goat cheese, it is a bit more refined and sophisticated, or at least that's what I think when I help myself to a huge piece. Trust me, make this cake if you've extended your stay somewhere, and your host will love you.

For the
ZUCCHINI CAKE

	Butter or nonstick cooking spray, for the pans
2½	cups (315 g) all-purpose flour, plus more for the pans
2	teaspoons baking powder
½	teaspoon baking soda
½	teaspoon salt
½	teaspoon ground cinnamon
½	teaspoon ground cardamom
¼	teaspoon freshly grated nutmeg
½	cup plus 2 tablespoons (150 ml) grapeseed oil
1½	cups (300 g) granulated sugar
2	teaspoons finely grated lemon zest
3	large eggs
1½	cups (225 g) grated zucchini, drained
3	tablespoons buttermilk
1	teaspoon fresh lemon juice

For the
GOAT CHEESE FROSTING

4	ounces (115 g) soft goat cheese, at room temperature
½	cup (1 stick / 115 g) unsalted butter, at room temperature
3	cups (375 g) confectioners' sugar, sifted
2	to 3 teaspoons whole milk
½	teaspoon pure vanilla extract

For the
LEMON GLAZE

1	cup (125 g) confectioners' sugar, sifted
2	to 3 tablespoons fresh lemon juice
2	teaspoons finely grated lemon zest

lemony zucchini cake

MAKES ONE FOUR-LAYER 6-INCH (15-CM) CAKE; SERVES 10 TO 12

Make the
ZUCCHINI CAKE

1. Preheat the oven to 350°F (175°C). Grease and flour four 6-inch (15-cm) cake pans and set aside.

2. Sift together the flour, baking powder, baking soda, salt, cinnamon, cardamom, and nutmeg and set aside.

3. In the bowl of a stand mixer fitted with the paddle attachment, beat together the oil, sugar, and lemon zest on medium speed for 2 minutes. With the mixer on medium-low, add the eggs one at a time. Stop the mixer and scrape down the bowl.

4. Turn the mixer to low and add the flour mixture in two batches until incorporated. Add the zucchini, buttermilk, and lemon juice. Mix on medium for no more than 30 seconds.

5. Evenly divide the batter among the prepared pans. Bake for 24 to 26 minutes, or until a toothpick inserted into the center of the cakes comes out clean. Let them cool on a wire rack for 10 to 15 minutes before removing the cakes from their pans.

Make the
GOAT CHEESE FROSTING

6. In the bowl of a stand mixer fitted with the paddle attachment, beat the goat cheese and butter together until smooth. With the mixer on low, gradually add the confectioners' sugar, milk, and vanilla until incorporated. Turn the mixer up to medium-high and mix until the frosting is fluffy.

ASSEMBLE THE CAKE

7. Once the cakes have completely cooled, level them and choose which layer will be at the bottom. Place it on a cake plate or serving dish. Spread on one-third of the goat cheese frosting with an offset spatula. Top with the next layer of cake and repeat twice with the frosting, ending with the fourth layer.

Make the
LEMON GLAZE

8. In a small bowl, whisk together the sugar, 2 tablespoons of the lemon juice, and the lemon zest until the sugar has dissolved. Add more lemon juice until the glaze is thick yet able to drip over the sides of the cake. Pour the lemon glaze onto the center of the top of the cake. Spread it with an offset spatula and let it drip over the edges.

BAKER'S NOTES

If making in advance, store the cake wrapped in plastic in the fridge. Make the glaze just before serving. Leftovers will keep in the fridge for up to 3 days (see page 25).

honey fig cake

MAKES ONE TWO-LAYER 6-INCH (15-CM) CAKE; SERVES 6 TO 8

WHEN I WAS SEVEN YEARS OLD, my family had a foreign exchange student from Italy stay with us for a few weeks. Pablo came into our lives more than two decades ago and has always seemed like another older brother to me. I still remember him asking my mom where the pasta shop was (we did not have one in the 'burbs) and that he made the most delicious carbonara for us all before heading back home.

　　We all stayed in touch over the years, getting together in Rome, Milan, and whenever he came back to the United States. As a thank-you for hosting him all those years ago, his mother prepared us the most spectacular nine-course traditional Italian dinner I have ever experienced. Later on in my twenties, Pablo treated my friend and me to drinks and small plates in a secret rooftop café overlooking il Duomo di Milano and the entire Cathedral Square. Fast-forward to my wedding: Pablo and his wife came all the way out to California and he even said a prayer in Italian during our ceremony. This cake is a tribute to my "Italian brother."

For the
HONEY YOGURT

1	(32-ounce / 907-g) container full-fat plain Greek yogurt
2	to 3 tablespoons honey

For the
POLENTA OLIVE OIL CAKE

	Butter or nonstick cooking spray, for the pans
1¼	cups (155 g) all-purpose flour, plus more for the pans
1½	teaspoons baking powder
¼	teaspoon salt
¾	cup (135 g) medium- or fine-ground cornmeal
¼	cup (½ stick / 55 g) unsalted butter, at room temperature
½	cup (100 g) granulated sugar
¼	cup (60 ml) olive oil
¼	cup (60 ml) honey
2	large eggs
2	large egg yolks
¼	cup plus 1 tablespoon (75 ml) whole milk

For the
THYME SYRUP

⅓	cup (65 g) granulated sugar
5	to 8 sprigs fresh thyme

For the
ASSEMBLY

6	to 8 fresh figs, halved and quartered

Make the
HONEY YOGURT

1. Line a mesh strainer with a double layer of cheesecloth and place it over a bowl. Empty the entire container of yogurt into the strainer. Refrigerate for about 4 hours, stirring halfway through. After the majority of the liquid has drained from the yogurt, squeeze out any remaining liquid by bundling and twisting the ends of the cheesecloth and giving it a good squeeze by hand. Be sure not to lose any of the yogurt in the process. Discard the liquid.

2. Stir the honey into the strained yogurt.

Make the
POLENTA OLIVE OIL CAKE

3. Preheat the oven to 350°F (175°C). Grease and flour two 6-inch (15-cm) cake pans and set aside.

4. Sift together the flour, baking powder, and salt and stir in the cornmeal. Set aside.

5. In the bowl of a stand mixer fitted with the paddle attachment, beat the butter on medium speed until smooth. Add the sugar, oil, and honey. Turn the mixer to medium-high and mix for 3 to 5 minutes. Stop the mixer and scrape down the bowl.

6. Turn the mixer to medium-low and add the eggs and egg yolks one at a time. Stop the mixer and scrape down the bowl.

7. Turn the mixer to low and add the flour mixture in three batches, alternating with the milk, beginning and ending with the flour mixture. Mix on medium for no more than 30 seconds after the last streaks of the dry ingredients are combined.

8. Evenly divide the batter between the prepared pans. Bake for 23 to 25 minutes, or until a toothpick inserted into the center of the cakes comes out clean. Let them cool on a wire rack for 10 to 15 minutes before removing the cakes from their pans.

Make the
THYME SYRUP

9. Place ⅓ cup (80 ml) water and the sugar in a saucepan and bring them to a boil over medium-high heat. Reduce the heat to maintain a simmer and add the thyme. Simmer for about 8 minutes. Remove from the heat and let steep until cool. Strain the syrup before use and discard the thyme.

ASSEMBLE THE CAKE

10. Once the cakes have completely cooled, choose which layer will be at the bottom. Place it on a cake plate or serving dish. Spread on half the yogurt with a spoon or offset spatula. Top with the next layer of cake and frost the top with the remaining yogurt. Place the figs on top and generously brush the cut sides with the thyme syrup. Drizzle another tablespoon of the syrup over the top of the cake.

BAKER'S NOTES

The thyme syrup may be made in advance and stored in a glass jar in the refrigerator for up to 1 week. Once assembled, eat the cake immediately or keep refrigerated, for up to 2 days, until 30 minutes before serving (see page 25).

GOT LEFTOVERS?

Use the thyme syrup to sweeten iced tea or lemonade or make a refreshing cocktail.

gâteau aux framboises

MY LOVE AFFAIR WITH FRANCE did not start until a decade after my first visit. When I was fifteen years old, I traveled across Europe with my family for the summer. My brother, our folks, grandparents, and I were quite the spectacle traveling by train for three weeks. Between my Filipino grandfather attempting his best German accent and the terror my brother endured riding a wobbly gondola in Venice, I'm not sure how we all survived.

I was too young to really appreciate all the things I've come to love about French culture today. I remember arriving at the train station and not even knowing what the colorful French macarons were. (Little did I know that I would later be determined to master them.) I have yet to make it back to France, but its art, fashion, and especially pastry have become major influences on both my professional and personal lives. I once saw Paris through the eye of a teenager being dragged around with her eccentric family; now I yearn to explore the city as a pastry chef. In the meantime, I will enjoy this *Gâteau aux Framboises*. This cake combines the classic French flavors of almond, pistachio, and fresh raspberry, reminiscent of many pastries found at a tea salon or Parisian bakery.

For the
ALMOND SPONGE CAKE

	Butter or nonstick cooking spray, for the pan
⅔	cup (85 g) confectioners' sugar, sifted
4	large eggs
1	teaspoon pure vanilla extract
1	cup (115 g) almond flour
½	cup (65 g) all-purpose flour
1	teaspoon baking powder
⅛	teaspoon salt
1	teaspoon finely grated lemon zest
2	tablespoons unsalted butter, melted
4	large egg whites
¼	cup (50 g) granulated sugar
¾	teaspoon cream of tartar

For the
PISTACHIO BUTTERCREAM

2	cups (480 ml) Vanilla Swiss Meringue Buttercream (page 41)
¼	cup (60 ml) pistachio paste

For the
ASSEMBLY

1½	pints (375 g) fresh raspberries
	Confectioners' sugar, for dusting

Make the
ALMOND SPONGE CAKE

1. Preheat the oven to 375°F (190°C). Grease a 10 by 15-inch (25 by 38-cm) rectangular cake pan (see Baker's Notes) and line it with parchment paper, letting the parchment paper overhang the edges by a couple of inches.

2. In a large bowl, whisk together the confectioners' sugar, eggs, and vanilla until pale ribbons form. Sift in the flours, baking powder, and salt. Add the lemon zest and mix until combined. Stir in the butter.

3. In the clean bowl of a stand mixer fitted with the whisk attachment, whisk the egg whites on medium-low until they start to foam. Add the granulated sugar and cream of tartar and turn the mixer to high. Whisk until stiff peaks form.

4. Carefully but deliberately fold the egg whites into the almond cake batter. Pour the batter into the prepared pan and evenly spread it out with an offset spatula. Bake for 5 to 10 minutes, or until springy to the touch. Let the cake cool on a wire rack for 10 to 15 minute.

Make the
PISTACHIO BUTTERCREAM

5. In the bowl of a stand mixer fitted with the paddle attachment, mix the buttercream until silky smooth. Separately, thoroughly whisk the pistachio paste until smooth. Stir the pistachio paste into the buttercream until combined.

ASSEMBLE THE CAKE

6. Once the cake has completely cooled, carefully lift it out of the cake pan using the edges of the parchment paper. Invert it onto a large cutting board or clean work surface. Peel back the parchment paper and discard. Using a 6-inch (15-cm) cake ring, cut out three rounds of cake.

7. Place the cake ring on a cake board or plate. Place the bottom cake layer inside the cake ring. Fill a pastry bag fitted with a round piping tip with the pistachio buttercream. Pipe about ½ cup (120 ml) of the buttercream on top of the cake, pressing it into the side of the cake ring to fill any gaps.

8. Place a layer of raspberries snugly on top of the buttercream. Pipe another ½ cup (120 ml) of the buttercream on top of the raspberries, filling in the gaps between the berries. Top with the second layer of cake and repeat with the buttercream and raspberries. Top the final layer of buttercream with the third layer of cake and refrigerate, loosely covered, until the buttercream sets, about 20 to 30 minutes.

9. Once set, carefully remove the cake ring. Dust the top of the cake with confectioners' sugar before serving.

BAKER'S NOTES

Carefully slide a metal spatula between the cake and cake ring and go around the cake to help release it. You will be able to cut out exactly three 6-inch (15-cm) round cake layers using a 10 by 15-inch (25 by 38-cm) cake pan. If using a standard 9 by 13-inch (23 by 33-cm) quarter-sheet cake pan, you will need to cut out two 6-inch (15-cm) round cake layers and two half circles or use the remaining cake "scraps" to piece together the third 6-inch (15-cm) round. Use this round as the middle layer of cake. The cake will keep in the fridge for up to 3 days (see page 25).

sweet tea cake

—

MAKES ONE THREE-LAYER 6-INCH (15-CM) CAKE; SERVES 10 TO 12

A FEW YEARS BACK, I WENT OUT TO NASHVILLE to help a friend with one of her own cookbooks. I've hardly spent any time in that part of the country, and I was eager to experience the food and allure of the South. Unfortunately, the trip was quick and nearly all business, so I am still uncertain of what the South is really like.

One thing I know for sure is that my hostess was as delightful as this little cake, with its vanilla-flecked frosting and candied lemon slices, but with a pinch of sass like the slight bite from the Sweet Tea Buttercream filling. While all Southerners may not sip sweet tea on their back porches every day, this cake embodies my romanticized vision of late, sunny afternoons in that region.

For the
CANDIED LEMONS

2	lemons, thinly sliced and seeded
1½	cups (300 g) granulated sugar

For the
LEMON BUTTER CAKE

	Butter or nonstick cooking spray, for the pans
2¼	cups (295 g) cake flour, plus more for the pans
2½	teaspoons baking powder
½	teaspoon baking soda
½	teaspoon salt
1½	cups (300 g) granulated sugar
2	tablespoons finely grated lemon zest
¾	cup (1½ sticks / 170 g) unsalted butter
1	teaspoon pure vanilla extract
4	large egg yolks
1	cup (240 ml) buttermilk

For the
SWEET TEA BUTTERCREAM

½	cup (100 g) granulated sugar
5	black tea bags, paper tags removed
1	medium recipe Vanilla Swiss Meringue Buttercream (page 41)

For the
VANILLA BEAN BUTTERCREAM

	Remaining Vanilla Swiss Meringue Buttercream
½	teaspoon vanilla bean paste

Make the
CANDIED LEMONS

1. Prepare an ice bath and set it aside.

2. Place 1½ cups (360 ml) water in a large shallow saucepan and bring it to a boil. Blanch the lemon slices in the boiling water for about 1 minute, then use a slotted spoon to transfer them to the ice bath.

3. Reduce the heat to bring the water to a simmer. Add the sugar and stir to dissolve. Return the blanched lemons to the pan and simmer for about 30 minutes, or until translucent. Place the lemons on a wire rack to drain. Let them dry completely on a piece of parchment paper for 2 to 4 hours, or overnight.

Make the
LEMON BUTTER CAKE

4. Preheat the oven to 350°F (175°C). Grease and flour three 6-inch (15-cm) cake pans and set aside.

5. Sift together the flour, baking powder, baking soda, and salt and set aside.

6. Place the sugar and lemon zest in a small bowl. Rub them together between your fingertips until fragrant.

7. In the bowl of a stand mixer fitted with the paddle attachment, beat the butter on medium speed until smooth. Add the sugar mixture and mix on medium-high until the butter is light and fluffy, 3 to 5 minutes. Stop the mixer and scrape down the bowl.

8. Turn the mixer to medium-low and add the vanilla and egg yolks, one at a time. Stop the mixer and scrape down the bowl.

9. Turn the mixer to low and add the flour mixture in three batches, alternating with the buttermilk, beginning and ending with the flour mixture. Mix on medium for no more than 30 seconds after the last streaks of the dry ingredients are combined.

10. Evenly divide the batter among the prepared pans. Bake for 22 to 24 minutes, or until a toothpick inserted into the center of the cakes comes out clean. Let them cool on a wire rack for 10 to 15 minutes before removing the cakes from their pans.

Make the
SWEET TEA BUTTERCREAM

11. Place 1 cup (240 ml) water and the sugar in a saucepan and bring them to a boil over medium-high heat. Reduce the heat to maintain a simmer and add the tea bags. Simmer for about 8 minutes. Carefully remove the tea bags and continue to cook until the syrup has reduced to about ¼ cup (60 ml), 20 to 30 minutes. Remove from the heat and let cool.

12. In the bowl of a stand mixer fitted with the paddle attachment, mix 1½ cups (360 ml) of the buttercream until silky smooth. Add 3 tablespoons of the syrup and mix until combined. Transfer to a separate bowl and set aside. Wipe out the mixer bowl.

Make the
VANILLA BEAN BUTTERCREAM

13. In the bowl of the stand mixer fitted with a paddle attachment, mix the remaining buttercream with the vanilla bean paste until silky smooth.

ASSEMBLE THE CAKE

14. Once the cakes have completely cooled, level them and choose which layer will be at the bottom. Place it on a cake plate or serving dish. Spread on half of the sweet tea buttercream with an offset spatula. Top with the next layer of cake and repeat with the sweet tea buttercream, ending with the third layer. Frost the cake with the vanilla bean buttercream and decorate with candied lemons.

BAKER'S NOTES

The cake will keep in the fridge for up to 4 days; it may also be frozen (see page 25). Store the candied lemons separately.

Smoothly frost the cake with the Vanilla Bean Buttercream. Fill a piping bag fitted with a small round tip with any remaining butter-cream. Pipe buttercream stripes (see page 37) around the sides of the cake. To do so, start piping your stripe on the top of the cake. Pipe with even pressure and gently pull out and over the top edge of the cake. As a "string" of buttercream is piped, bring the piping bag down and attach the string to the side of the cake. The buttercream should hover slightly before adhering to the side of the cake, as opposed to being piped directly on the surface. Finish off each stripe by piping a dot (see page 37) on the top and bottom. Continue to pipe stripes around the entire cake, ¼ to ½ inch (6 to 12 mm) apart. Fan out the can-died lemons on the top of the cake or serve one with each slice.

I HAVE A LOVE-HATE RELATIONSHIP with peaches, and I have come to accept that they are not all created equal. Perhaps it is where I live, but I swear sometimes even the most gorgeous peach doesn't ripen the way I want it to. However, when I do find a juicy, fragrant peach, it is the most delicious treat ever!

    I wanted to create a cake that really showcased those ripe gems—a cake to enjoy after a successful late-summer trip to the farmers' market. I've kept the peaches pure, placing them on top of the cake instead of baking them down. The peach glaze elevates the spice cake, and the rosemary pine nuts add an addictive savory crunch.

For the SPICE CAKE

	Butter or nonstick cooking spray, for the pans
2¾	cups (360 g) cake flour, plus more for the pans
1	tablespoon unsweetened cocoa powder
1	tablespoon ground cinnamon
2	teaspoons baking powder
1	teaspoon ground ginger
1	teaspoon baking soda
½	teaspoon salt
½	teaspoon freshly grated nutmeg
¼	teaspoon ground cloves
¾	cup (1½ sticks / 170 g) unsalted butter, at room temperature
¼	cup (60 ml) grapeseed oil
2	cups (400 g) granulated sugar
1	teaspoon pure vanilla extract
4	large eggs
1¼	cups (300 ml) buttermilk

For the PEACH GLAZE

1	cup (240 ml) peach jam
½	teaspoon ground cinnamon
½	teaspoon ground ginger
⅛	teaspoon freshly grated nutmeg

For the ROSEMARY PINE NUTS

½	cup (65 g) pine nuts
1	tablespoon honey
1	teaspoon dried rosemary
¼	teaspoon salt

For the CARAMEL CREAM CHEESE FROSTING

4	ounces (115 g) cream cheese, softened
2	cups (480 ml) Vanilla Swiss Meringue Buttercream (page 41)
¼	cup (60 ml) Salted Caramel Sauce (page 43)

For the ASSEMBLY

| 1 | to 2 ripe peaches, sliced |

peach spice cake

MAKES ONE TWO-LAYER 8-INCH (20-CM) CAKE; SERVES 12 TO 15

Make the
SPICE CAKE

1. Preheat the oven to 350°F (175°C). Grease and flour two 8-inch (20-cm) springform cake pans (see Baker's Notes) and set aside.

2. Sift together the flour, cocoa powder, cinnamon, baking powder, ginger, baking soda, salt, nutmeg, and cloves and set aside.

3. In the bowl of a stand mixer fitted with the paddle attachment, beat the butter on medium speed until smooth. Add the oil and sugar. Turn the mixer to medium-high and mix for 3 minutes. With the mixer on medium-low, add the vanilla and eggs, one at a time. Stop the mixer and scrape down the bowl.

4. Turn the mixer to low and add the flour mixture in three batches, alternating with the buttermilk, beginning and ending with the flour mixture. Mix on medium-low for no more than 30 seconds, or until combined.

5. Evenly divide the batter between the prepared pans. Bake for 25 to 28 minutes, or until a toothpick inserted into the center of the cakes comes out clean.

Make the
PEACH GLAZE

6. While the cakes are baking, combine the jam, cinnamon, ginger, and nutmeg in a saucepan. Heat over medium heat until the jam melts, 5 to 8 minutes. When the mixture is syrup-like, strain it through a fine-mesh sieve set over a bowl to remove any solids.

7. Evenly pour the warm peach glaze over the top of the two cakes just after they come out of the oven. Let them cool completely on a wire rack before removing the cakes from their pans.

Make the
ROSEMARY PINE NUTS

8. Heat a heavy-bottomed skillet over medium-high heat. Reduce the heat to medium and dry-roast the nuts until browned and fragrant, 3 to 5 minutes. Add the honey, rosemary, and salt and stir until the pine nuts are evenly coated. Cook, stirring, for an additional 3 to 5 minutes. Remove from the heat and spread the pine nuts on a piece of parchment paper to cool and dry, about 10 minutes.

Make the
CARAMEL CREAM CHEESE
FROSTING

9. In the bowl of a stand mixer fitted with the paddle attachment, beat the cream cheese on medium speed until smooth. Add the buttercream and caramel sauce and mix until combined.

ASSEMBLE THE CAKE

10. Level the layers and choose which one will be at the bottom. Place it on a cake plate or serving dish. Spread on half the frosting with an offset spatula. Top with the next layer of cake and frost the top with the remaining frosting. Arrange the peach slices on top and garnish with a generous handful of the rosemary pine nuts.

BAKER'S NOTES

The cakes are baked in springform pans for easier removal due to the peach glaze. If using regular cake pans, line them with parchment paper and gently lift the cakes out instead of flipping them upside-down. The cake will keep in the fridge for up to 3 days (see page 25). Store the peaches and pine nuts separately.

---

apricot carrot cake

—

MAKES ONE TWO-LAYER 6-INCH (15-CM) CAKE; SERVES 6 TO 8

I DON'T HAVE TOO MANY HARD-AND-FAST RULES when it comes to baking. Of course there is some science involved but, whenever possible, I try not to restrict my recipe development or creativity. My cooking philosophy? Cook with the seasons and the best possible ingredients available to you. It just makes sense that if the ingredients taste great, then the final recipe will taste even better. Pretty simple, right?

I love going to my local market and being inspired by fresh, seasonal produce. When I found some gorgeous rainbow carrots, I knew I had to take them home. This carrot cake is the result. Made with yogurt and soft spelt flour, it is studded with apricots and sweetened with honey. The spiced frosting made with mascarpone (cream cheese's sophisticated cousin) is unbelievably creamy and worthy of turning an ordinary day into a mini celebration.

	For the **APRICOT CARROT CAKE**
	Butter or nonstick cooking spray, for the pans
1¾	cups (225 g) white spelt or all-purpose flour, plus more for the pans
1	teaspoon baking powder
1	teaspoon ground cinnamon
½	teaspoon baking soda
½	teaspoon salt
¼	cup (15 g) oat bran
1	cup (240 ml) full-fat plain yogurt
⅔	cup (160 ml) honey
6	tablespoons (¾ stick / 85 g) unsalted butter, melted
1	large egg
2	tablespoons grapeseed oil
1	teaspoon vanilla bean paste or pure vanilla extract
1½	cups (165 g) shredded carrots
⅓	cup (45 g) finely chopped dried apricots

	For the **CINNAMON MASCARPONE FROSTING**
4	tablespoons (½ stick / 55 g) unsalted butter, at room temperature
1	cup (125 g) confectioners' sugar, sifted
1	teaspoon vanilla bean paste
¼	teaspoon ground cinnamon
⅔	cup (160 ml) mascarpone, softened

	For the **HONEY CARAMEL**
½	cup (100 g) granulated sugar
¼	cup (60 ml) honey
½	cup (120 ml) heavy cream
2	tablespoons unsalted butter, diced
½	teaspoon vanilla bean paste

Make the
APRICOT-CARROT CAKE

1. Preheat the oven to 350°F (175°C). Grease and flour two 6-inch (15-cm) pans and set aside.

2. Sift together the flour, baking powder, cinnamon, baking soda, and salt. Whisk in the oat bran and set aside.

3. In a large bowl, stir together the yogurt, honey, butter, egg, grape-seed oil, and vanilla until combined. In two batches, stir in the dry ingredients. Fold in the carrots and apricots.

4. Evenly divide the batter between the prepared pans. Bake for 26 to 28 minutes, or until a toothpick inserted into the center of the cakes comes out clean. Let them cool on a wire rack for 10 to 15 minutes before removing the cakes from their pans.

Make the
CINNAMON MASCARPONE
FROSTING

5. In the bowl of a stand mixer fitted with the paddle attachment, beat the butter on medium speed until smooth. With the mixer on low, gradually add the confectioners' sugar, vanilla, and cinnamon until incorporated. Turn the mixer to medium-high and mix the frosting until combined and fluffy. Turn the mixer off and scrape down the bowl. Add the mascarpone and mix on low until combined. Do not overmix.

Make the
HONEY CARAMEL

6. Place the sugar, honey, and 1 tablespoon water in a saucepan. Heat over medium heat until it turns a medium amber color and the bubbles subside (about 305°F / 152°C on a candy thermometer). Remove from the heat and carefully whisk in the cream. Add the butter and vanilla and stir until melted. Transfer to a heat-safe container and let it cool to room temperature.

ASSEMBLE THE CAKE

7. Once the cakes have completely cooled, choose which layer will be at the bottom. Place it on a cake plate or serving dish. Spread on half the mascarpone frosting with an offset spatula or spoon. Top with the next layer of cake and frost the top with the remaining frosting. Drizzle the top with ¼ cup (60 ml) of the caramel.

8. Serve slices of cake with more honey caramel, if desired.

BAKER'S NOTES

The cake will keep in the fridge for up to 3 days (see page 25).

GOT LEFTOVERS?

Store honey caramel in the refrigerator. Use it to pour over ice cream or stir into coffee!

THIS CAKE HAS BECOME ONE OF MY NEW FAVORITES. Using white sugar and white flour alternatives, I feel a little less guilty enjoying this proper companion to a cup of coffee on a casual afternoon. The contrasting flavors of tangy sour cream and bittersweet espresso pair perfectly in this not-too-sweet cake combination. The cake itself is dense, yet moist at the same time, and brilliantly nutty.

For the
ESPRESSO GANACHE

½	cup (120 ml) heavy cream
1½	tablespoons coarsely ground or chopped espresso or coffee beans
1	cup (6 ounces / 170 g) chopped bittersweet chocolate

For the
ESPRESSO WALNUT CAKE

	Butter or nonstick cooking spray, for the pans
2	cups (240 g) whole wheat pastry flour, plus more for the pans
1	cup (130 g) white spelt or all-purpose flour
2½	teaspoons baking powder
½	teaspoon salt
½	cup (40 g) ground walnuts
¾	cup (180 ml) strong-brewed coffee
¼	cup (60 ml) whole milk
1	cup (2 sticks / 225 g) unsalted butter, at room temperature
½	cup (110 g) firmly packed brown sugar
1	cup (240 ml) brown rice syrup (see Baker's Notes, page 145)
1	teaspoon vanilla bean paste
2	large eggs
1	large egg yolk
¾	cup (90 g) chopped walnuts

For the
SOUR CREAM BUTTERCREAM

1	medium recipe Vanilla Swiss Meringue Buttercream (page 41)
⅓	cup (80 ml) sour cream
¼	teaspoon ground cardamom

For the
ESPRESSO BUTTERCREAM

	Remaining Vanilla Swiss Meringue Buttercream
2	tablespoons cooled espresso

For the
ASSEMBLY

	Chocolate-covered espresso beans (*optional*)

espresso walnut cake

—

MAKES ONE THREE-LAYER 8-INCH (20-CM) CAKE; SERVES 10 TO 12

Make the
ESPRESSO GANACHE

1. Place the cream in a saucepan over medium-low heat and bring it to a simmer. Add the ground or chopped espresso beans and remove the pan from the heat. Transfer the mixture to a heat-safe container and let it steep in the refrigerator for 2 to 3 hours.

2. Strain the cream back into the saucepan. Heat it over medium-low heat until the cream begins to simmer. Place the chocolate in a heat-safe bowl. Remove the cream from the heat and pour it over the chocolate. Let stand for 30 seconds, then whisk to combine. Let cool to thicken before use.

Make the
ESPRESSO WALNUT CAKE

3. Preheat the oven to 350°F (175°C). Grease and flour three 8-inch (20-cm) cake pans and set aside.

4. Sift together the flours, baking powder, and salt and stir in the ground walnuts. Set aside.

5. Combine the coffee and milk and set aside.

6. In the bowl of a stand mixer fitted with the paddle attachment, beat the butter on medium speed until smooth. Add the brown sugar and mix for 2 to 3 minutes. Add the brown rice syrup and mix until combined. Stop the mixer and scrape down the bowl.

7. Turn the mixer to medium-low and add the vanilla, then add the eggs and egg yolk one at a time. Stop the mixer and scrape down the bowl.

8. Turn the mixer to low and add the flour mixture in three batches, alternating with the coffee mixture, beginning and ending with the flour mixture. Mix on medium for no more than 30 seconds after the last streaks of the dry ingredients are combined. Fold in the chopped walnuts.

9. Evenly divide the batter among the prepared pans. Bake for 24 to 26 minutes, or until a toothpick inserted into the center of the cakes comes out clean. Let them cool on a wire rack for 10 to 15 minutes before removing the cakes from their pans.

Make the
SOUR CREAM BUTTERCREAM

10. In the bowl of a stand mixer fitted with the paddle attachment, mix 1¼ cups (300 ml) of the buttercream until silky smooth. Add the sour cream and cardamom and mix until combined. Transfer to a separate bowl and set aside. Wipe out the mixer bowl.

Make the
ESPRESSO BUTTERCREAM

11. In the bowl of the stand mixer fitted with the paddle attachment, mix the remaining vanilla buttercream until silky smooth. Add 3 tablespoons of the espresso ganache and the cooled espresso and mix until combined.

ASSEMBLE THE CAKE

12. Once the cakes have completely cooled, level them and choose which layer will be at the bottom. Place it on a cake plate or serving dish. Spread on half of the remaining ganache with an offset spatula. Spread half of the sour cream buttercream on top. Top with the next layer of cake and repeat with the remaining ganache and sour cream buttercream. Place the last layer on top. Frost the top and sides of the cake with the espresso buttercream and decorate with the chocolate-covered espresso beans, if using.

DECORATE IT

Use a small offset spatula to create a wave pattern. Follow the technique for the swirl finish (see page 31), but hold the spatula horizontally and create a wave motion with the tip as you move it up the side of the cake. Keep the top frosted smooth or with a swirl finish (see page 31). For even placement, place the first chocolate-covered coffee bean at 12 o'clock on the top of the cake. Put the next bean directly across at 6 o'clock, and then place the next two at 3 and 9 o'clock. Space the remaining beans evenly in between.

BAKER'S NOTES

The brown rice syrup may be replaced with ¾ cup (150 g) granulated sugar plus ¼ cup (60 ml) maple syrup. Bake for 23 to 25 minutes, or until a toothpick inserted into the center of the cakes comes out clean. The cake will keep in the fridge for up to 3 days; it may also be frozen (see page 25).

THIS CAKE IS LIVELY AND VIBRANT, INSIDE AND OUT. I aimed to make something that was not too sweet and was perfect for sharing at a summer brunch or on a sunny afternoon among friends. I love incorporating fresh herbs in dessert recipes. The thyme and citrus create a dynamic flavor palette against the canvas of a brown sugar buttermilk cake and blushed raspberry filling. Plus, the thyme creates a beautiful crown for the impressive yet simple cake, don't you think?

For the
**BROWN SUGAR
BUTTERMILK CAKE**

	Butter or nonstick cooking spray, for the pans
2¼	cups (295 g) cake flour, plus more for the pans
1½	teaspoons baking powder
½	teaspoon salt
¼	teaspoon baking soda
¾	cup (1½ sticks / 170 g) unsalted butter, at room temperature
¾	cup plus 2 tablespoons (190 g) firmly packed brown sugar
½	cup (100 g) granulated sugar
1½	tablespoons finely grated blood orange zest (see Baker's Notes, page 149)
1	teaspoon pure vanilla extract
3	large eggs
1	large egg yolk
¾	cup plus 2 tablespoons (210 ml) buttermilk

For the
**RASPBERRY
BUTTERCREAM**

½	cup (60 g) fresh raspberries
2	teaspoons granulated sugar
2	cups (480 ml) or a little less than ½ medium recipe Vanilla Swiss Meringue Buttercream (page 41)

For the
**BLOOD ORANGE
THYME SYRUP**

½	cup (120 ml) fresh blood orange juice (from 2 to 3 oranges; see Baker's Notes, page 149)
½	cup (100 g) granulated sugar
5	to 8 sprigs fresh thyme

For the
BLOOD ORANGE GLAZE

1¼	cups (155 g) confectioners' sugar, sifted, plus more as needed
2	tablespoons plus 1 teaspoon fresh blood orange juice (see Baker's Notes, page 149)

For the
ASSEMBLY

	Sprigs of fresh thyme (*optional*)

blood orange thyme cake

MAKES ONE THREE-LAYER 6-INCH (15-CM) CAKE; SERVES 10 TO 12

GOT LEFTOVERS?

Use blood orange thyme syrup to sweeten cocktails or iced tea.

Make the
BROWN SUGAR BUTTERMILK CAKE

1. Preheat the oven to 350°F (175°C). Grease and flour three 6-inch (15-cm) cake pans and set aside.

2. Sift together the flour, baking powder, salt, and baking soda and set aside.

3. In the bowl of a stand mixer fitted with the paddle attachment, beat the butter on medium speed until smooth. Add the sugars and orange zest. Turn the mixer to medium-high and mix until the butter is light and fluffy, 3 to 5 minutes. Stop the mixer and scrape down the bowl.

4. Turn the mixer to medium-low and add the vanilla, then add the eggs and egg yolk one at a time. Stop the mixer and scrape down the bowl.

5. Turn the mixer to low and add the flour mixture in three batches, alternating with the buttermilk, beginning and ending with the flour mixture. Mix on medium for no more than 30 seconds after the last streaks of the dry ingredients are combined.

6. Evenly divide the batter among the prepared pans. Bake for 23 to 25 minutes, or until a toothpick inserted into the center of the cakes comes out clean. Let them cool on a wire rack for 10 to 15 minutes before removing the cakes from their pans.

Make the
RASPBERRY BUTTERCREAM

7. Blend the raspberries and sugar together in a food processor until combined. If you prefer to remove the seeds, strain the puree through a mesh sieve set over a bowl.

8. In the bowl of a stand mixer fitted with the paddle attachment, mix the buttercream until silky smooth. Add ¼ cup (60 ml) of the pureed raspberries and mix until combined.

Make the
BLOOD ORANGE THYME SYRUP

9. Place the orange juice and sugar in a saucepan and bring them to a boil over medium-high heat. Reduce the heat to maintain a simmer and add the thyme. Simmer for about 8 minutes. Remove from the heat and let steep until cool. Strain the syrup before use and discard the thyme.

ASSEMBLE THE CAKE

10. Once the cakes have completely cooled, level them and choose which layer will be at the bottom. Generously brush the cake layers with the blood orange thyme syrup. Place the bottom layer on a cake plate or serving dish. Spread on ¾ cup (180 ml) of the raspberry buttercream with an offset spatula. Top with the next layer of cake and repeat with the buttercream, ending with the third layer. Use the remaining buttercream to fill in any gaps between layers and give the cake a rustic coat of icing.

Make the
BLOOD ORANGE GLAZE

11. In a small bowl, whisk the confectioners' sugar and orange juice together until the sugar has dissolved. If a thicker glaze is desired, stir in more sugar, a few tablespoons at a time. Pour the glaze onto the center of the top of the cake. Spread it evenly with an offset spatula and let it drip over the edges. Decorate the top with thyme, if using.

BAKER'S NOTES

Try regular oranges or even a grapefruit if blood oranges are not in season. If making in advance, store the cake wrapped in plastic in the fridge. Make the glaze and garnish just before serving. Leftovers will keep in the fridge for up to 3 days (see page 25).

POPULAR IN THE SOUTH, A HUMMINGBIRD CAKE is a banana-pineapple spice cake that tastes dynamite with fluffy cream cheese frosting. Even farther south, the cake is often thought to be named after the Jamaican national fowl or "doctor bird." No matter what you call it, this cake is always a hit.

It whips up fairly fast and is perfect for entertaining on a casual afternoon. The banana, pineapple, and grapeseed oil make this cake supermoist and extremely flavorful. I like to toss chopped pecans in mine, and dress it up with dried pineapple flowers and maple candied pecans.

For the
DRIED PINEAPPLE FLOWERS

1   large pineapple

For the
HUMMINGBIRD CAKE

Butter or nonstick cooking spray, for the pans

3   cups (375 g) all-purpose flour, plus more for the pans

2   teaspoons ground cinnamon

2   teaspoons baking powder

1   teaspoon baking soda

½   teaspoon salt

¾   cup (180 ml) grapeseed oil

1   cup (200 g) granulated sugar

¾   cup (165 g) firmly packed brown sugar

2   teaspoons pure vanilla extract

4   large eggs

3   ripe bananas, mashed

1   (8-ounce / 225-g) can crushed pineapple, drained

1   cup (120 g) chopped pecans, toasted

For the
CREAM CHEESE FROSTING

12   ounces (340 g) cream cheese, softened

1   cup (2 sticks / 225 g) unsalted butter, at room temperature

4½   cups (565 g) confectioners' sugar, sifted

3   tablespoons whole milk

2   teaspoons vanilla bean paste

For the
MAPLE CANDIED PECANS

1   teaspoon unsalted butter

2½   tablespoons maple syrup

¼   cup (55 g) firmly packed brown sugar

1   cup (100 g) whole pecans

¼   teaspoon ground cinnamon

⅛   teaspoon salt

hummingbird cake

MAKES ONE TWO-LAYER 8-INCH (20-CM) CAKE; SERVES 12 TO 15

Make the
DRIED PINEAPPLE FLOWERS

1. Preheat the oven to 225°F (110°C). Line two baking sheets with parchment paper.

2. Remove the top and bottom of the pineapple and cut away the skin. Using a paring knife or small melon baller, remove the "eyes." Cut the pineapple crosswise into thin slices, no more than ¼ inch (6 mm) thick.

3. Place the slices on the lined baking sheets and bake for about 2 hours, or until dried out, flipping them over halfway through. Remove from the oven. While the slices are still warm, carefully place each one into the well of a cupcake tin. Gently press them into the wells to form a "cup" shape. Let the slices dry completely for a couple of hours or overnight in order to best retain a flowerlike shape.

Make the
HUMMINGBIRD CAKE

4. Preheat the oven to 350°F (175°C). Grease and flour two 8-inch (20-cm) cake pans and set aside.

5. Sift together the flour, cinnamon, baking powder, baking soda, and salt and set aside.

6. In the bowl of a stand mixer fitted with the paddle attachment, beat the oil and sugars together on medium speed for 2 minutes. Turn the mixer to medium-low and add the vanilla and eggs one at a time. Stop the mixer and scrape down the bowl.

7. Turn the mixer to low and add the flour mixture in two batches. Add the bananas and pineapple and mix until combined. Fold in the pecans.

8. Evenly divide the batter between the prepared pans. Bake for 24 to 26 minutes, or until a toothpick inserted into the center of the cakes comes out clean. Let them cool on a wire rack for 10 to 15 minutes before removing the cakes from their pans.

Make the
CREAM CHEESE FROSTING

9. In the bowl of a stand mixer fitted with the paddle attachment, beat the cream cheese and butter together until smooth. With the mixer on low, gradually add the confectioners' sugar, milk, and vanilla until incorporated. Turn the mixer to medium-high and mix until the frosting is fluffy.

Make the
MAPLE CANDIED PECANS

10. Line a baking sheet with parchment paper.

11. Melt the butter in a saucepan over medium heat. Add the maple syrup and brown sugar and stir until the sugar has dissolved. Add the pecans, cinnamon, and salt and stir with a wooden spoon to coat the pecans. Cook over medium-low heat for about 5 minutes. Remove from the heat and spread the pecans on the lined baking sheet to cool and dry, about 10 minutes.

ASSEMBLE THE CAKE

12. Once the cakes have completely cooled, level them and choose which layer will be at the bottom. Place it on a cake plate or serving dish. Spread on ¾ to 1 cup (180 to 240 ml) of the frosting with an offset spatula. Top with the second layer of cake. Frost the top and sides with the remaining frosting and decorate with the candied pecans and pineapple flowers.

DECORATE IT

Place pecans and pineapple flowers in rings around the top and base of the cake. Alternatively, make patterns on the sides or top of the cake with the pecans or serve each slice of cake with a pineapple flower on top.

BAKER'S NOTES

The cake will keep in the fridge for up to 3 days (see page 25). Store the pineapple flowers separately.

GOT LEFTOVERS?

Store the maple candied pecans in an airtight container and eat them as a sweet snack, chop and sprinkle them over salad or yogurt, or add to trail mix.

WHIMSICAL CAKES

Many of the cakes in this section boast flavors reminiscent of other classic desserts, but in the form of layer cakes. From cinnamon roll to banana split, the inspirations behind these cakes are fun and are intended to evoke feelings of joy and nostalgia. They are youthful in nature, but can be enjoyed by all ages. The flavors are bright and lively, with playful twists and even some cookie dough. Grab your favorite sprinkles and a blowtorch, and let the party begin!

WHAT'S A BOOK ABOUT LAYER CAKES without a rainbow cake? Despite the absence of an ultra-imaginative flavor combination, this cake is just plain fun. The cake itself is a yellow butter cake dyed all sorts of whimsical colors. Covered in sprinkles that conceal a rainbow surprise inside, this cake is guaranteed to make you smile.

For the
RAINBOW BUTTER CAKE

	Butter or nonstick cooking spray, for the pans
4½	cups (585 g) cake flour, plus more for the pans
1½	tablespoons baking powder
1	teaspoon salt
1½	cups (3 sticks / 340 g) unsalted butter, at room temperature
3	cups (600 g) granulated sugar
1	tablespoon pure vanilla extract
9	large egg yolks
2¼	cups (540 ml) whole milk
	Assorted gel food colorings (*I used 6 colors*)

For the
ASSEMBLY

1	medium recipe Vanilla Swiss Meringue Buttercream (page 41)
1	to 1½ cups (180 to 270 g) sprinkles

Make the
RAINBOW BUTTER CAKE

1. Preheat the oven to 350°F (175°C). Grease and flour six 6-inch (15-cm) cake pans (see Baker's Notes) and set aside.

2. Sift together the flour, baking powder, and salt and set aside.

3. In the bowl of a stand mixer fitted with the paddle attachment, beat the butter on medium speed until smooth. Add the sugar and mix on medium-high until the butter is light and fluffy, 3 to 5 minutes. Stop the mixer and scrape down the bowl.

4. Turn the mixer to medium-low and add the vanilla and egg yolks one at a time. Stop the mixer and scrape down the bowl.

5. Turn the mixer to low and add the flour mixture in three batches, alternating with the milk, beginning and ending with the flour mixture. Mix on medium until just after the last streaks of the dry ingredients are combined.

6. Evenly divide the batter among six small bowls. Tint the batter in each bowl a different color, starting with a couple of drops of gel coloring at a time and stirring to combine. Add more gel until the desired colors are achieved.

7. Place one dyed batter in each prepared pan. Bake for 20 to 24 minutes, or until a toothpick inserted into the center of the cakes comes out clean. Rotate pans halfway through baking. Let them cool on a wire rack for 10 minutes before removing the cakes from their pans.

ASSEMBLE THE CAKE

8. Once the cakes have completely cooled, level them and choose which layer will be at the bottom. Place it on a cake plate or serving dish. Spread on ½ cup (120 ml) of the buttercream with an offset spatula. Top with the next layer of cake and repeat with the buttercream and layers. Smoothly frost the top and sides of the cake with the remaining buttercream.

9. Over a baking sheet or large piece of parchment paper, press handfuls of sprinkles against the sides of the cake. Continue around the cake, using the sprinkles that fall off as you go, until the cake is completely covered.

DECORATE IT

Fill a piping bag fitted with an open star piping tip with the remaining buttercream and create a spiral border (see page 37) around the top. Garnish with extra sprinkles. Alternatively, cover the top of the cake with sprinkles as well. For more tips on decorating with sprinkles, see "Edible Garnishes" on page 39. You can also use Homemade Sprinkles (page 188).

BAKER'S NOTES

If you do not have six 6-inch (15-cm) pans, work in batches. Just bake two or three colors at a time, then wash the pans and bake the remaining colors of batter. The cake will keep in the fridge for up to 4 days; it may also be frozen (see page 25).

---

rainbow sprinkle cake

MAKES ONE SIX-LAYER 6-INCH (15-CM) CAKE; SERVES 12 TO 15

MY HUSBAND, BRETT, AND HIS SIBLINGS were often treated to cinnamon rolls on the weekends. Brett is the youngest child by many years and always got to select which roll he wanted first. Being the big sweet tooth that he is, he remembers always picking the one from the middle of the pan—the one with the most frosting. Clever kid! I developed this cake with him and the roll in the middle of the pan in mind. The cream cheese in this Cinnamon Roll Cake makes it extra rich and velvety, while the ribbons of cinnamon throughout give it a punch of flavor. Serve it as a special weekend breakfast treat or to celebrate with any cinnamon roll enthusiast.

For the
CINNAMON SWIRL CAKE

	Butter or nonstick cooking spray, for the pans
2¼	cups (295 g) cake flour, plus more for the pans
2	teaspoons baking powder
½	teaspoon salt
¼	cup (60 ml) sour cream
½	cup (120 ml) whole milk
1	cup (2 sticks / 225 g) unsalted butter, at room temperature
4	ounces (115 g) cream cheese, softened
1½	cups (300 g) granulated sugar
2	teaspoons vanilla bean paste
3	large eggs
1	large egg yolk
4	tablespoons (½ stick / 55 g) butter, melted
¼	cup (55 g) firmly packed brown sugar
2	teaspoons ground cinnamon

For the
CINNAMON CRUMBLE

½	cup (65 g) all-purpose flour
⅓	cup (75 g) firmly packed brown sugar
4	tablespoons (½ stick / 55 g) unsalted butter, at room temperature
1	tablespoon honey
2	teaspoons ground cinnamon

For the
CREAM CHEESE FROSTING

8	ounces (225 g) cream cheese, softened
¾	cup (1½ sticks / 170 g) unsalted butter, at room temperature
3	cups (375 g) confectioners' sugar, sifted
2	tablespoons whole milk
1½	teaspoons vanilla bean paste

For the
CINNAMON SYRUP

½	cup (100 g) granulated sugar
½	teaspoon ground cinnamon
⅛	teaspoon salt
1	tablespoon unsalted butter
1	tablespoon all-purpose flour

cinnamon roll cake

—

MAKES ONE TWO-LAYER 8-INCH (20-CM) CAKE; SERVES 10 TO 12

Make the
CINNAMON SWIRL CAKE

1. Preheat the oven to 350°F (175°C). Grease and flour two 8-inch (20-cm) cake pans and set aside.

2. Sift together the flour, baking powder, and salt and set aside.

3. Stir together the sour cream and milk and set aside.

4. In the bowl of a stand mixer fitted with the paddle attachment, beat the butter and cream cheese on medium speed until smooth. Add the granulated sugar and mix on medium-high until light and fluffy, 3 to 5 minutes. Stop the mixer and scrape down the bowl.

5. Turn the mixer to medium-low and add the vanilla, then add the eggs and egg yolk one at a time. Stop the mixer and scrape down the bowl.

6. Turn the mixer to low and add the flour mixture in three batches, alternating with the milk mixture, beginning and ending with the flour mixture. Mix on medium for no more than 30 seconds after the last streaks of the dry ingredients are combined.

7. In a small bowl, mix together the melted butter, brown sugar, and cinnamon.

8. Pour one-quarter of the batter into each of the prepared pans. Spoon one-quarter of the cinnamon mixture on top of the batter in each pan and use a wooden skewer or the tip of a knife to gently swirl it. Divide the remaining batter between the pans. Divide the remaining cinnamon mixture between

the pans and gently swirl it. Bake for 24 to 26 minutes, or until a toothpick inserted into the center of the cakes comes out clean. Let them cool on a wire rack for 10 to 15 minutes before removing the cakes from their pans.

Make the
CINNAMON CRUMBLE

9. While the oven is still at 350°F (175°C), line a baking sheet with parchment paper.

10. In a medium bowl, mix together the flour, brown sugar, butter, honey, and cinnamon with a wooden spoon until combined. The mixture should resemble little clumps of sand. Sprinkle them over the lined baking sheet and bake for 8 to 10 minutes, stirring halfway through, or until golden brown. Let the crumble cool before use.

Make the
CREAM CHEESE FROSTING

11. In the bowl of a stand mixer fitted with the paddle attachment, beat the cream cheese and butter together on medium speed until smooth. With the mixer on low, gradually add the confectioners' sugar, milk, and vanilla until incorporated. Turn the mixer up to medium-high and mix until the frosting is fluffy.

Make the
CINNAMON SYRUP

12. Just before assembling the cake, in a saucepan, place 2 tablespoons water with the sugar, cinnamon, and salt. Heat over medium-high until the sugar has completely dissolved and the mixture starts to

simmer. Remove the pan from the heat and stir in the butter until melted. Mix in the flour until combined.

13. Let the syrup cool slightly, then use it immediately before it thickens.

ASSEMBLE THE CAKE

14. Once the cakes have completely cooled, level them and choose which layer will be at the bottom. Place it on a cake plate or serving dish. Spread on half of the cream cheese frosting with an offset spatula. Sprinkle it with the cinnamon crumble pieces. Drizzle half the cinnamon syrup over the top. Top with the second layer of cake and repeat with the remaining frosting. Use a spoon and a zigzag motion to drizzle the remaining cinnamon syrup across the top layer of cake, letting it drip over the edges. Discard any extra syrup.

BAKER'S NOTES

The cinnamon crumble may be made in advance and stored in an airtight container for up to 1 week. The cake will keep in the fridge for up to 3 days (see page 25).

GOT LEFTOVERS?

Sprinkle extra cinnamon crumble over ice cream!

oatmeal cookie cake

—

MAKES ONE TWO-LAYER 8-INCH (20-CM) CAKE; SERVES 12 TO 15

ONE OF MY GUILTY PLEASURES is eating a handful of those thin, packaged oatmeal cookies with glaze on top. The crispy texture is probably my favorite part, yet I still have the desire to dunk them in milk to create the perfect crispy-yet-soggy bite. I've never been able to replicate the recipe, and usually end up settling for eating the dough straight from the bowl. This Oatmeal Cookie Cake combines those childlike behaviors with a sophisticated muscovado cake to create one incredible dessert for all ages.

The muscovado sugar in this cake creates a rich, dark molasses flavor that balances out the playful cookie dough filling perfectly. Serve it with the cream cheese glaze and a tall glass of cold milk.

For the
MUSCOVADO CAKE

	Butter or nonstick cooking spray, for the pans
3¼	cups (425 g) cake flour, plus more for the pans
2	teaspoons baking powder
1	teaspoon baking soda
½	teaspoon salt
1	cup (2 sticks / 225 g) unsalted butter, at room temperature
1	cup (185 g) firmly packed muscovado sugar
½	cup (100 g) granulated sugar
2	tablespoons honey
1	tablespoon molasses
2	teaspoons pure vanilla extract
3	large eggs
2	large egg yolks
1	cup plus 2 tablespoons (270 ml) buttermilk

For the
OATMEAL COOKIE DOUGH FROSTING

½	cup (1 stick / 115 g) unsalted butter, at room temperature
⅓	cup (75 g) firmly packed brown sugar
⅓	cup (30 g) quick-cooking oats, slightly toasted
¼	cup (30 g) all-purpose flour
¼	cup (45 g) mini chocolate chips
1	teaspoon plus 2 tablespoons whole milk
½	teaspoon pure vanilla extract
½	teaspoon ground cinnamon
¼	teaspoon salt
¼	teaspoon pure almond extract
1	cup (125 g) confectioners' sugar, sifted

For the
CREAM CHEESE GLAZE

4	ounces (115 g) cream cheese, softened
½	cup (65 g) confectioners' sugar, sifted
1	teaspoon vanilla bean paste
1½	teaspoons whole milk, plus more as needed

Make the
MUSCOVADO CAKE

1. Preheat the oven to 350°F (175°C). Grease and flour two 8-inch (20-cm) pans and set aside.

2. Sift together the flour, baking powder, baking soda, and salt and set aside.

3. In the bowl of a stand mixer fitted with the paddle attachment, beat the butter on medium speed until smooth. Add the sugars and mix on medium-high until the butter is light and fluffy, 3 to 5 minutes. Stop the mixer and scrape down the bowl.

4. Turn the mixer to medium-low and add the honey, molasses, vanilla, and the eggs and egg yolks, one at a time, until combined. Stop the mixer and scrape down the bowl.

5. Turn the mixer to low and add the flour mixture in three batches, alternating with the buttermilk, beginning and ending with the flour mixture. Mix on medium for no more than 30 seconds after the last streaks of the dry ingredients are combined.

6. Evenly divide the batter between the prepared pans. Bake for 25 to 28 minutes, or until a toothpick inserted into the center of the cakes comes out clean. Let them cool on a wire rack for 10 to 15 minutes before removing the cakes from their pans.

Make the
OATMEAL COOKIE DOUGH FROSTING

7. Combine ¼ cup (½ stick / 55 g) of the butter with the brown sugar, oats, flour, chocolate chips, 1 teaspoon of the milk, the vanilla, cinnamon, salt, and almond extract in a bowl with a wooden spoon and stir until combined.

8. Place the remaining butter in the bowl of a stand mixer fitted with the paddle attachment and beat it on medium speed until smooth. With the mixer on low, gradually add the confectioners' sugar and remaining 2 tablespoons milk until incorporated. Turn the mixer to medium-high and mix until the frosting is fluffy. Stop the mixer and scrape down the bowl. Add the oatmeal cookie dough mixture and mix until combined.

ASSEMBLE THE CAKE

9. Once the cakes have completely cooled, choose which layer will be at the bottom. Place it on a cake plate or serving dish. Spread on all of the cookie dough frosting with an offset spatula. Invert the second cake and place it on top, bottom-side up.

Make the
CREAM CHEESE GLAZE

10. Stir the cream cheese with a wooden spoon until smooth and free from any lumps. Whisk in the confectioners' sugar, vanilla, and milk until thick but spreadable. Add a splash more milk, as needed, if the glaze is too thick to spread over the top of the cake.

11. Spread the glaze over the top of the cake, letting it run down over the sides.

BAKER'S NOTES

If making in advance, store the cake wrapped in plastic in the fridge. Make the glaze just before serving. Leftovers will keep in the fridge for up to 3 days (see page 25).

MY MEMORIES OF VISITING FAMILY IN HAWAII mostly revolve around food. My childhood was made up of eating *hulihuli* chicken, hunting down sugary *malasadas* from Leonard's Bakery, licking cones full of sticky shaved ice, and lunching at the now-famous shrimp trucks. I remember rolling *lumpia* with my aunties and making butter cookies by the dozen—everyone singing, laughing, and sharing family recipes, except for my aunt Mila's secret mango pie recipe. Her recipe is not mine to share, but this Mango Coconut Cream Cake is its jovial cake cousin. The vanilla-flecked coconut cake is tender and aromatic, while the white chocolate mango ganache is mellow yet enticing—all blanketed in fluffy coconut.

For the
VANILLA COCONUT CAKE

	Butter or nonstick cooking spray, for the pans
3¼	cups (425 g) cake flour, plus more for the pans
1	tablespoon baking powder
½	teaspoon salt
1	cup (240 ml) coconut milk
⅓	cup (80 ml) whole milk
½	cup (1 stick / 115 g) unsalted butter, at room temperature
½	cup (120 ml) melted coconut oil
2	cups (400 g) granulated sugar
	Seeds of 1 vanilla bean (see Baker's Notes, page 169)
2	teaspoons pure coconut extract
6	large egg yolks

For the
MANGO GANACHE

2	cups (12 ounces / 340 g) chopped white chocolate
½	cup (120 ml) mango puree (see Baker's Notes, page 169)
1	tablespoon unsalted butter, diced

For the
COCONUT CREAM
CHEESE FROSTING

6	ounces (170 g) cream cheese, softened
¾	cup (1½ sticks / 170 g) unsalted butter, at room temperature
4	cups (500 g) confectioners' sugar, sifted
3	tablespoons coconut cream (see Baker's Notes, page 169)
½	teaspoon pure coconut extract
	Splash of coconut milk or whole milk, if needed

For the
ASSEMBLY

| 2 | to 2½ cups (170 to 215 g) shredded sweetened coconut |

mango coconut cream cake

MAKES ONE THREE-LAYER 8-INCH (20-CM) CAKE; SERVES 12 TO 15

Make the
VANILLA COCONUT CAKE

1. Preheat the oven to 350°F (175°C). Grease and flour three 8-inch (20-cm) cake pans and set aside.

2. Sift together the flour, baking powder, and salt and set aside.

3. Stir together the coconut milk and whole milk. Set aside.

4. In the bowl of a stand mixer fitted with the paddle attachment, beat the butter, coconut oil, and sugar on medium-high speed until light and fluffy, 3 to 5 minutes. Add the vanilla bean seeds and mix for another minute. Stop the mixer and scrape down the bowl.

5. Turn the mixer to medium-low and add the coconut extract and egg yolks one at a time. Stop the mixer and scrape down the bowl.

6. Turn the mixer to low and add the flour mixture in three batches, alternating with the milk mixture, beginning and ending with the flour mixture. Mix on medium for no more than 30 seconds after the last streaks of the dry ingredients are combined.

7. Evenly divide the batter among the prepared pans. Bake for 23 to 25 minutes, or until a toothpick inserted into the cakes comes out clean. Let them cool on a wire rack for 10 to 15 minutes before removing the cakes from their pans.

Make the
MANGO GANACHE

8. Place the white chocolate in a heat-safe bowl and set aside. In a medium saucepan, bring the mango puree to a slow simmer over medium-low heat. Remove it from the heat and pour it over the chocolate. Let sit for 30 seconds, then whisk together until smooth. Add the butter and stir until combined (see Baker's Notes).

Make the
COCONUT CREAM CHEESE FROSTING

9. In the bowl of a stand mixer fitted with the paddle attachment, beat the cream cheese and butter on medium-low speed for 2 minutes. With the mixer on low, gradually add the confectioners' sugar, coconut cream, and coconut extract until everything starts to incorporate. Turn the mixer to medium-high and mix until the frosting is light and fluffy. Add a splash of milk if the frosting seems a bit thick, or until it reaches a spreadable consistency, if necessary.

ASSEMBLE THE CAKE

10. Once the cakes have completely cooled, level them and choose which layer will be at the bottom. Place it on a serving dish. Spread on half of the ganache with an offset spatula. Top with the next layer of cake and repeat with the ganache, ending with the third layer. Frost the top and sides of the cake with the coconut cream cheese frosting. Cover the cake with shredded coconut (see page 39).

BAKER'S NOTES

If the white chocolate and butter do not completely melt, place the bowl over a saucepan of simmering water until everything is melted and combined. Use an immersion blender to thoroughly incorporate, if necessary. If making your own mango puree, I highly recommend using Ataulfo mangoes. They have a thinner skin and smaller pit, and I find them to be much sweeter and more flavorful than other mangoes. If coconut cream is unavailable, you may substitute coconut milk. If using canned coconut milk and it separates, use the coconut solids that rise to the top of the can. Two teaspoons vanilla bean paste may substituted for vanilla bean seeds. The cake will keep in the fridge for up to 3 days (see page 25).

banana cream cake

——

MAKES ONE TWO-LAYER 8-INCH (20-CM) CAKE; SERVES 12 TO 15

WHEN I WAS IN COLLEGE, MY MOTHER AND I went to New York City every spring. We saw Broadway shows and hit up as many bakeries as we could find to test out new pastries. I'd heard about this itty-bitty corner bakery down on Bleecker Street. I was told they had the best cupcakes, and although I hadn't had a cupcake since I was a kid, we decided to check it out. This was before cupcakes got trendy and iPhone maps directed you to your destination's doorstep. I remember taking the subway down to the West Village and getting all turned around. We almost gave up until I saw a cupcake wrapper on the sidewalk. A little farther down, I saw that someone had devastatingly dropped a nearly whole cupcake on the ground. Then we rounded the corner and found a line out the door for Magnolia Bakery. What I didn't know was that they were also known for their banana pudding. Rich and creamy, the layers of bananas, crushed cookies, and thick vanilla custard were out of this world. This recipe combines a rich vanilla butter cake (much like the cupcake I enjoyed years ago) and my adaptation of Magnolia Bakery's Famous Banana Pudding.

For the
BANANA CUSTARD

2	cups (480 ml) whole milk, plus more as needed
1	vanilla bean, split lengthwise
2	ripe bananas, sliced crosswise
⅔	cup (135 g) granulated sugar
5	egg yolks
6	tablespoons (45 g) cornstarch
2	tablespoons unsalted butter

For the
VANILLA BEAN BUTTER CAKE

	Butter or nonstick cooking spray, for the pans
3¼	cups (425 g) cake flour, plus more for the pans
1	tablespoon plus ½ teaspoon baking powder
¾	teaspoon salt
1	cup (2 sticks / 225 g) unsalted butter, at room temperature
2	cups (400 g) granulated sugar
	Seeds of 1 vanilla bean
½	teaspoon pure vanilla extract
6	large egg yolks
1½	cups (360 ml) whole milk

For the
ASSEMBLY

1	medium recipe Vanilla Swiss Meringue Buttercream (page 41)
	Gel food coloring (*optional*)
10	to 15 vanilla wafer cookies, broken but not crumbled

Make the
BANANA CUSTARD

1. In a medium sauce-pan, combine the milk, vanilla bean seeds and scraped-out pod, and sliced bananas and place over low heat. Bring to a simmer and cook for 3 to 5 minutes. Remove the pan from the heat and pour the mixture into a heat-safe container. Refrigerate it for 12 to 24 hours.

2. Strain the banana milk through a mesh sieve into a measuring cup, discarding the solids in the sieve. Top off the measure with enough milk to make 2 cups (480 ml) total. Pour it into a saucepan and slowly bring it to a simmer over medium-low heat, being careful not to burn the milk.

3. Meanwhile, combine the sugar, egg yolks, and corn-starch in a mixing bowl with a balloon whisk.

4. Once the milk is hot, temper it into the bowl by whisking a small amount at a time into the egg mixture to slowly raise the temperature of the eggs. Transfer everything back to the saucepan.

5. Place the saucepan back on the stove and cook the custard over low heat. Whisk the mixture until it thickens and starts to bubble. Remove the pan from the heat and stir in the butter until smooth.

6. Transfer the custard to a bowl and cover it with plastic wrap, pressing it directly against the sur-face of the custard to pre-vent a skin from forming. Refrigerate it until cool and thick, or overnight.

Make the
VANILLA BEAN BUTTER CAKE

7. Preheat the oven to 350°F (175°C). Grease and flour two 8-inch (20-cm) cake pans and set aside.

8. Sift together the flour, baking powder, and salt and set aside.

9. In the bowl of a stand mixer fitted with the pad-dle attachment, beat the butter on medium speed until smooth. Add the sugar and mix on medium-high until the butter is light and fluffy, 3 to 5 min-utes. Stop the mixer and scrape down the bowl.

10. Turn the mixer to medium-low and add the vanilla bean seeds, vanilla extract, and egg yolks one at a time. Stop the mixer and scrape down the bowl.

11. Turn the mixer to low and add the flour mixture in three batches, alternating with the milk, beginning and ending with the flour mixture. Mix on medium for no more than 30 sec-onds after the last streaks of the dry ingredients are combined.

12. Evenly divide the batter between the prepared pans. Bake for 25 to 28 minutes, or until a tooth-pick inserted into the center of the cakes comes out clean. Let them cool on a wire rack for 10 to 15 minutes before removing the cakes from their pans.

ASSEMBLE THE CAKE

13. Tint the buttercream with the food coloring of your choice, if using. Transfer the buttercream to a pastry bag fitted with a medium round tip.

14. Once the cakes have completely cooled, level them and choose which layer will be at the bottom. Place it on a cake plate or serving dish. Pipe a double-height ring of but-tercream around the top edge of the cake to create a dam 1½ inches (4 cm) tall (see page 27). Whisk the custard to loosen it, if necessary, and transfer it to a pastry bag fitted with a medium round tip. Pipe half the custard inside the buttercream ring. Place the cookies on top and cover them with the remaining custard. Top with the second layer of cake.

15. Crumb coat the sides with the buttercream to seal in the custard. Frost with the remaining buttercream.

DECORATE IT

Using your desired color palette, frost the cake with a watercolor ombré finish (see page 34). Alternatively, use any of the but-tercream finishes (see pages 30 to 35) to frost the cake.

BAKER'S NOTES

The banana custard may be pre-pared up to 3 days ahead of time and stored separately and tightly covered in the refrigerator. Once assembled, eat the cake immedi-ately or keep refrigerated for up to 2 days, until 30 minutes before serving (see page 25).

---

blueberry pancake cake

MAKES ONE THREE-LAYER 8-INCH (20-CM) CAKE; SERVES 12 TO 15

MY MOM'S FAVORITE MEAL TO EAT OUT IS BREAKFAST. As the main cook in our house when I was growing up, she always remarked on how difficult it was to get breakfast on the table for everyone at the same time. Whether it is made-to-order eggs, pancakes, or waffles, the cook definitely gets the short end of the stick—not being able to enjoy her own meal until after everyone else is served. I usually snack on the ugly pancakes next to the stove when I cook breakfast, so I totally understand Mom's point. For all of you short-order cooks out there, make this Blueberry Pancake Cake and enjoy a slice with the rest of your guests at your next brunch or special breakfast.

For the
**BLUEBERRY
BUTTERMILK CAKE**

	Butter or nonstick cooking spray, for the pans
3	cups plus 2 tablespoons (405 g) cake flour, plus more for the pans
2	teaspoons baking powder
1	teaspoon ground cinnamon
½	teaspoon baking soda
½	teaspoon salt
1	cup (2 sticks / 225 g) unsalted butter, at room temperature
2	cups (400 g) granulated sugar
2	teaspoons finely grated lemon zest
1	teaspoon pure vanilla extract
3	large eggs
2	large egg yolks
1¼	cups (300 ml) buttermilk
1½	cups (220 g) fresh blueberries (see Baker's Notes, page 175)

For the
**MAPLE BROWN SUGAR
BUTTERCREAM**

½	cup plus 2 tablespoons (150 ml) large egg whites
1	cup (220 g) firmly packed brown sugar
1	teaspoon pure vanilla extract
1	cup (2 sticks / 225 g) unsalted butter, at room temperature, cubed
3	to 4 tablespoons (45 to 60 ml) maple syrup

For the
**CINNAMON
WHIPPED CREAM**

2	cups (480 ml) cold heavy cream
3	tablespoons granulated sugar
1	teaspoon pure vanilla extract
¾	teaspoon ground cinnamon

Make the
BLUEBERRY BUTTERMILK CAKE

1. Preheat the oven to 350°F (175°C). Grease and flour three 8-inch (20-cm) cake pans and set aside.

2. Sift together 3 cups (390 g) of the flour, the baking powder, cinnamon, baking soda, and salt and set aside.

3. In the bowl of a stand mixer fitted with the paddle attachment, beat the butter on medium speed until smooth. Add the sugar and lemon zest. Turn the mixer to medium-high and mix until the butter is light and fluffy, 3 to 5 minutes. Stop the mixer and scrape down the bowl.

4. Turn the mixer to medium-low and add the vanilla, then add the eggs and egg yolks one at a time. Stop the mixer and scrape down the bowl.

5. Turn the mixer to low and add the flour mixture in three batches, alternating with the buttermilk, beginning and ending with the flour mixture. Mix on medium for no more than 30 seconds after the last streaks of the dry ingredients are combined.

6. Toss the blueberries in the remaining 2 tablespoons of the flour. Gently fold about 1 cup (145 g) of the blueberries into the batter.

7. Evenly divide the batter among the prepared pans. Sprinkle the remaining berries on top of the batter, dividing them evenly. Bake for 23 to 25 minutes, or until a toothpick inserted into the center of the cakes comes out clean. Let them cool on a wire rack for 10 to 15 minutes before removing the cakes from their pans.

Make the
MAPLE BROWN SUGAR BUTTERCREAM

8. Place the egg whites and brown sugar in the bowl of a stand mixer. Whisk them together by hand to combine. Fill a medium saucepan with a few inches of water and place it over medium-high heat. Place the mixer bowl on top of the saucepan to create a double boiler. The bottom of the bowl should not touch the water. Whisking intermittently, heat the egg mixture until it registers 160°F (70°C) on a candy thermometer or is hot to the touch. Once hot, carefully fit the mixer bowl onto the stand mixer.

9. With the whisk attachment, beat the egg white mixture on high speed for 8 to 10 minutes, until it holds medium-stiff peaks. When done, the outside of the mixer bowl should return to room temperature and no residual heat should be escaping the meringue out of the top of the bowl. Stop the mixer and swap out the whisk for the paddle attachment.

10. With the mixer on low speed, add the vanilla and butter, a couple of cubes at a time (see Baker's Notes). Add the syrup and turn the mixer to medium-high. Beat until the buttercream is silky smooth, 3 to 5 minutes.

Make the
CINNAMON WHIPPED CREAM

11. In the bowl of a stand mixer fitted with the whisk attachment, whisk the cream on medium speed until it starts to thicken. Add the sugar, vanilla, and cinnamon. Whisk on high until medium peaks form.

For best results, whip the cream just before assembling or store separately in the refrigerator (see Baker's Notes).

ASSEMBLE THE CAKE

12. Once the cakes have completely cooled, level them and choose which layer will be at the bottom. Place it on a cake plate or serving dish. Spread on half the buttercream with an offset spatula. Top with the next layer of cake and repeat with the buttercream, finishing with the last layer. Frost the top and sides with the cinnamon whipped cream, using an offset spatula to create a rustic finish (see page 31).

BAKER'S NOTES

If the buttercream starts to look "curdled" after adding the butter, just keep mixing. The butter is probably too cold and will need more time to incorporate (see "Tips and Troubleshooting" section, page 42). If fresh blueberries are unavailable, you may substitute frozen blueberries. Quickly rinse and dry the berries, but do not thaw them. The whipped cream may be made up to 8 hours ahead of time and stored separately and tightly covered in the refrigerator. Once assembled, eat the cake immediately or keep refrigerated, for up to 2 days, until 30 minutes before serving (see page 25).

AS SOON AS WE LAND ON OAHU TO VISIT FAMILY, we always stop for a local lunch and stock up on our favorite treats. Whether we are eating breakfast on the lanai or preparing lunch for the beach, each of us has our go-to snacks that are easier to find on the islands. My stash always includes Hawaiian soda crackers, orange and passion fruit juice, and guava jam, not to mention fresh coconut, *li hing* pickled mango, and papaya from the Kahuku farm stand. Needless to say, I definitely have an appetite for tropical flavors and exotic treats, especially the tart, vibrant passion fruit filling in this dessert. It brilliantly complements the tender butter cake speckled with poppy seeds and aromatic orange zest. The cake is frosted with tinted vanilla buttercream to resemble the many island sunsets I've been fortunate to witness over the years.

For the
ORANGE POPPY SEED CAKE

	Butter or nonstick cooking spray, for the pans
2¼	cups (295 g) cake flour, plus more for the pans
1	teaspoon baking powder
½	teaspoon baking soda
¼	teaspoon salt
¾	cup (1½ sticks / 170 g) unsalted butter, at room temperature
1½	cups (300 g) granulated sugar
2	tablespoons finely grated orange zest
4	large egg whites
¼	cup (60 ml) fresh orange juice (from 1 to 2 oranges)
¾	cup (180 ml) buttermilk
2	teaspoons poppy seeds

For the
PASSION FRUIT BUTTERCREAM

1	medium recipe Vanilla Swiss Meringue Buttercream (page 41)
2	to 3 tablespoons passion fruit concentrate (see Baker's Notes, page 179)

For the
ASSEMBLY

Remaining Vanilla Swiss Meringue Buttercream

Gel food coloring (*optional*)

Sprinkles and/or sugar pearls (*optional*)

orange passion fruit cake

MAKES ONE THREE-LAYER 6-INCH (15-CM) CAKE; SERVES 8 TO 10

Make the
ORANGE POPPY SEED CAKE

1. Preheat the oven to 350°F (175°C). Grease and flour three 6-inch (15-cm) cake pans and set aside.

2. Sift together the flour, baking powder, baking soda, and salt and set aside.

3. In the bowl of a stand mixer fitted with the paddle attachment, beat the butter on medium speed until smooth. Add the sugar and orange zest. Mix on medium-high until the butter is light and fluffy, 3 to 5 minutes. Stop the mixer and scrape down the bowl.

4. Turn the mixer to medium-low, then gradually add the egg whites and mix until incorporated. Add the orange juice and mix until combined. Stop the mixer and scrape down the bowl.

5. Turn the mixer to low and add the flour mixture in three batches, alternating with the buttermilk, beginning and ending with the flour mixture. Add the poppy seeds. Mix on medium for no more than 30 seconds after the last streaks of the dry ingredients are combined.

6. Evenly divide the batter among the prepared pans. Bake for 22 to 25 minutes, or until a toothpick inserted into the center of the cakes comes out clean. Let them cool on a wire rack for 10 to 15 minutes before removing the cakes from their pans.

Make the
PASSION FRUIT BUTTERCREAM

7. In the bowl of a stand mixer fitted with the paddle attachment, mix 1½ cups (360 ml) of the buttercream until silky smooth. Add the passion fruit concentrate and mix until combined.

ASSEMBLE THE CAKE

8. Tint the remaining vanilla buttercream with the food coloring of your choice, if using.

9. Once the cakes have completely cooled, level them and choose which layer will be at the bottom. Place it on a cake plate or serving dish. Spread on half the passion fruit buttercream with an offset spatula. Top with the next layer of cake and repeat with the passion fruit buttercream, finishing with the final layer. Frost the cake with the tinted buttercream and garnish with sprinkles and sugar pearls, if using.

DECORATE IT

Select your desired color palette and frost the cake with the remaining buttercream to create a smooth ombré finish (see page 34). Scatter or place sugar pearls and sprinkles on top of the cake, letting them fall onto the sides, if desired. Alternatively, use any of the buttercream finishes (see pages 30 to 35) to frost the cake.

BAKER'S NOTES

Look for passion fruit concentrate online or even at your local grocery store. If you are having trouble sourcing it, you can reduce passion fruit juice by simmering 1 cup (240 ml) until it reduces to about ¼ cup (60 ml). The cake will keep in the fridge for up to 4 days; it may also be frozen (see page 25).

s'mores cake

MAKES ONE THREE-LAYER 8-INCH (20-CM) CAKE; SERVES 12 TO 15

I GREW UP IN A PART-SUBURBAN, PART-COUNTRY neighborhood. Our yard backed up to a horse ranch and was large enough to camp out in during the summer. I remember toasting marshmallows and making homemade s'mores under the stars with all the neighborhood kids. As adults, my husband, Brett, and I decided to sacrifice the square footage and big backyards to have a chic city apartment. It is sad to think that our children may only experience toasted marshmallows from the gas fireplace. If you are in the same boat, let me introduce you to the kitchen torch. Not only is it good for a multitude of pastry needs, but it is great for toasting up a marshmallowy meringue. Layers of cinnamon buttermilk cake and creamy chocolate are slathered with fluffy meringue icing. A quick torch, and voilà—instant indoor s'mores flavor for all you city dwellers.

For the
CINNAMON BUTTERMILK CAKE

	Butter or nonstick cooking spray, for the pans
3	cups (390 g) cake flour, plus more for the pans
2	teaspoons baking powder
2	teaspoons ground cinnamon
½	teaspoon freshly grated nutmeg
½	teaspoon baking soda
½	teaspoon salt
1	cup (2 sticks / 225 g) unsalted butter, at room temperature
1¼	cups (250 g) granulated sugar
½	cup (110 g) firmly packed light brown sugar
2	teaspoons pure vanilla extract
3	large eggs
2	large egg yolks
1¼	cups (300 ml) buttermilk

For the
MILK CHOCOLATE FUDGE FROSTING

½	cup (1 stick / 115 g) unsalted butter, at room temperature
2	cups (250 g) confectioners' sugar, sifted
3	tablespoons unsweetened cocoa powder
⅛	teaspoon salt
½	teaspoon pure vanilla extract
2	tablespoons heavy cream or whole milk
6	ounces (170 g) milk chocolate, melted and cooled

For the
MERINGUE FROSTING

¾	cup (180 ml) large egg whites
1½	cups (300 g) granulated sugar
2	teaspoons pure vanilla extract

Make the
CINNAMON BUTTERMILK CAKE

1. Preheat the oven to 350°F (175°C). Grease and flour three 8-inch (20-cm) cake pans and set aside.

2. Sift together the flour, baking powder, cinnamon, nutmeg, baking soda, and salt and set aside.

3. In the bowl of a stand mixer fitted with the paddle attachment, beat the butter on medium speed until smooth. Add the sugars and mix on medium-high until the butter is light and fluffy, 3 to 5 minutes. Stop the mixer and scrape down the bowl.

4. Turn the mixer to medium-low and add the vanilla, then add the eggs and egg yolks one at a time. Stop the mixer and scrape down the bowl.

5. Turn the mixer to low and add the flour mixture in three batches, alternating with the buttermilk, beginning and ending with the flour mixture. Mix on medium for no more than 30 seconds after the last streaks of the dry ingredients are combined.

6. Evenly divide the batter among the prepared pans. Bake for 23 to 25 minutes, or until a toothpick inserted into the center of the cakes comes out clean. Let them cool on a wire rack for 10 to 15 minutes before removing the cakes.

Make the
MILK CHOCOLATE FUDGE FROSTING

7. In the bowl of a stand mixer fitted with the paddle attachment, beat the butter on medium speed until smooth. With the mixer on low, gradually add the confectioners' sugar, cocoa powder, salt, and vanilla. Pour in the cream and mix until everything starts to incorporate. Turn the mixer to medium and mix until the frosting is light and fluffy. Stop the mixer and scrape down the bowl. Add the cooled chocolate and mix until smooth.

ASSEMBLE THE CAKE

8. Once the cakes have completely cooled, level them and choose which layer will be at the bottom. Place it on a serving dish. Spread on half the fudge frosting with an offset spatula. Top with the next layer of cake and repeat with the frosting, finishing with the final layer.

Make the
MERINGUE FROSTING

9. Place the egg whites and sugar in the bowl of a stand mixer. Whisk them together by hand to combine. Fill a medium saucepan with a few inches of water and place it over medium-high heat. Place the mixer bowl on top of the saucepan to create a double boiler. The bottom of the bowl should not touch the water. Whisking, heat the mixture until it registers 160°F (70°C) on a candy thermometer. Carefully fit the bowl onto the stand mixer.

10. With the whisk attachment, beat the egg white mixture on high until medium-stiff, glossy peaks form. Add the vanilla and mix until combined. When done, the outside of the mixer bowl should return to room temperature and no residual heat should be escaping from the meringue.

11. With a large offset spatula, frost the top and sides of the cake with the meringue frosting. Use a fluffy, rustic finish (see page 31) to create a textured surface for toasting. Lightly toast with a kitchen torch (see Baker's Notes).

BAKER'S NOTES

Try holding the torch 4 to 6 inches (10 to 15 cm) away from the meringue when toasting. Keep the torch moving and do not leave the flame in one spot for too long. Experiment with distance and length of the flame until the desired look is achieved. Once assembled, eat the cake within 90 minutes or keep refrigerated, for up to 2 days, until 30 minutes before serving (see page 25).

banana split ice cream cake

MAKES ONE THREE-LAYER 6-INCH (15-CM) CAKE; SERVES 10 TO 12

FOR MY TENTH BIRTHDAY, my parents took my friends and me to the water park. I have a June birthday, so I always looked forward to celebrating with an outdoor activity. For some reason, that year I insisted on having an ice cream cake. My accommodating mother fulfilled my wish by transporting a giant ice cream cake all the way to the water park. All seemed well until it was time to cut the cake. I'm sure you can only imagine what happened when we tried to serve and eat it under the hot California sun . . .

Not all ice cream cakes need to become ice cream soup. In fact, making an ice cream cake is not as complicated as you might imagine. And while I don't recommend taking one to a pool party, the allure of getting ice cream and cake in one slice is definitely worth giving this recipe a shot. Plus, the Roasted Banana Chip Cake is killer, especially when paired with this malty chocolate filling. Not into frozen treats? Ditch the ice cream and sub in some Strawberry Cream filling (page 188).

For the
ROASTED BANANA CHIP CAKE

3	ripe bananas, halved lengthwise
1	cup (220 g) firmly packed brown sugar
1	tablespoon grapeseed oil
¼	teaspoon salt
	Butter or nonstick baking spray, for the pan
1½	cups plus 2 tablespoons (205 g) all-purpose flour, plus more for the pan
¾	teaspoon baking powder
½	teaspoon baking soda
¼	teaspoon salt
½	cup (120 ml) sour cream
¼	cup (60 ml) whole milk
½	cup (1 stick / 115 g) unsalted butter, at room temperature
½	cup (100 g) granulated sugar
2	teaspoons vanilla bean paste
2	large eggs
½	cup (90 g) mini chocolate chips

For the
CHOCOLATE MALT POWDER

5	tablespoons plus 1 teaspoon (35 g) dry milk powder
1	teaspoon malt powder
1	teaspoon unsweetened cocoa powder

For the
CHOCOLATE MALT FILLING

10	tablespoons (1¼ sticks / 140 g) unsalted butter, at room temperature
6	tablespoons (40 g) Chocolate Malt Powder (*see above*)
1½	cups (190 g) confectioners' sugar, sifted
½	teaspoon pure vanilla extract
1	to 2 tablespoons whole milk

For the
HONEYED PEANUT TOPPING

½	cup (75 g) whole roasted peanuts, unsalted, chopped
1	teaspoon honey
1	tablespoon granulated sugar
⅛	teaspoon fine salt

For the
ASSEMBLY

1	(1.5-quart / 1.4-L) container strawberry ice cream

For the
WHIPPED CREAM FROSTING

2	cups (480 ml) cold heavy cream
3	tablespoons granulated sugar
1	teaspoon pure vanilla extract
	Gel food coloring (*optional*)
	Sprinkles, for decorating (*optional*)

Make the
ROASTED BANANA CHIP CAKE

1. Preheat the oven to 400°F (205°C). Place the bananas, cut-sides up, in a baking pan. Sprinkle them with ¼ cup (55 g) of the brown sugar, the oil, and the salt. Roast, flipping them over halfway through, until caramelized, 10 to 15 minutes. Remove from the oven and let cool. In a bowl, mash the roasted bananas with a potato masher or large fork and set aside.

2. Reduce the oven temperature to 350°F (175°C). Grease and flour a 10 by 15-inch (25 by 38-cm) rectangular cake pan and set aside (see Baker's Notes).

3. Sift together the flour, baking powder, baking soda, and salt and set aside.

4. Stir together the sour cream and milk and set aside.

5. In the bowl of a stand mixer fitted with the paddle attachment, beat the butter on medium speed until smooth. Add the remaining ¾ cup (165 g) brown sugar and the granulated sugar and mix on medium-high until the butter is light and fluffy, 3 to 5 minutes. Stop the mixer and scrape down the bowl.

6. With the mixer on medium-low, add the vanilla and eggs, one at a time, and mix until combined.

7. Turn the mixer to low and add the flour mixture in three batches, alternating with the milk mixture, beginning and ending with the flour mixture. Add the mashed roasted bananas and mix on medium for no more than 30 seconds. Fold in the chocolate chips.

8. Spread the batter in the prepared pan. Bake for 22 to 24 minutes, or until a toothpick inserted into the center of the cake comes out clean. Let the cake cool on a wire rack.

Make the
CHOCOLATE MALT POWDER

9. Sift together the dry milk powder, malt powder, and cocoa powder. Set aside.

Make the
CHOCOLATE MALT FILLING

10. In the bowl of a stand mixer fitted with the paddle attachment, beat the butter on medium speed until smooth. With the mixer on low, gradually add the chocolate malt powder, confectioners' sugar, vanilla, and 1 tablespoon of the milk until everything starts to incorporate. Turn the mixer to medium-high and mix until the filling is light and fluffy. If the mixture looks too thick, add the remaining 1 tablespoon milk and continue to mix until the filling is spreadable.

Make the
HONEYED PEANUT TOPPING

11. Place the chopped peanuts in a small zip-top plastic bag. Drizzle in the honey and give the bag a good shake until the peanuts are evenly coated. Add the sugar and salt. Shake again until evenly distributed. Spread out the peanuts on a piece of parchment paper and let them dry slightly, 10 to 15 minutes, or until they are no longer too sticky to handle.

ASSEMBLE THE CAKE

12. Trim a piece of parchment paper to about 6 by 19 inches (15 by 48 cm).

13. Remove the ice cream from the freezer to soften slightly, but not melt. Line two 6-inch (15-cm) cake pans with plastic wrap, letting it overhang the sides by several inches. Remove the ice cream from its container and slice it into 1½-inch (4-cm) slabs. Press the ice cream into the prepared pans, filling in the gaps to create an even layer. Fold over the edges of the plastic wrap and press down to create even discs of ice cream. Freeze until solid.

14. Once the cake has completely cooled, use a cake ring to cut out three 6-inch (15-cm) rounds of cake.

15. Place the bottom cake layer in a 6-inch (15-cm) ring mold on top of a cake board or in a 6-inch (15-cm) springform pan. Tuck the strip of parchment between the cake and the pan to create a collar and extend the sides. Secure with tape, if needed.

16. Spread on ¾ cup (180 ml) of the malt filling with an offset spatula or the back of a large spoon.

17. Remove one of the frozen ice cream discs and unmold it from the cake pan. Place the ice cream layer on top of the malt filling. Top with the next layer of cake and repeat with the malt filling and ice cream, then with the final layer of cake.

18. Cover the assembled cake with plastic wrap and let it set in the freezer for 20 to 30 minutes.

Make the
WHIPPED CREAM FROSTING

19. Meanwhile, in the bowl of a stand mixer fitted with the whisk attachment, whisk the cream on medium speed until it starts to thicken. Add the sugar and vanilla and whisk on high until it holds medium peaks. Add the gel food coloring, if using, when the whipped cream reaches soft peaks and continue to whip until it holds medium peaks.

20. Just before serving, frost the top and sides of the cake with the whipped cream frosting. Garnish by gently pressing the peanut topping around the sides of the cake and top it with sprinkles, if using.

BAKER'S NOTES

You will be able to cut out exactly three 6-inch (15-cm) round cake layers using a 10 by 15-inch (25 by 38-cm) cake pan. If using a standard 9 by 13-inch (23 by 33-cm) quarter-sheet cake pan, you will need to cut out two 6-inch (15-cm) round cake layers and two half circles or use the remaining cake "scraps" to piece together the third 6-inch (15-cm) round. Use this round as the middle layer of cake. Try not to overwork the whipped cream when frosting or it will lose its structure. During the last stage of assembly, do not let the cake completely freeze or it will become very difficult to slice. However, if you prefer to have a more solid cake and ice cream combo, then freeze it thoroughly. If you're having trouble cutting the cake, run the knife under hot water. I find it easier to cut uniform ice cream slabs from the types that come in a box, but choose whatever ice cream you desire. Once assembled, eat the cake within 20 minutes or freeze for up to 2 days (see page 25).

SHORTCUT

Use store-bought chocolate malt powder and/or honey-roasted peanuts.

DECORATE IT

To tint the whipped cream frosting different colors, stop the mixer when the cream reaches soft peaks. Remove a small amount (¾ to 1 cup / 180 to 240 ml) and place it in a separate bowl. Add gel food coloring and whisk by hand until it holds medium peaks. Transfer it to a pastry bag fitted with an open star tip. Tint the remaining whipped cream left in the mixer bowl with a different color, continue to whip until it hold medium peaks, and use it to frost the cake. Pipe a shell border (see page 37) on the top and bottom edges of the cake. Decorate with sprinkles.

IS IT FACT OR JUST MY ASSUMPTION THAT EVERYONE'S favorite boxed cake is the kind with the sprinkles in it? It was for me when I was twelve years old, at least, especially in cupcake form, topped with frosting that was laced with sprinkles as well. I get it, really. The ease of everything premeasured, almost foolproof directions, and bits of sugary confetti in every bite. But let's get real—it's not 1996 anymore. We've graduated beyond the box. It's increasingly common for home bakers and DIY-ers to make desserts from scratch these days (insert happy dance here). If you picked up this book, then you probably agree. And what if I told you that you could make your own confetti cake that tastes even better than the boxed version? It's true. (Plus, strawberries. You won't ever find that kind of freshness on a grocery store shelf.) So set your playlist to your favorite nineties hits and let's get rockin'!

For the
HOMEMADE SPRINKLES

2   large egg whites (⅜ cup / 90 ml)

4   cups (500 g) confectioners' sugar, sifted

½   teaspoon pure vanilla extract (see Baker's Notes, page 191)

Gel food coloring, as many colors as desired

For the
STRAWBERRY PUREE

12   to 15 medium-large strawberries, hulled and quartered

1   tablespoon granulated sugar

¼   teaspoon salt

For the
STRAWBERRY CONFETTI CAKE

Butter or nonstick cooking spray, for the pans

1½   cups plus 2 tablespoons (215 g) cake flour, plus more for the pans

1½   teaspoons baking powder

½   cup (1 stick / 115 g) unsalted butter, at room temperature

1   cup (200 g) granulated sugar

2   teaspoons pure vanilla extract (see Baker's Notes, page 191)

3   large egg yolks

2   tablespoons milk

For the
VANILLA CONFETTI CAKE

Butter or nonstick cooking spray, for the pans

1½   cups plus 2 tablespoons (215 g) cake flour, plus more for the pans

1½   teaspoons baking powder

½   cup (1 stick / 115 g) unsalted butter, at room temperature

1   cup (200 g) granulated sugar

1½   teaspoons pure vanilla extract (see Baker's Notes, page 191)

½   teaspoon pure almond extract

3   large egg yolks

¾   cup (180 ml) milk

For the
STRAWBERRY CREAM

4   ounces (115 g) cream cheese, softened

½   cup (1 stick / 115 g) unsalted butter, at room temperature

3   cups (375 g) confectioners' sugar, sifted

3   to 4 tablespoons Strawberry Puree *(see above)*

For the
CONFETTI BUTTERCREAM

4   ounces (115 g) cream cheese, softened

2 ½   cups (600 ml) Vanilla Swiss Meringue Buttercream (page 41)

½   teaspoon pure almond extract

For the
ASSEMBLY

Remaining Homemade Sprinkles *(see above)*

strawberry confetti cake

MAKES ONE FOUR-LAYER 6-INCH (15-CM) CAKE; SERVES 10 TO 12

4. Preheat the oven to 350°F (175°C). Grease and flour two 6-inch (15-cm) cake pans and set aside.

5. Sift together the flour and baking powder and set aside.

6. In the bowl of a stand mixer fitted with the paddle attachment, beat the butter on medium speed for 2 minutes. Add the sugar and mix on medium-high until the butter is light and fluffy, 3 to 5 minutes. Stop the mixer and scrape down the bowl.

7. Turn the mixer to medium-low and add the egg yolks one at a time, the vanilla, and ¾ cup (180 ml) of the strawberry puree (reserve the rest for the strawberry cream). Stop the mixer and scrape down the bowl.

8. Turn the mixer to low and add the flour mixture in two batches. Add the milk. Mix on medium for no more than 30 seconds after the last streaks of the dry ingredients are combined. Fold in ½ cup (70 g) of the homemade sprinkles.

9. Evenly divide the batter between the prepared pans. Bake for 23 to 25 minutes, or until a toothpick inserted into the center of the cakes comes out clean. Let them cool on a wire rack for 10 to 15 minutes before removing the cakes from their pans.

Make the
HOMEMADE SPRINKLES

1. In the bowl of a stand mixer fitted with the whisk attachment, whisk the egg whites on medium-low speed until foamy. Gradually add the confectioners' sugar and increase the speed to medium-high. Continue to whisk until stiff, glossy peaks form. Add the vanilla and mix until combined.

2. Divide the icing mixture into as many small bowls as you like and color as desired with the food coloring. Place each color of icing in a small piping bag

fitted with a small round tip. Pipe out small dots (see page 37) on a piece of parchment paper. Use a clean, damp paintbrush or fingertip to flatten out any small peaks that may form. Repeat with the remaining colors. Let the sprinkles dry for at least 2 hours before use.

Make the
STRAWBERRY PUREE

3. Place the strawberries, sugar, and salt in a food processor and process until smooth. Set aside.

Make the VANILLA CONFETTI CAKE

10. While the strawberry cakes bake, grease and flour two 6-inch (15-cm) cake pans and set aside.

11. Sift together the flour and baking powder and set aside.

12. In the bowl of a stand mixer fitted with the paddle attachment, beat the butter on medium speed for 2 minutes. Add the granulated sugar and mix on medium-high until the butter is light and fluffy, 3 to 5 minutes. Stop the mixer and scrape down the bowl.

13. Turn the mixer to medium-low and add the vanilla, almond extract, and egg yolks, one at a time. Stop the mixer and scrape down the bowl.

14. Turn the mixer to low and add the flour mixture in three batches, alternating with the milk, beginning and ending with the flour mixture. Mix on medium for no more than 30 seconds after the last streaks of the dry ingredients are combined. Fold in ½ cup (70 g) of the homemade sprinkles.

15. Evenly divide the batter between the prepared pans. Bake for 23 to 25 minutes, or until a toothpick inserted into the cakes comes out clean. Let them cool on a wire rack for 10 to 15 minutes before removing the cakes from their pans.

Make the STRAWBERRY CREAM

16. In the bowl of a stand mixer fitted with the paddle attachment, beat the cream cheese and butter on medium speed until smooth. With the mixer on low, gradually add the confectioners' sugar and 3 to 4 tablespoons of the reserved strawberry puree until incorporated. Turn the mixer to medium-high and mix until smooth and creamy. Transfer to a separate bowl and set aside. Wipe out the mixer bowl.

Make the CONFETTI BUTTERCREAM

17. In the bowl of the stand mixer fitted with the paddle attachment, beat the cream cheese on medium-low for 2 minutes. Add the buttercream and almond extract and mix on medium until smooth. Fold in ¾ to 1 cup (105 to 140 g) of the homemade sprinkles.

ASSEMBLE THE CAKE

18. Once the cakes have completely cooled, level them and choose which layer will be at the bottom. Place it on a cake plate or serving dish. Spread on ½ cup (120 ml) of the strawberry cream with an offset spatula. Top with next cake layer, being sure to alternate between vanilla and strawberry cakes, and repeat twice with the strawberry cream, ending with the fourth layer. Frost the top and sides of the cake with the confetti buttercream and decorate with the remaining homemade sprinkles.

DECORATE IT

Fill a piping bag fitted with an open star piping tip with the remaining buttercream and create shell and spiral borders (see pages 37) on the top and bottom edges of the cake.

BAKER'S NOTES

For a nostalgic taste that is more like the beloved boxed version, use clear imitation vanilla in place of pure vanilla extract throughout the recipe. To make homemade jimmies, pipe the sprinkle mixture in long, thin lines instead of dots. Cut into short pieces after drying. The cake will keep in the fridge for up to 4 days; it may also be frozen (see page 25).

SHORTCUT

Use all store-bought sprinkles instead of making your own. Feel free to use whatever shape or color you'd like, or a combination of your favorites—jimmies and quins (flat sprinkles) work best.

ADVENTUROUS CAKES

These cakes are not your usual suspects. From booze to savory spices, these recipes will excite and amuse even the most sophisticated palate. Ignite your inner explorer with exotic flavors like yuzu, pink peppercorn, and chai. Any one of these "wow"-worthy cakes, like the Red Wine Blackberry Cake or Lavender Olive Oil Cake, is sure to thrill party guests or anyone lucky enough to taste a bite.

raspberry stout cake

MAKES ONE SIX-LAYER 6-INCH (15-CM) CAKE; SERVES 10 TO 12

IT WAS SUMMERTIME, AND I WAS ON A QUEST to pair the rich nuttiness of a chocolate stout cake with something light but not too sweet, when I thought of raspberries. Heavy, thick stout beer does not scream "refreshing summer beverage," but I had a hunch we'd be in business if I used it in an extra-moist cake brushed with sweet raspberry sauce and filled with tangy raspberry cheesecake frosting.

Now that we are getting crazy combining dark beer and fresh raspberries, why not take this cake creation to a whole new level with a chocolate-raspberry-pretzel bark garnish?! The tartness of the freeze-dried raspberries balances the dark chocolate beautifully, while the pretzels add the perfect amount of salt and crunch. And pretzels, duh—we are still talking about a perfect beer pairing here.

For the
CHOCOLATE STOUT CAKE

	Butter or nonstick cooking spray, for the pans
2	cups (250 g) all-purpose flour, plus more for the pans
1¼	teaspoons baking soda
1	teaspoon baking powder
½	teaspoon salt
1	cup (240 ml) stout beer, such as Guinness
¾	cup (1½ sticks / 170 g) unsalted butter
⅔	cup (160 ml) sour cream
2	large eggs
2	teaspoons pure vanilla extract
1	cup (220 g) firmly packed dark brown sugar
¾	cup (150 g) granulated sugar
¾	cup (70 g) unsweetened cocoa powder
1	tablespoon instant espresso powder

For the
RASPBERRY COULIS

2½	cups (310 g) fresh or frozen raspberries
2	to 4 tablespoons granulated sugar
1	teaspoon fresh lemon juice

For the
RASPBERRY CHEESECAKE FILLING

4	ounces (115 g) cream cheese, softened
1	small recipe Vanilla Swiss Meringue Buttercream (page 41)
1¼	cup (60 ml) Raspberry Coulis (*see above*), or to taste

For the
RASPBERRY CHOCOLATE BARK

8	ounces (225 g) dark chocolate
3	ounces (85 g) white chocolate
½	cup (20 g) freeze-dried raspberries, chopped
½	cup (25 g) chopped mini twist or small rod pretzels

For the
ASSEMBLY

| ½ | recipe Dark Chocolate Ganache (page 41) |
| ½ | cup (60 g) fresh raspberries (*optional*) |

Make the
CHOCOLATE STOUT CAKE

1. Preheat the oven to 350°F (175°C). Grease and flour three 6-inch (15-cm) cake pans and set aside.

2. Sift together the flour, baking soda, baking powder, and salt and set aside.

3. Place the stout and butter in a medium-large saucepan over medium heat until the butter has melted.

4. Meanwhile, combine the sour cream, eggs, and vanilla in a separate bowl and set aside.

5. Whisk the sugars, cocoa powder, and espresso powder into the stout mixture until combined. Remove from the heat and stir in the sour cream mixture. Whisk in the dry ingredients until smooth.

6. Evenly divide the batter among the prepared pans. Bake for 22 to 24 minutes, or until a toothpick inserted into the center of the cakes comes out clean. Let them cool on a wire rack for 10 to 15 minutes before removing the cakes from their pans.

Make the
RASPBERRY COULIS

7. Combine the raspberries, 2 tablespoons of the sugar, and the lemon juice in a saucepan and heat over medium-high until the juices begin to bubble. Reduce the heat to low and simmer until the raspberries break down, about 10 minutes. Taste and add more sugar, if needed. Strain the sauce through a fine-mesh sieve set over a bowl and discard the seeds and solids. Let the coulis cool.

Make the
RASPBERRY CHEESECAKE FILLING

8. In the bowl of a stand mixer fitted with the paddle attachment, beat the cream cheese on medium speed until soft and creamy. Add the buttercream and ¼ cup (60 ml) of the cooled raspberry coulis, or to taste, and mix until smooth.

Make the
RASPBERRY CHOCOLATE BARK

9. Line a baking sheet with parchment paper or a nonstick silicone mat.

10. Melt the dark chocolate in the top portion of a double boiler. Meanwhile, place the white chocolate in a heat-safe bowl and microwave it at half power in 20- to 30-second intervals until melted.

11. Pour the dark chocolate onto the lined baking sheet. Smooth it into a ¼-inch (6-mm) layer with an offset spatula. Spoon dollops of the white chocolate on top and swirl them with a wooden skewer. Sprinkle with the raspberries and pretzels. Let the bark cool and set, then break it into pieces.

ASSEMBLE THE CAKE

12. Once the cakes have completely cooled, carefully halve them horizontally to make six even layers. Level the cakes and choose which layer will be at the bottom. Place it on a cake plate or serving dish. Brush it with raspberry coulis and spread on ½ cup (120 ml) of the raspberry cheesecake filling with an offset spatula. Top with the next layer and repeat with the coulis and filling, finishing with the final layer.

13. Frost the top of the cake with the ganache by placing a large dollop on the top and gently smoothing it around with an offset spatula until just before you reach the edge of the cake. Before the ganache sets, gently stick the ends of the bark into the cake. Arrange the bark and fresh raspberries, if using, so that the top of the cake looks random and abstract.

BAKER'S NOTES

The chocolate bark should be made the same day as serving and kept separately in a cool, dry place until ready to use. The cake will keep in the fridge (without the chocolate bark) for up to 3 days (see page 25).

SHORTCUT

Use warmed and strained raspberry preserves from a jar instead of making the raspberry coulis.

lavender olive oil cake

MAKES ONE TWO-LAYER 8-INCH (20-CM) CAKE; SERVES 10 TO 12

I WAS ONE OF THOSE LUCKY KIDS WHO HAD A BEST FRIEND just two doors down growing up—the kind whose house you ride your bike to and spend literally all day playing with, whose parents almost seem like your own. We had countless sleepovers, and I enjoyed many meals prepared by my "second mom."

Before there was such a thing as a "foodie," there was my friend's mother. She is an excellent cook, sourcing the best, freshest ingredients for her family even back in the day. With the most impeccable taste, she was always the perfect hostess and could throw a dinner party like no one else. She always used the finest olive oil in a kitchen that smelled of fresh lavender and citrus, and so the unforgettable scent of this elegant cake reminds me of her.

For the
CITRUS OLIVE OIL CAKE

Butter or nonstick cooking spray, for the pans

2¼ cups (280 g) all-purpose flour, plus more for the pans

1¼ teaspoons baking powder

1 teaspoon baking soda

½ teaspoon salt

½ teaspoon ground cardamom

¾ cup (180 ml) good-quality olive oil

1½ cups (300 g) granulated sugar

1 tablespoon finely grated lemon zest

3 large eggs

¾ cup (180 ml) buttermilk

For the
LAVENDER SIMPLE SYRUP

½ cup (100 g) granulated sugar

1½ teaspoons dried culinary lavender

For the
LAVENDER CREAM

2 cups (480 ml) cold heavy cream

2 teaspoons dried culinary lavender

2 tablespoons granulated sugar

1 teaspoon pure vanilla extract

Make the
CITRUS OLIVE OIL CAKE

1. Preheat the oven to 350°F (175°C). Grease and flour two 8-inch (20-cm) cake pans and set aside.

2. Sift together the flour, baking powder, baking soda, salt, and cardamom and set aside.

3. In the bowl of a stand mixer fitted with the paddle attachment, mix the oil, sugar, and lemon zest on medium speed until combined. Turn the mixer to medium-low and add the eggs one at a time. Stop the mixer and scrape down the bowl.

4. Turn the mixer to low and add the flour mixture in three batches, alternating with the buttermilk, beginning and ending with the flour mixture. Mix on medium for no more than 30 seconds after the last streaks of the dry ingredients are combined.

5. Evenly divide the batter between the prepared pans. Bake for 24 to 26 minutes, or until a toothpick inserted into the center of the cakes comes out clean. Let them cool on a wire rack for 10 to 15 minutes before removing the cakes from their pans.

Make the
LAVENDER SIMPLE SYRUP

6. Place ½ cup (120 ml) water and the sugar in a saucepan over medium-high heat and bring them to a boil. Reduce the heat to low and add the lavender. Simmer until the mixture is reduced and syrup-like, 8 to 10 minutes. Remove from the heat and let steep until cool. Strain the syrup through a fine-mesh sieve set over a bowl and discard the lavender.

Make the
LAVENDER CREAM

7. In a saucepan, combine the cream and lavender and slowly bring them to a simmer over medium-low heat. Cook for about 5 minutes, then remove the pan from the heat and let the lavender steep for about 20 minutes. Strain the cream through a fine-mesh sieve set over a bowl and discard the lavender. Cover and refrigerate it until cold.

8. Once cold, transfer the cream to the bowl of a stand mixer fitted with the whisk attachment and whisk it on medium speed until it starts to thicken. Add the sugar and vanilla and whisk on high until it holds medium peaks. For best results, store the whipped cream in the refrigerator until ready to use and assemble the cake just before serving.

ASSEMBLE THE CAKE

9. Once the cakes have completely cooled, generously brush each layer with the simple syrup. Choose which layer will be at the bottom and place it on a cake plate or serving dish. Spread on half of the lavender cream and top it with the next layer of cake. Use an offset spatula to create a rustic finish (see page 31) on the top of the cake with the remaining lavender cream.

BAKER'S NOTES

The lavender simple syrup may be made in advance and stored in a glass jar in the refrigerator for up to 1 week. The whipped cream may be made up to 8 hours ahead of time and stored separately and tightly covered in the refrigerator. Once assembled, eat the cake immediately or keep refrigerated, for up to 2 days, until 30 minutes before serving (see page 25).

GOT LEFTOVERS?

Use lavender simple syrup to sweeten iced tea.

PERHAPS IT IS BECAUSE WINTER SPORTS AND AMBER-COLORED LIQUORS tend to be synonymous with colder climates, but the chilly Canadian months have me yearning to watch hockey by the fire and craving a slice of this Butterscotch Bourbon Cake. I'm not a huge fan of drinking bourbon, but put it in a cake and it's an entirely different story. There is nothing like adding some butter and sugar to transform the oaky, sweet, and caramel flavors of that liquor into dessert. The bourbon butterscotch topping is like liquid gold—making for the best boozy buttercream with which to smother a cake.

For the
BOURBON CAKE

	Butter or nonstick cooking spray, for the pans
2¼	cups (295 g) cake flour, plus more for the pans
1½	teaspoons baking powder
¾	teaspoon baking soda
½	teaspoon salt
½	teaspoon freshly grated nutmeg
¾	cup (1½ sticks / 170 g) unsalted butter, at room temperature
¾	cup (150 g) granulated sugar
½	cup plus 2 tablespoons (140 g) firmly packed brown sugar
1	teaspoon pure vanilla extract
2	large eggs
2	large egg yolks
1	cup (240 ml) buttermilk
¼	cup (60 ml) bourbon

For the
BOURBON BUTTERSCOTCH

6	tablespoons (¾ stick / 80 g) unsalted butter
¾	cup (165 g) firmly packed brown sugar
1	teaspoon corn syrup
½	teaspoon salt
¼	cup (60 ml) heavy cream
½	teaspoon pure vanilla extract
3	tablespoons bourbon

For the
BOURBON BUTTERSCOTCH
BUTTERCREAM

1	medium recipe Vanilla Swiss Meringue Buttercream (page 41)
½	cup (120 ml) cooled Bourbon Butterscotch (see above), or to taste

butterscotch bourbon cake

MAKES ONE THREE-LAYER 6-INCH (15-CM) CAKE; SERVES 10 TO 12

Make the
BOURBON CAKE

1. Preheat the oven to 350°F (175°C). Grease and flour three 6-inch (15-cm) cake pans and set aside.

2. Sift together the flour, baking powder, baking soda, salt, and nutmeg and set aside.

3. In the bowl of a stand mixer fitted with the paddle attachment, beat the butter on medium speed until smooth. Add the sugars and mix on medium-high until the butter is light and fluffy, 3 to 5 minutes. Stop the mixer and scrape down the bowl.

4. Turn the mixer to medium-low and add the vanilla, then add the eggs and egg yolks one at a time. Stop the mixer and scrape down the bowl.

5. Turn the mixer to low and add the flour mixture in three batches, alternating with the buttermilk, beginning and ending with the flour mixture. Turn the mixer to medium and gradually add the bourbon. Mix for no more than 30 seconds.

6. Evenly divide the batter among the prepared pans. Bake for 22 to 25 minutes, or until a toothpick inserted into the center of the cakes comes out clean. Let them cool on a wire rack for 10 to 15 minutes before removing the cakes from their pans.

Make the
BOURBON BUTTERSCOTCH

7. In a heavy-bottomed saucepan, melt the butter over medium heat. Stir in the brown sugar, corn syrup, and salt. Raise the heat to medium-high and stir continuously with a wooden spoon for about 5 minutes, or until the sugar completely melts and no longer looks like wet sand.

8. Remove the pan from the heat and, while whisking, carefully pour in the cream (see Baker's Notes). Return the pan to low heat and simmer, continuously stirring with a whisk, for 8 minutes. Pour the butterscotch into a heat-safe container. Stir in the vanilla and bourbon. Set it aside to cool to room temperature. The butterscotch should thicken slightly as it cools.

Make the
BOURBON BUTTERSCOTCH BUTTERCREAM

9. In the bowl of a stand mixer fitted with the paddle attachment, mix the buttercream until silky smooth. Add ½ cup (120 ml) of the cooled bourbon butterscotch (or to taste) and mix until combined.

ASSEMBLE THE CAKE

10. Once the cakes have completely cooled, level them and choose which layer will be at the bottom. Place it on a cake plate or serving dish. Spread on ¾ cup (180 ml) of the bourbon buttercream with an offset spatula. Top with the next layer of cake and repeat with the buttercream, finishing with the final layer. Frost the top and sides of the cake with the remaining buttercream and refrigerate until set, 15 to 20 minutes. Reheat the remaining butterscotch, if necessary, until thick and syrup-like. Carefully pour it onto the center of the top of the cake and use an offset spatula or spoon to spread it so it drips over the edges.

DECORATE IT

Use an icing comb to create a striped finish (see page 30) for the butterscotch to ripple over. Finish the cake with a pearl or braided border (see page 37) around the bottom of the cake.

BAKER'S NOTES

Use caution when adding the cream to the butterscotch, as the contents may start to bubble up rather quickly. Pour slowly and keep whisking. Not sure if the butterscotch is the correct temperature for drizzling? Try a few practice drips on the side of the cake that will be turned to the back. Reheat or cool as needed. The cake will keep in the fridge for up to 4 days; it may also be frozen (see page 25). Store the butterscotch separately.

GOT LEFTOVERS?

Reheat and pour extra bourbon butterscotch over a homemade ice cream sundae.

ONE BENEFIT OF MAKING CAKES FOR FAMILY and friends is that each occasion is an opportunity to experiment with new flavors and recipes. This Pink Peppercorn Cherry Cake is one of my favorite experiments yet, especially since it was hastily planned and happened sort of by accident.

This was supposed to be a pistachio cake. It was a friend's birthday, and I wanted to combine her favorite flavor of pistachio and love of crispy meringues. Come birthday week, there was no pistachio paste to be found. Instead, I found myself without a plan B stranded at Gourmet Warehouse. The Gourmet Warehouse in Vancouver is every chef's dream, with thousands upon thousands of spices, oils, teas, sprinkles, etc. It was information overload and the clock was ticking. I was doing a quick mental search of my baking to-do list, a running catalog of interesting flavors and desserts that I wanted to try, when I ran right into a jar of bright pink peppercorns.

Pink peppercorns! *Yes,* I thought, *this is something I always wanted to incorporate into a dessert and will surely impress—if all goes well . . .* And what does pink peppercorn go well with? My brain flashed to my favorite strawberry–black pepper jam and figured any red fruit would balance the sweet spice of peppercorn. I grabbed a jar of tart cherry preserves and ran home to bake up this beauty.

For the
ALMOND BUTTER CAKE

	Butter or nonstick cooking spray, for the pans
2	cups (260 g) cake flour
1	cup (125 g) all-purpose flour
1	tablespoon baking powder
¾	teaspoon salt
⅔	cup (80 g) almond meal
1¼	cups (2½ sticks / 285 g) unsalted butter, at room temperature
2	cups (400 g) granulated sugar
2½	teaspoons almond extract
1	teaspoon vanilla extract
4	eggs
1⅓	cups (315 ml) whole milk

For the
PINK PEPPERCORN BUTTERCREAM

1	medium recipe Vanilla Swiss Meringue Buttercream (page 41)
2	to 3 teaspoons finely crushed pink peppercorns
⅛	teaspoon salt
2	or 3 drops pink gel food coloring (*optional*)

For the
CHERRY JAM

1½	pounds (680 g) whole cherries, pitted and halved
3	tablespoons fresh lemon juice
1	cup (200 g) granulated sugar
1	to 2 teaspoons balsamic vinegar (*optional*)

For the
CRISPY MERINGUE KISSES

¼	cup (60 ml) large egg whites
½	cup (100 g) granulated sugar
	Pinch of salt
⅛	teaspoon cream of tartar
¼	teaspoon pure vanilla extract

pink peppercorn cherry cake

MAKES ONE THREE-LAYER 8-INCH (20-CM) CAKE; SERVES 12 TO 15

Make the
ALMOND BUTTER CAKE

1. Preheat the oven to 350°F (175°C). Grease three 8-inch (20-cm) cake pans (see Baker's Notes), then line the bottoms with parchment paper and set aside.

2. Sift together the flours, baking powder, and salt and whisk in the almond meal. Set aside.

3. In the bowl of a stand mixer fitted with the paddle attachment, beat the butter on medium speed until smooth. Add the sugar and beat on medium-high until the mixture is light and fluffy, 3 to 5 minutes. Stop the mixer and scrape down the bowl.

4. Turn the mixer to medium-low and add the almond extract, vanilla, and eggs one at a time. Stop the mixer and scrape down the bowl.

5. Turn the mixer to low and add the flour mixture in three batches, alternating with the milk, beginning and ending with the flour mixture. Mix on medium for no more than 30 seconds after the last streaks of the dry ingredients are combined.

6. Evenly divide the batter among the prepared pans. Bake for 25 to 28 minutes, or until a toothpick inserted into the center of the cakes comes out clean. Let them cool on a wire rack for 10 to 15 minutes before removing the cakes from their pans.

Make the
PINK PEPPERCORN
BUTTERCREAM

7. In the bowl of a stand mixer fitted with the paddle attachment, mix the buttercream until silky smooth. Add the peppercorns, salt, and food coloring, if using, and mix on medium-high until incorporated.

Make the
CHERRY JAM

8. Place the cherries and lemon juice in a large nonreactive pot or saucepan. Stirring intermittently, cook over medium-high heat until the fruit has softened, about 10 minutes. Stir in the sugar and continue to cook over medium heat until the bubbles from the juice start to subside and the jam has thickened. Remove the pan from the heat and stir in the vinegar (if using) for an extra-tart, sweet tang. Store the jam in a heat-safe container until cooled and thickened.

Make the
CRISPY MERINGUE KISSES

9. Preheat the oven to 215°F (100°C). Line a baking sheet with parchment paper.

10. Place the egg whites, sugar, and salt in the bowl of a stand mixer. Whisk them together by hand to combine. Fill a medium saucepan with a few inches of water and place it over medium-high heat. Place the mixer bowl on top of the saucepan to create a double boiler. The bottom of the bowl should not touch the water. Whisking intermittently, heat until the mixture is warm to the touch and the sugar has dissolved, 2 to 3 minutes.

11. Carefully transfer the bowl back to the stand mixer. With the whisk attachment, beat the egg white mixture on high speed until the outside of the mixing bowl returns to room temperature. Add the cream of tartar and vanilla and mix until medium-stiff, glossy peaks form.

12. Fill a pastry bag fitted with a large round piping tip with the meringue and pipe small kisses (see page 105) onto the lined baking sheet.

13. Bake for 30 to 60 minutes, depending on the size of the meringues. The meringues are done when they are dry to the touch and can easily be removed from the parchment paper, but are still slightly chewy inside. A meringue kiss with a 2-inch (5-cm) base requires 45 to 60 minutes of baking time.

ASSEMBLE THE CAKE

14. Once the cakes have completely cooled, level them and choose which layer will be at the bottom. Place it on a cake plate or serving dish. Fill a pastry bag fitted with a round piping tip with the buttercream. Pipe a ring of buttercream around the top edge of the cake to create a dam (see page 27). Fill in the buttercream ring with 1/3 to 1/2 cup (80 to 120 ml) of the cherry jam. Top with the next layer and repeat with the buttercream and jam. Frost the top and sides of the cake with the remaining buttercream. Before serving, decorate with the meringue kisses, placing them around the top edge of the cake and then filling in the middle until completely covered.

BAKER'S NOTES

It is better to undercook the jam than to let the sugars caramelize and ruin the whole batch. The jam should thicken once cooled. The cherry jam may be made in advance and stored in a glass jar in the refrigerator for 2 to 4 weeks. The Crispy Meringue Kisses may be made in advance and stored in an airtight container in a cool, dry place for up to 1 week. The cake will keep in the fridge for up to 4 days; it may also be frozen (see page 25). Store the meringues separately.

SHORTCUT

Use your favorite store-bought cherry jam.

GOT LEFTOVERS?

Dip the bottoms of the Crispy Meringue Kisses into melted chocolate. Let them set, and enjoy!

DECORATE IT

Frost the cake using a smooth, striped, or swirl (as pictured) finish (see pages 26, 32, and 31).

I IMAGINE PARADING AROUND THIS boozy banana espresso cake at an intimate dinner party—a gathering set outside under strings of twinkly lights. The layers of meticulously piped mascarpone topped with gooey caramel and a blanket of chocolate curls will evoke whispers from the other guests upon my arrival, and their curiosity about such a stunning creation will linger in their minds until after the entrée is served. The vanilla-specked chiffon layers are light, tender, and brushed with espresso rum syrup. Creamy mascarpone, fresh bananas, and decadent salted caramel make this cake truly irresistible, even after everyone has wined and dined to their hearts' desire. And I will be the dessert superhero for bringing such a showstopper, or at least that's how I envision it all in my mind. A cross between the classic English banoffee pie and an Italian tiramisu (or "pick me up," as the word means in Italian), this cake is the perfect dessert to serve after dinner. Think of it as a digestif, but cake—and with bananas.

For the
VANILLA ESPRESSO CHIFFON CAKE

Butter or nonstick cooking spray, for the pans

2 cups (260 g) cake flour

1 tablespoon instant espresso powder

2 teaspoons baking powder

½ teaspoon salt

½ cup (120 ml) grapeseed oil

1¼ cups plus 2 tablespoons (275 g) granulated sugar

Seeds of 1 vanilla bean

6 large egg yolks

½ cup (120 ml) whole milk

8 large egg whites

¾ teaspoon cream of tartar

For the
RUM-ESPRESSO SOAK

½ cup (100 g) granulated sugar

2 teaspoons instant espresso powder

¼ cup (60 ml) dark rum

For the
MASCARPONE BUTTERCREAM

½ cup plus 2 tablespoons (150 ml) large egg whites

1¼ cups (250 g) granulated sugar

1½ cups (3 sticks / 340 g) unsalted butter, at room temperature, cubed

¾ cup (180 ml) mascarpone, softened

1 tablespoon dark rum

1 teaspoon pure vanilla extract

For the
ASSEMBLY

2 to 3 ripe bananas, sliced on the bias ½ inch (12 mm) thick

1 recipe Salted Caramel Sauce (page 43)

Chocolate Curls for sprinkling (optional; see page 72)

banoffee tiramisu cake

MAKES ONE THREE-LAYER 8-INCH (20-CM) CAKE; SERVES 12 TO 15

Make the
VANILLA ESPRESSO CHIFFON CAKE

1. Preheat the oven to 350°F (175°C). Line the bottoms of three 8-inch (20-cm) cake pans with parchment paper and set aside.

2. Sift together the flour, espresso powder, baking powder, and salt and set aside.

3. In the bowl of a stand mixer fitted with the paddle attachment, beat together the oil, 1¼ cups (250 g) of the sugar, and the vanilla bean seeds on medium speed for 1 minute. Add the egg yolks one at a time and mix for about 3 minutes. The mixture will increase in volume and be pale in color. Stop the mixer and scrape down the bowl.

4. Turn the mixer to low and add the flour mixture in three batches, alternating with the milk, beginning and ending with the flour mixture. Mix on medium for no more than 30 seconds after the last streaks of the dry ingredients are combined. Pour the batter into a large bowl and set aside.

5. Clean the mixer bowl thoroughly and dry it well. In the clean bowl of the stand mixer fitted with the whisk attachment, whip the egg whites on medium-low speed until foamy. Add the remaining 2 tablespoons of the sugar and the cream of tartar and whisk on high until stiff peaks form.

6. Stop the mixer and carefully but deliberately fold the egg whites into the cake batter. Evenly divide the batter among the prepared pans. Bake for 23 to 25 minutes, or until a toothpick inserted into the center of the cakes comes out clean. Let them rest on a wire rack until cool before running a paring knife or metal spatula around the edges of the cakes and removing the them from their pans.

Make the
RUM-ESPRESSO SOAK

7. Combine the sugar, espresso powder, and ¼ cup (60 ml) water in a saucepan. Bring them to a boil, then reduce the heat to low and simmer for about 5 minutes. Remove the pan from the heat and stir in the rum. Let the liquid cool slightly before use, about 5 minutes.

Make the
MASCARPONE BUTTERCREAM

8. Place the egg whites and sugar in the bowl of a stand mixer. Whisk them together by hand to combine. Fill a medium saucepan with a few inches of water and place it over medium-high heat. Place the mixer bowl on top of the saucepan to create a double boiler. The bottom of the bowl should not touch the water.

9. Whisking intermittently, heat the egg mixture until it registers 160°F (70°C) on a candy thermometer or is hot to the touch. Once hot, carefully fit the mixer bowl onto the stand mixer.

10. With the whisk attachment, beat the egg white mixture on high speed for 8 to 10 minutes, until it holds medium-stiff peaks. When done, the outside of the mixer bowl should return to room temperature and no residual heat should be escaping from the meringue. Stop the mixer and swap out the whisk attachment for the paddle. With the mixer on low speed, add the butter, a few cubes at a time (see Baker's Notes). Once incorporated, turn the mixer to medium-high and beat until the buttercream is silky smooth, 3 to 5 minutes. Reduce the speed to medium-low and add in the mascarpone, rum, and vanilla. Mix until combined.

ASSEMBLE THE CAKE

11. Fill a pastry bag fitted with a round piping tip with some of the buttercream and set aside.

12. Once the cakes are completely cooled, level them and generously brush each cake with the rum- espresso soak. Choose which layer will be at the bottom and place it on a serving dish. Spread on ½ cup (120 ml) of the buttercream with an offset spatula. Using the piping bag, pipe kisses (see page 105) of buttercream in a circle around the outer edge of the cake. Fill the ring of buttercream with half of the bananas and ¼ cup (60 ml) salted caramel. Top with the next layer of cake and repeat with the buttercream, bananas, and caramel, topping with the last cake layer. Frost the top of the cake with the remaining buttercream. Finish with a blanket of chocolate curls, if desired. Serve with an extra drizzle of salted caramel sauce.

BAKER'S NOTES

If the buttercream starts to look "curdled" after adding the butter, just keep mixing. The butter is probably too cold and will need more time to incorporate (see "Tips and Techniques" section, page 42). The cake will keep in the fridge for up to 3 days (see page 25).

LIVING IN AN INTERNATIONAL CITY OPENS UP so many opportunities, especially when it comes to cuisine. Within walking distance from our home you can find a dozen Japanese restaurants, Korean barbecue, a Ukrainian cafe, African food, and ramen on every corner. In addition to all the fresh and local produce, there is a store down the street devoted to spices, and there are Asian markets galore. The cooking opportunities with all these fine ingredients are endless!

One fruit that I recently started working with is yuzu. This highly aromatic citrus originated in East Asia, but has become more available worldwide over the last decade. With tartness similar to a grapefruit, it is characterized as a cross between a mandarin orange and a lemon. The juice and zest tend to be a bit stronger than other citrus, making it the perfect ingredient for vibrant, exotic baked goods.

For the YUZU CURD	
7	tablespoons (100 g) unsalted butter, at room temperature, diced
1	cup (200 g) granulated sugar
¼	cup (60 ml) fresh yuzu juice (see Baker's Notes, page 215)
3	tablespoons fresh lemon juice
1	large egg
3	large egg yolks

For the YUZU CAKE	
	Butter or nonstick cooking spray, for the pans
3¼	cups (425 g) cake flour, plus more for the pans
2	teaspoons baking powder
¾	teaspoon baking soda
¼	teaspoon salt
2	cups (400 g) granulated sugar
2	tablespoons finely grated yuzu or grapefruit zest
1	cup (2 sticks / 225 g) unsalted butter, at room temperature
6	egg whites
3	tablespoons fresh yuzu juice (see Baker's Notes, page 215)
¼	cup (60 ml) fresh grapefruit juice (from 1 grapefruit)
1	cup (240 ml) whole milk

For the ASSEMBLY	
1	large recipe Swiss Meringue Buttercream (page 41)
	Gel food coloring (*optional*)

yuzu citrus cake

—

MAKES ONE THREE-LAYER 8-INCH (20-CM) CAKE; SERVES 12 TO 15

Make the
YUZU CURD

1. Place the butter in a heat-safe bowl and set aside.

2. In a medium saucepan, whisk together the sugar, yuzu and lemon juices, egg, and egg yolks. Cook over medium heat, stirring continuously to prevent the eggs from curdling, until the mixture is thick enough to coat the back of a spoon, or registers 160°F (70°C) on a candy thermometer, 6 to 8 minutes.

3. Remove the pan from the heat and strain the curd through a fine-mesh sieve over the bowl containing the butter. Stir to combine. Cover the curd with plastic wrap, pressing it directly against the surface of the curd to prevent a skin from forming, and refrigerate it until set, at least 4 hours or overnight.

Make the
YUZU CAKE

4. Preheat the oven to 350°F (175°C). Grease and flour three 8-inch (20-cm) cake pans and set aside.

5. Sift together the flour, baking powder, baking soda, and salt and set aside.

6. Place the sugar and yuzu zest in a small bowl. Rub them together with your fingertips until fragrant.

7. In the bowl of a stand mixer fitted with the paddle attachment, beat the butter on medium speed until smooth. Add the sugar mixture and mix on medium-high until the butter is light and fluffy, 3 to 5 minutes. Stop the mixer and scrape down the bowl.

8. Turn the mixer to medium-low and gradually add the egg whites until incorporated. Add the yuzu and grapefruit juices and mix until combined. Stop the mixer and scrape down the bowl.

9. Turn the mixer to low and add the flour mixture in three batches, alternating with the milk, beginning and ending with the flour mixture. Mix on medium for no more than 30 seconds after the last streaks of the dry ingredients are combined.

10. Evenly divide the batter among the prepared pans. Bake for 23 to 25 minutes, or until a toothpick inserted into the center of the cakes comes out clean. Let them cool on a wire rack for 10 to 15 minutes before removing the cakes from their pans.

ASSEMBLE THE CAKE

11. Tint the buttercream with the food coloring of your choice, if using.

12. When the cakes have completely cooled, level them and choose which layer will be at the bottom. Place it on a cake plate or serving dish. Fill a piping bag fitted with a medium round tip with some of the buttercream. Pipe a ring of buttercream around the top edge of the bottom layer to create a dam (see page 27). Fill in the middle with half of the curd. Top with the next layer of cake and repeat with the buttercream and remaining curd, finishing with the final layer. Frost the top and sides of the cake with the remaining buttercream.

DECORATE IT

To create a petal finish (see page 33) in a pattern similar to the cake pictured, you will need a large recipe Vanilla Swiss Meringue (page 41) and three pastry bags—one for each color. Crumb coat the cake then divide the remaining buttercream into separate mixing bowls and tint each one separately. Transfer the buttercream colors to individual pastry bags fitted with round tips. When piping the bulbs or kisses (see page 33) of buttercream, alternate colors as you progress down each row. Continue with the same color pattern all the way around the cake. For a simpler finish, a medium recipe of buttercream will do.

BAKER'S NOTES

Use bottled yuzu juice if the whole fruit is unavailable or out of season. Some yuzu juice can be a bit salty, so be sure to taste it prior to baking with it or use with caution. If you decide to use less yuzu juice, supplement with extra grapefruit juice. Look for yuzu juice at Asian markets or online. The yuzu curd may be made in advance and will keep for up to 1 month stored in an airtight container in the refrigerator. The cake will keep in the fridge for up to 3 days (see page 25).

MY HUSBAND AND I HAD OUR WEDDING RECEPTION in the stylish, five-story atrium of the Sacramento Library. With an entire wall of windows, it gave the illusion of being outdoors while keeping us protected from the summer heat. We decorated the elegant space with tropical flowers and other subtle hints of my Hawaiian heritage. To match, we decided to serve refreshing signature cocktails—I chose coconut mojitos to go with Brett's pick of Mai Tais. While this cake reminds me of our wedding day, the fresh and tropical flavors will surely send you off daydreaming of sea breezes and white sandy beaches. The tantalizing flavors of zesty lime and cool mint pair excellently with the creamy Coconut Rum Buttercream. The Lime Mint Sugar is flirty and festive, like sugar or salt on the rim of a cocktail glass—making this cake perfect for serving at a wedding celebration or any fun occasion.

For the
LIME MINT SUGAR

- ½ cup (100 g) granulated sugar
- 1 tablespoon loosely packed chopped fresh mint leaves
- 1 teaspoon finely grated lime zest

For the
LIME CAKE

- Butter or nonstick cooking spray, for the pans
- 5 large egg whites
- 1 teaspoon pure vanilla extract
- ¾ cup (180 ml) whole milk
- 2½ cups (325 g) cake flour, plus more for the pans
- 1½ cups (300 g) granulated sugar
- 1 tablespoon baking powder
- ¾ teaspoon salt
- 1½ tablespoons finely grated lime zest
- ¾ cup (1½ sticks / 170 g) unsalted butter, at room temperature, diced

For the
MINT RUM SIMPLE SYRUP

- ½ cup (100 g) granulated sugar
- ¼ cup (60 ml) white rum
- 1 cup (30 g) loosely packed fresh mint leaves

For the
LIME FILLING

- 2 ounces (55 g) cream cheese, softened
- 1 medium recipe Vanilla Swiss Meringue Buttercream (page 41)
- 2 teaspoons fresh lime juice
- 1 teaspoon finely grated lime zest
- Green gel food coloring (*optional*)

For the
COCONUT RUM BUTTERCREAM

- ¼ cup (60 ml) coconut cream (see Baker's Notes, page 219)
- 1½ tablespoons white rum

coconut mojito cake

MAKES ONE THREE-LAYER 6-INCH (15-CM) CAKE; SERVES 8 TO 10

Make the
LIME MINT SUGAR

1. Combine the sugar, mint, and lime zest in the bowl of a food processor and pulse until the mint is minced. Spread the sugar on a piece of parchment paper and let it dry overnight before use.

Make the
LIME CAKE

2. Preheat the oven to 350°F (175°C). Grease and flour three 6-inch (15-cm) cake pans and set aside.

3. Stir together the egg whites, vanilla, and ¼ cup (60 ml) of the milk in a small bowl and set aside.

4. Sift together the flour, sugar, baking powder, and salt into the bowl of a stand mixer. Add in the lime zest. With the paddle attachment, mix on low until combined. Add the butter and remaining ½ cup (120 ml) milk and mix on low until the dry ingredients are moistened. Turn the mixer to medium-high and mix for about 1 minute, until combined. Stop the mixer and scrape down the bowl.

5. Turn the mixer to medium. Add the egg white mixture in three additions, mixing for about 20 seconds and stopping and scraping down the bowl after each addition.

6. Evenly divide the batter among the prepared pans. Bake for 23 to 25 minutes, or until a toothpick inserted into the center of the cakes comes out clean. Let them cool on a wire rack for 10 to 15 minutes before removing the cakes from their pans.

Make the
MINT RUM SIMPLE SYRUP

7. Place the sugar, rum, and ¼ cup (60 ml) water in a saucepan. Stir to combine. Bring to a boil over medium-high heat. Meanwhile, muddle the mint leaves in a bowl.

8. Reduce the heat to maintain a simmer and add the mint leaves. Simmer for about 10 minutes, until the mixture has reduced to a syrup. Remove the pan from the heat and let steep until the syrup is cool. Strain the syrup through a fine-mesh sieve set over a bowl and discard the mint leaves.

Make the
LIME FILLING

9. In the bowl of a stand mixer fitted with the paddle attachment, beat the cream cheese on medium speed until smooth. Add 1¼ cups (300 ml) of the buttercream, the lime juice and zest, and food coloring (if using) and mix until combined. Transfer to a separate bowl and set aside. Wipe out the mixer bowl.

Make the
COCONUT RUM
BUTTERCREAM

10. In the bowl of the stand mixer fitted with the paddle attachment, mix 2½ cups (600 ml) of the vanilla buttercream until silky smooth. Add the coconut cream and rum and mix until combined.

ASSEMBLE THE CAKE

11. Once the cakes have completely cooled, level them and choose which layer will be at the bottom. Generously brush the layers with the simple syrup. Place the bottom layer on a cake plate or serving dish. Spread on half of the lime filling with an offset spatula. Top with the next layer of cake and repeat with the filling, finishing with the final layer. Frost the top and sides of the cake with the coconut rum buttercream and decorate with the lime mint sugar.

DECORATE IT

Use an offset spatula to create a swirl finish (see page 31) and sprinkle the Lime Mint Sugar in a concentrated ring around the top edge of the cake.

BAKER'S NOTES

If coconut cream is unavailable, you may substitute 3 tablespoons coconut milk. If using canned coconut milk and it separates, use ¼ cup (60 ml) of the coconut solids that rise to the top of the can. The cake will keep in the fridge for up to 3 days; it may also be frozen (see page 25).

GOT LEFTOVERS?

Store the Lime Mint Sugar in an airtight container. Use the sugar to rim glasses and use any extra Mint Rum Simple Syrup as a sweetener to make fresh and fruity cocktails.

ONE OF MY FAVORITE WEEKEND ACTIVITIES is to go the farmers' market. In the summer, in particular, I am always attracted to all the colors, especially in the form of vibrant rhubarb and juicy berries. The earthy tang of rhubarb always goes well with the sweetness of perfectly sun-ripened strawberries, especially when cooked together in a jam or pie.

This cake plays on those compatible flavors, all paired with the crispness of sweet Riesling, forming my version of a Champagne and strawberry cake. The oat crumble adds a bit of texture, mimicking that of a baked fruit crisp. Serve this summer treat with a side of extra compote and/or a cool glass of Riesling.

For the
RIESLING CAKE

Butter or nonstick cooking spray, for the pans

3¼ cups (425 g) cake flour, plus more for the pans

1 tablespoon plus ½ teaspoon baking powder

¾ teaspoon salt

1 cup (2 sticks / 225 g) unsalted butter, at room temperature

2 cups (400 g) granulated sugar

2 teaspoons pure vanilla extract

6 large egg whites

1½ cups (360 ml) sweet Riesling

For the
RHUBARB STRAWBERRY COMPOTE

1¾ cup (8 ounces / 225 g) fresh strawberries, hulled and quartered

1 cup (4 ounces / 115 g) fresh rhubarb, cut into ¼-inch (6-mm) pieces

¼ cup (50 g) granulated sugar

2 tablespoons fresh lemon juice

For the
RHUBARB BUTTERCREAM

2 medium recipes Vanilla Swiss Meringue Buttercream (page 41)

½ cup (120 ml) Rhubarb-Strawberry Compote (*see above*)

For the
OAT CRUMBLE

½ cup (45 g) quick-cooking oats

¼ cup (25 g) sliced almonds

¼ cup (55 g) firmly packed brown sugar

¼ cup (30 g) all-purpose flour

3 tablespoons unsalted butter, at room temperature

2 tablespoons honey

½ teaspoon ground cinnamon

¼ teaspoon salt

For the
ASSEMBLY

Gel food coloring (*optional*)

Remaining Vanilla Swiss Buttercream

Fresh strawberries for decorating (*optional*)

Remaining Rhubarb Strawberry Compote, for serving (*optional*)

riesling rhubarb crisp cake

—

MAKES ONE THREE-LAYER 8-INCH (20-CM) CAKE; SERVES 12 TO 15

Make the
RIESLING CAKE

1. Preheat the oven to 350°F (175°C). Grease and flour three 8-inch (20-cm) cake pans and set aside.

2. Sift together the flour, baking powder, and salt and set aside.

3. In the bowl of a stand mixer fitted with the paddle attachment, beat the butter on medium speed until smooth. Add the sugar and mix on medium-high until the butter is light and fluffy, 3 to 5 minutes. Stop the mixer and scrape down the bowl.

4. Turn the mixer to medium-low and gradually add the vanilla and egg whites until combined. Stop the mixer and scrape down the bowl.

5. Turn the mixer to low and add the flour mixture in three batches, alternating with the Riesling, beginning and ending with the flour mixture. Mix on medium for no more than 30 seconds after the last streaks of the dry ingredients are combined.

6. Evenly divide the batter among the prepared pans. Bake for 23 to 25 minutes, or until a toothpick inserted into the center of the cakes comes out clean. Let them cool on a wire rack for 10 to 15 minutes before removing the cakes from their pans.

Make the
RHUBARB STRAWBERRY COMPOTE

7. Combine the strawberries, rhubarb, sugar, and lemon juice in a medium saucepan and cook them over medium-high heat, stirring intermittently with a wooden spoon, until the juices start to bubble. Reduce the heat to maintain a simmer and cook for 8 to 10 minutes, or until the fruit starts to break down. Remove the pan from the heat and let cool.

Make the
RHUBARB BUTTERCREAM

8. In the bowl of a stand mixer fitted with the paddle attachment, mix 2 cups (480 ml) of the buttercream until silky smooth. Add ½ cup (120 ml) of the cooled rhubarb compote and mix until combined.

Make the
OAT CRUMBLE

9. Preheat the oven to 375°F (190°C). Line a baking sheet with parchment paper.

10. In a medium bowl, mix together the oats, almonds, brown sugar, flour, butter, honey, cinnamon, and salt with a wooden spoon until combined. The mixture should resemble clumps of sand. Sprinkle it over the lined baking sheet and bake, stirring halfway through, for 8 to 10 minutes, or until golden brown. Let it cool and crumble the mixture into smaller pieces, if necessary.

ASSEMBLE THE CAKE

11. Once the cakes have completely cooled, level them and choose which layer will be at the bottom. Place it on a cake plate or serving dish. Spread on 1 cup (240 ml) of the rhubarb buttercream with an offset spatula. Sprinkle it with ½ to ¾ cup (50 to 75 g) of the oat crumble. Top with the next layer of cake and repeat with the buttercream and remaining crumble, finishing with the final layer.

12. Add the gel food coloring, if using, to the remaining vanilla buttercream. Use it to frost the top and sides of the cake. Top with fresh strawberries, if using, and serve with the remaining compote.

DECORATE IT

To create the ruffle design in the photo, fill a pastry bag fitted with a petal tip with buttercream. Starting at the top of the cake, pipe rows of continuous, horizontal ruffle swags (see page 36) around the cake. Invert the swag by keeping the narrow end of the petal tip facing upward. Start the second row slightly overlapping the bottom of the top row and continue around and down the cake. For a simpler finish, 1 large recipe of buttercream will do.

BAKER'S NOTES

The cake will keep in the fridge for up to 4 days; it may also be frozen (see page 25).

---

red wine blackberry cake

———

MAKES ONE THREE-LAYER 6-INCH (15-CM) CAKE; SERVES 8 TO 10

THE FROSTED CAKE SHOP, MY OLD BAKERY, was sandwiched between a local winery and one of the most popular in-house coffee roasters in town. We all moved in and opened at the same time, hustling day and night to get our businesses rolling.

I was so spoiled to have amazing coffee being freshly brewed every day just steps away from my front door. It was a no-brainer to use their different roasts in my recipes, but it took me a bit longer to realize that the local wine could be just as delicious in cake. Using a sweet but full-bodied red wine from my trusted neighbor, I created this decadent, chocolate red wine cake. Succulent blackberries and rich, dark chocolate finish off this robust, flavor-packed dessert.

For the RED WINE CAKE

Butter or nonstick cooking spray, for the pans

1½ cups (190 g) all-purpose flour, plus more for the pans

½ cup plus 1 tablespoon (55 g) natural unsweetened cocoa powder

¾ teaspoon baking soda

½ teaspoon baking powder

½ teaspoon salt

¾ cup (1½ sticks / 170 g) unsalted butter, at room temperature

1½ cups (300 g) granulated sugar

1 teaspoon pure vanilla extract

2 large eggs

1 large egg yolk

1 cup (240 ml) full-bodied red wine, such as a Cabernet, Malbec, or Syrah

For the BLACKBERRY GANACHE

3 cups (15 ounces / 420 g) whole fresh blackberries

2 tablespoons granulated sugar

1 cup (6 ounces / 170 g) chopped bittersweet chocolate

¾ cup (95 g) confectioners' sugar, sifted

For the ASSEMBLY

½ to 1 cup (70 to 140 g) whole fresh blackberries

Make the
RED WINE CAKE

1. Preheat the oven to 350°F (175°C). Grease and flour three 6-inch (15-cm) cake pans and set aside.

2. Sift together the flour, cocoa powder, baking soda, baking powder, and salt and set aside.

3. In the bowl of a stand mixer fitted with the paddle attachment, beat the butter on medium speed until smooth. Add the sugar and mix on medium-high until the butter is light and fluffy, 3 to 5 minutes. Stop the mixer and scrape down the bowl.

4. Turn the mixer to medium-low and add the vanilla, then add the eggs and egg yolk one at a time. Stop the mixer and scrape down the bowl.

5. Turn the mixer to low and add the flour mixture in three batches, alternating with the red wine, beginning and ending with the flour mixture. Mix on medium for no more than 30 seconds after the last streaks of the dry ingredients are combined.

6. Evenly divide the batter among the prepared pans. Bake for 23 to 25 minutes, or until a toothpick inserted into the center of the cakes comes out clean. Let them cool on a wire rack for 10 to 15 minutes before removing the cakes from their pans.

Make the
BLACKBERRY GANACHE

7. Place the blackberries and granulated sugar in a saucepan. Heat over medium-high until the berries start to break down and expel their juices, about 10 minutes. Remove the pan from the heat and strain the juice through a fine-mesh sieve set over a bowl. Discard the solids.

8. Place the chocolate in a heat-safe bowl and set aside. Reheat 6 tablespoons (90 ml) of the blackberry juice in the saucepan until it begins to simmer (reserve the remaining blackberry juice for finishing the cake). Pour the hot juice over the chocolate. Let sit for 30 seconds, then whisk until combined. Set aside until the ganache cools to room temperature but is still spreadable.

9. Once the ganache has cooled, whisk to loosen it and stir in the confectioners' sugar until smooth.

ASSEMBLE THE CAKE

10. Once the cakes have completely cooled, level them and choose which layer will be at the bottom. Generously brush the layers with the remaining blackberry juice. Place the bottom layer on a cake plate or serving dish. Spread on about ⅓ cup (80 ml) of the blackberry ganache with an offset spatula (see Baker's Notes). Top with the next layer of cake and repeat with the ganache, finishing with the final layer. Frost the top and sides of the cake with the remaining ganache and top with the whole blackberries.

DECORATE IT

For contrast with the refined flavors, do not fully frost the cake to create an unfinished, rustic look (see page 31). Randomly pile on the blackberries before serving.

BAKER'S NOTES

If the ganache starts to set and is difficult to frost with, gradually reheat it in the microwave at half power in no more than 20-second intervals. The cake will keep in the fridge for up to 4 days; it may also be frozen (see page 25). Store the blackberries separately.

SHORTCUT

Use store-bought blackberry nectar instead of making blackberry juice for the ganache.

pumpkin vanilla chai cake

MAKES ONE THREE-LAYER 6-INCH (15-CM) CAKE; SERVES 8 TO 10

IS IT ME, OR COME SEPTEMBER, ARE WE LIVING in a pumpkin-obsessed culture these days? I, for one, love pumpkin recipes (sweet and savory) and look forward to my pumpkin fix each fall. And while I feel that I still haven't gotten enough yet, I do have the need to give these flavors a modern twist.

As mentioned before, I am a big tea lover. One of my favorites is a bold chai tea latte. With warm cinnamon, vibrant cardamom, spicy ginger, and nutmeg, I feel that chai flavors embody fall and pair perfectly with creamy pumpkin. Topped off with spiced homemade marshmallows, this Pumpkin-Vanilla Chai Cake is the best way to elevate a typical fall treat.

For the
SPICED MARSHMALLOWS

	Butter or nonstick cooking spray, for the pan
	Confectioners' sugar, for dusting
	Cornstarch, for dusting
3	(2½-teaspoon / 7-g) envelopes unflavored gelatin
1½	cups (300 g) granulated sugar
1	cup (240 ml) light corn syrup
¼	teaspoon salt
	Seeds of 1 vanilla bean
½	teaspoon ground cinnamon
½	teaspoon freshly grated nutmeg

For the
VANILLA CHAI CAKE

1	cup (240 ml) whole milk
1	tablespoon loose chai tea
	Butter or nonstick cooking spray, for the pans
2¼	cups (295 g) cake flour, plus more for the pans
2	teaspoons baking powder
1	teaspoon ground cinnamon
1	teaspoon ground ginger
½	teaspoon salt
½	teaspoon ground cardamom
¼	teaspoon freshly grated nutmeg
¾	cup (1½ sticks / 170 g) unsalted butter, at room temperature
1½	cups (300 g) granulated sugar
2	teaspoons vanilla bean paste
4	large egg yolks

For the
PUMPKIN GANACHE

2	cups (12 ounces / 340 g) chopped white chocolate
¼	teaspoon ground cinnamon
⅛	teaspoon freshly grated nutmeg
5	tablespoons (75 ml) pumpkin puree
2½	tablespoons heavy cream
1	teaspoon corn syrup
1	tablespoon unsalted butter

For the
PUMPKIN CHAI BUTTERCREAM

¾	cup (1½ sticks / 170 g) unsalted butter
2	tablespoons loose chai tea
3½	cups (440 g) confectioners' sugar, sifted
⅓	cup (80 ml) pumpkin puree
2	tablespoons whole milk
1	teaspoon vanilla bean paste
½	teaspoon ground cinnamon
½	teaspoon ground ginger
¼	teaspoon freshly grated nutmeg

Make the
SPICED MARSHMALLOWS

1. Grease a 9 by 13-inch (23 by 33-cm) baking pan and then generously dust it with a mixture of one part confectioners' sugar to one part cornstarch.

2. Place the gelatin and ½ cup (120 ml) water in the bowl of a stand mixer and set aside.

3. In a saucepan, combine the granulated sugar, corn syrup, salt, and ½ cup (120 ml) water and heat over high heat until the mixture reaches 238°F (114°C) on a candy thermometer. Remove from the heat.

4. Put the bowl with the gelatin on the stand mixer and fit it with the whisk attachment. Turn the mixer on high speed. While it is running, carefully pour the sugar mixture into the gelatin. Continue to mix on high until the outside of the bowl cools to room temperature, 8 to 10 minutes. Add the vanilla bean seeds, cinnamon, and nutmeg until combined.

5. Coat a spatula with nonstick cooking spray and scoop out the marshmallow mixture into the prepared pan. Working carefully but quickly, smooth out the top. Dust the top with confectioners' sugar. Cover the surface with plastic wrap and set the pan aside until the marshmallow has set, about 3 hours.

6. Coat the blade of a knife with nonstick cooking spray and cut the marshmallow into squares. Toss each marshmallow square in confectioners' sugar to prevent it from sticking.

Make the
VANILLA CHAI CAKE

7. In a saucepan, bring the milk to a slow simmer over medium-low heat. Add the tea and remove the pan from the heat. Let steep for 8 to 10 minutes. Strain it through a fine-mesh sieve set over a bowl and discard the loose tea. Set it aside to cool.

8. Preheat the oven to 350°F (175°C). Grease and flour three 6-inch (15-cm) cake pans and set aside.

9. Sift together the flour, baking powder, cinnamon, ginger, salt, cardamom, and nutmeg and set aside.

10. In the bowl of a stand mixer fitted with the paddle attachment, beat the butter on medium speed until smooth. Add the sugar and mix on medium-high until the butter is light and fluffy, 3 to 5 minutes. Stop the mixer and scrape down the bowl.

11. Turn the mixer to medium-low and add the vanilla and egg yolks one at a time. Stop the mixer and scrape down the bowl.

12. Turn the mixer to low and add the flour mixture in three batches, alternating with the chai-infused milk, beginning and ending with the flour mixture. Mix on medium for no more than 30 seconds after the last streaks of the dry ingredients are combined.

13. Evenly divide the batter among the prepared pans. Bake for 23 to 25 minutes, or until a toothpick inserted into the center of the cakes comes out clean. Let them cool on a wire rack for 10 to 15 minutes before removing the cakes from their pans.

Make the
PUMPKIN GANACHE

14. Place the white chocolate in a heat-safe bowl. Sprinkle it with the cinnamon and nutmeg and set aside. In a saucepan, stir together the pumpkin, cream, and corn syrup and bring them to a simmer for a few minutes over medium-low heat.

15. Remove the pan from the heat and pour the pumpkin mixture over the white chocolate. Whisk until the white chocolate has melted. Add the butter and stir until smooth. Transfer to a heat-safe container and refrigerate it until cooled and slightly thickened to a spreadable consistency, stirring intermittently, for 1 to 2 hours.

Make the
PUMPKIN CHAI BUTTERCREAM

16. Place the butter in a medium saucepan with the tea. Heat them over medium until the butter melts. Reduce the heat to low and simmer for 5 minutes. Remove the pan from the heat and let steep for 5 minutes more. Strain the butter through a fine-mesh sieve into a bowl, discarding the tea, and chill the butter until it has the same consistency as softened butter, 20 to 30 minutes. Small bits of tea may remain in the butter.

17. Place the cooled butter in the bowl of a stand mixer fitted with the paddle attachment and beat it on medium speed until smooth. With the mixer on medium-low, carefully add the confectioners' sugar, pumpkin, milk, vanilla, cinnamon, ginger, and

nutmeg and mix until they are incorporated. Turn the mixer to medium-high and mix until the buttercream is light and fluffy.

ASSEMBLE THE CAKE

18. Once the cakes have completely cooled, level them and choose which layer will be at the bottom. Place it on a cake plate or serving dish. Spread on half of the pumpkin ganache with an offset spatula. Top with the next layer of cake and repeat with the ganache, finishing with the final layer. Frost the top and sides of the cake with the pumpkin buttercream and decorate with the marshmallows.

DECORATE IT

Since the pumpkin buttercream is not as silky smooth as Vanilla Swiss Meringue Buttercream, I recommend using an offset spatula to create a rustic finish (see page 31). Try creating swirls, diagonals, or whatever designs you'd like.

BAKER'S NOTES

Store the marshmallows in an airtight container for up to 1 week. The cake will keep in the fridge for up to 3 days (see page 25).

GOT LEFTOVERS?

Toss extra marshmallows in hot chocolate or eat them plain.

HOLIDAY CAKES

A holiday is a time to celebrate, and no celebration is complete without cake. Ring in the new year with a Golden Champagne Celebration Cake or kick off autumn with the cake version of a caramel apple. With seasonal flavors and a touch of sparkle, these crowd-pleasing cakes are perfect for life's many special occasions.

chocolate pomegranate
cake

—

MAKES ONE FOUR-LAYER 8-INCH (20-CM) CAKE; SERVES 12 TO 15

I KNOW IT'S RARE TO SAY, BUT I HAVE ONE of the sweetest mother-in-laws ever. Pink is extremely kind and has always welcomed me with open arms. Brett and I met in early fall, so when we decided to spend our first Christmas together, his family did not know me very well, and vice versa. I kept asking Brett what I could bring or make for Christmas dinner, and he kept saying nothing. I had heard that his mom was busy trying to get everything together, so I didn't know why my offers were being declined. After all, I did make desserts for a living.

The truth was, I secretly wanted to bring over an extravagant cake to impress them, while Pink was too polite to ask a new guest for help. She was more concerned with my enjoying the holidays and did not want to put any stress on me. I ended up bringing a dessert anyway, and have been asked to do so ever since. I gladly oblige and find joy in coming up with new, inventive cakes with alluring flavors for them to try each year. This festive pomegranate cake was one such creation. The intense pomegranate molasses moistens and elevates the complexity of the chocolate cake, while the piquancy of the pomegranate in the filling is balanced with silky sweet cheesecake buttercream. All layered with satiny dark chocolate ganache, it is sure to entice your holiday guests.

For the
SOUR CREAM CHOCOLATE CAKE

	Butter or nonstick cooking spray, for the pans
2½	cups (315 g) all-purpose flour, plus more for the pans
1	cup (95 g) unsweetened cocoa powder
2½	teaspoons baking powder
1	teaspoon baking soda
1	teaspoon salt
¾	cup (180 ml) grapeseed oil
1	cup (200 g) granulated sugar
¾	cup (165 g) firmly packed brown sugar
2	teaspoons pure vanilla extract
½	teaspoon pure almond extract
2	large eggs
1	large egg yolk
1	cup (240 ml) sour cream
1½	cups (360 ml) hot strong-brewed coffee

For the
POMEGRANATE MOLASSES

2	cups (480 ml) pomegranate juice
¼	cup (50 g) granulated sugar
2	teaspoons fresh lemon juice

For the
POMEGRANATE CHEESECAKE FILLING

3	ounces (85 g) cream cheese, softened
1	large recipe Vanilla Swiss Meringue Buttercream (page 41)
3	tablespoons Pomegranate Molasses (*see above*)

For the
ASSEMBLY

1	recipe Dark Chocolate Ganache (page 45)
	Remaining Vanilla Swiss Buttercream
	Pomegranate seeds (*optional*)

Make the
SOUR CREAM CHOCOLATE CAKE

1. Preheat the oven to 350°F (175°C). Grease and flour two 8-inch (20-cm) cake pans and set aside.

2. Sift together the flour, cocoa powder, baking powder, baking soda, and salt and set aside.

3. In the bowl of a stand mixer fitted with the paddle attachment, beat the oil and sugars together on medium speed for 2 minutes. With the mixer on, add the vanilla and almond extracts, then the eggs and yolk, one at a time. Stop the mixer and scrape down the bowl.

4. Turn the mixer to low and add the flour mixture in three batches, alternating with the sour cream, beginning and ending with the flour mixture. Stop the mixer and scrape down the bowl. With the mixer on low, stream in the coffee. Mix on medium-low for no more than 30 seconds, or until combined.

5. Evenly divide the batter between the prepared pans. Bake for 25 to 28 minutes, or until a toothpick inserted into the center of the cakes comes out clean. Let them cool on a wire rack for 10 to 15 minutes before removing the cakes from their pans.

Make the
POMEGRANATE MOLASSES

6. Combine the pomegranate juice, sugar, and lemon juice in a medium saucepan and stir. Bring to a boil over medium-high heat. Reduce the heat and simmer for about 45 minutes, or until the mixture has reduced to about ¾ cup (180 ml) and is thick and syrupy. Remove it from the heat and let it cool before using.

Make the
POMEGRANATE CHEESECAKE FILLING

7. In the bowl of a stand mixer fitted with the paddle attachment, beat the cream cheese until soft and smooth. Add 2 cups (480 ml) of the buttercream and 3 tablespoons of the pomegranate molasses and mix until combined.

ASSEMBLE THE CAKE

8. Once the cakes have completely cooled, halve them horizontally with a long serrated knife to create four even layers (see page 27). Level the cakes and choose which layer will be at the bottom. Generously brush each layer with pomegranate molasses. Place the bottom layer on a serving dish. Spread on ⅓ cup (80 ml) of the ganache with an offset spatula. Top with ⅔ cup (160 ml) of the cheesecake filling and spread until smooth. Place the next layer of cake on top and repeat with the ganache and cheesecake filling, finishing with the final layer. Frost the top and sides of the cake with the remaining buttercream and garnish with pomegranate seeds, if using.

DECORATE IT

Use an offset spatula to create a smooth, striped, or swirl finish (see pages 26, 32, and 31). Fill a pastry bag fitted with a small round top with any remaining buttercream to pipe a pearl border (see page 37) around the bottom of the cake. Finish with a crown of pomegranate seeds on the top of the cake.

BAKER'S NOTES

The cake will keep in the fridge for up to 3 days; it may also be frozen (see page 25).

SHORTCUT

Use store-bought pomegranate molasses.

GOT LEFTOVERS?

Use pomegranate molasses to sweeten iced tea or in a fruity sangria.

golden champagne celebration cake

—

MAKES ONE FOUR-LAYER 6-INCH (15-CM) CAKE; SERVES 10 TO 12

I HONESTLY CAN'T THINK OF ANYTHING BETTER to start off a new year than a pure, buttery vanilla cake. That, plus Champagne, of course! This velvety cake is rich with egg yolks, real butter, and vanilla bean seeds. The buttercream even tastes sparkling, especially after drinking a glass or two of Champagne. Truthfully, how could your year not be amazing following a slice of this beauty? So make this cake and start your resolutions afterward.

For the **VANILLA BEAN BUTTER CAKE**		*For the* **CHAMPAGNE BUTTERCREAM**		*For the* **ASSEMBLY**
	Butter or nonstick cooking spray, for the pans	1	medium recipe Vanilla Swiss Meringue Buttercream (page 41)	Edible gold leaf, sugar pearls, or metallic sprinkles (*optional*)
2¼	cups (295 g) cake flour, plus more for the pans	½	cup (120 ml) Champagne or sparkling wine	
2	teaspoons baking powder			
½	teaspoon salt			
¾	cup (1 ½ sticks / 170 g) unsalted butter, at room temperature			
1½	cups (300 g) granulated sugar			
	Seeds of 1 vanilla bean (see Baker's Note, page 241)			
4	large egg yolks			
1	cup (240 ml) whole milk			

Make the
VANILLA BEAN BUTTER CAKE

1. Preheat the oven to 350°F (175°C). Grease and flour four 6-inch (15-cm) cake pans and set aside.

2. Sift together the flour, baking powder, and salt and set aside.

3. In the bowl of a stand mixer fitted with the paddle attachment, beat the butter on medium speed until smooth. Add the sugar and vanilla bean seeds. Mix on medium-high until the butter is light and fluffy, 3 to 5 minutes. Stop the mixer and scrape down the bowl.

4. Turn the mixer to medium-low and add the egg yolks one at a time. Stop the mixer and scrape down the bowl.

5. Turn the mixer to low and add the flour mixture in three batches, alternating with the milk, beginning and ending with the flour mixture. Mix on medium for no more than 30 seconds after the last streaks of the dry ingredients are combined.

6. Evenly divide the batter among the prepared pans. Bake for 22 to 25 minutes, or until a toothpick inserted into the center of the cakes comes out clean. Let them cool on a wire rack for 10 to 15 minutes before removing the cakes from their pans.

Make the
CHAMPAGNE BUTTERCREAM

7. In the bowl of a stand mixer fitted with the paddle attachment, mix the buttercream until silky smooth. Slowly add the Champagne and mix until combined.

ASSEMBLE THE CAKE

8. Once the cakes have completely cooled, level them and choose which layer will be at the bottom. Place it on a cake plate or serving dish. Spread on ¾ cup (180 ml) of the buttercream with an offset spatula. Top with the next layer of cake and repeat with the buttercream, finishing with the final layer. Frost the cake with the remaining buttercream. Decorate with edible gold leaf (see Baker's Notes), sugar pearls, or metallic sprinkles, if using.

DECORATE IT

Use a small offset spatula to create a smooth, striped, or swirl finish (see pages 26–32). Garnish with the festive element of your choice.

BAKER'S NOTES

Use the tip of a paring knife or clean tweezers to apply the edible gold leaf so it doesn't stick to your fingers. Two teaspoons vanilla bean paste may be substituted for vanilla bean seeds. The cake will keep in the fridge for up to 3 days; it may also be frozen (see page 25).

MY HUSBAND, BRETT, AND I LIKE TO CELEBRATE Valentine's Day by cooking a meal together followed by homemade sweet treats instead of making reservations at a fancy restaurant or buying lavish gifts. Leading up to the occasion, we take the time to plan our menu and source our ingredients. And to finish, I always come up with a new, grand idea for dessert. My most memorable Valentine's Day so far was spent with our three-week-old son. While we miraculously carved out enough time to whip up something for dinner while tending to a newborn, I was forced to go a bit simpler with the dessert. I decided on this tried-and-true sour cream chocolate cake. It always comes out rich and extra moist. With just the addition of rose and fresh strawberries, this cake was transformed into something remarkable enough for the romantic occasion.

For the SOUR CREAM CHOCOLATE CAKE		*For the* STRAWBERRY ROSE BUTTERCREAM	
	Butter or nonstick cooking spray, for the pans	6	to 8 medium-large fresh strawberries, hulled and quartered
1¾	cups (220 g) all-purpose flour, plus more for the pans	2	tablespoons granulated sugar
¾	cup plus 2 tablespoons (80 g) unsweetened cocoa powder	⅛	teaspoon salt
1¾	teaspoons baking powder	1	medium recipe Vanilla Swiss Meringue Buttercream (see page 41)
¾	teaspoon baking soda	½	teaspoon rose extract
¾	teaspoon salt		
½	cup plus 1 tablespoon (135 ml) grapeseed oil		
¾	cup (150 g) granulated sugar		
¾	cup (165 g) firmly packed brown sugar		
2	large eggs		
1	teaspoon pure vanilla extract		
½	teaspoon pure almond extract		
1	cup (240 ml) sour cream		
¾	cup (180 ml) hot strong-brewed coffee		

strawberry rose
valentine cake

—

MAKES ONE THREE-LAYER 6-INCH (15-CM) CAKE; SERVES 8 TO 10

Make the
SOUR CREAM CHOCOLATE CAKE

1. Preheat the oven to 350°F (175°C). Grease and flour three 6-inch (15-cm) cake pans and set aside.

2. Sift together the flour, cocoa powder, baking powder, baking soda, and salt and set aside.

3. In the bowl of a stand mixer fitted with the paddle attachment, beat the oil and sugars on medium speed for 2 minutes. Add the eggs, vanilla, and almond extract. Stop the mixer and scrape down the bowl.

4. Turn the mixer to low and add the flour mixture in three batches, alternating with the sour cream, beginning and ending with the flour mixture. Stop the mixer and scrape down the bowl. With the mixer on low, stream in the coffee. Mix on medium-low for no more than 30 seconds, or until combined.

5. Evenly divide the batter among the prepared pans. Bake for 24 to 26 minutes, or until a toothpick inserted into the center of the cakes comes out clean. Let them cool on a wire rack for 10 to 15 minutes before removing the cakes from their pans.

Make the
STRAWBERRY ROSE BUTTERCREAM

6. Place the strawberries, sugar, and salt in the bowl of a food processor. Pulse until the strawberries are pureed.

7. In the bowl of a stand mixer fitted with the paddle attachment, mix the buttercream until silky smooth. Gradually add ½ cup (120 ml) of the strawberry puree and the rose extract. Mix until combined.

ASSEMBLE THE CAKE

8. Once the cakes have completely cooled, level them and choose which layer will be at the bottom. Place it on a cake plate or serving dish. Spread on ⅓ cup (80 ml) of the buttercream with an offset spatula. Top with the next layer of cake and repeat with the buttercream, finishing with the final layer. Frost the top and sides of the cake with the remaining buttercream.

DECORATE IT

To create the rose design in the photo, fill a pastry bag fitted with a medium-large star tip with buttercream. Pipe overlapping, staggered rosettes (see page 37) in rows around the sides and top of the cake. Fill in any gaps by piping plain stars (see page 37).

BAKER'S NOTES

The cake will keep in the fridge for up to 4 days; it may also be frozen (see page 25). If frosting the cake with a thinner smooth finish, increase the filling to ⅔ cup (165 ml) between the layers of cake.

SHORTCUT

Use strawberry jam or preserves instead of puree to make the buttercream. Start by adding in ¼ cup (60 ml) and adjust to taste.

CLASSIC, NO-FUSS, AND STRAIGHT TO THE GOOD STUFF. Many carrot cakes are studded with an array of nuts, raisins, and other hidden gems, but not this cake. A pinch of cinnamon and the addition of some crushed pineapple make this version superior to a basic carrot cake—a true favorite in my household. Between Easter celebrations with my own family and years of wedding cakes at the bakery, I've been making this recipe for nearly a decade. Lemon cream cheese frosting adds a hint of freshness and a subtle tang, making it the perfect cake for any spring gathering. Want to dress it up a bit? Throw on a spun-sugar bird's nest for that "wow" factor!

For the
CARROT CAKE

Butter or nonstick cooking spray, for the pans

2¼ cups (280 g) all-purpose flour, plus more for the pans

2 teaspoons baking powder

2 teaspoons baking soda

2 teaspoons ground cinnamon

¾ teaspoon salt

¾ cup (180 ml) grapeseed oil

1¼ cups (250 g) granulated sugar

½ cup (110 g) firmly packed brown sugar

4 large eggs

3 cups (330 g) shredded carrots

1 (8-ounce / 227-g) can crushed pineapple, drained

For the
LEMON CREAM CHEESE FROSTING

4 ounces (115 g) cream cheese, softened

½ cup (1 stick / 115 g) unsalted butter, at room temperature

3½ to 4 cups (440 to 500 g) confectioners' sugar, sifted

2 teaspoons finely grated lemon zest

2 teaspoons fresh lemon juice

½ teaspoon pure vanilla extract

For the
ASSEMBLY

1 medium recipe Vanilla Swiss Meringue Buttercream (page 41)

Gel food coloring (*optional*)

For the
SPUN-SUGAR BIRD'S NEST
(*OPTIONAL*)

2 cups (400 g) granulated sugar

½ cup (120 ml) light corn syrup

lemony carrot cake

MAKES ONE THREE-LAYER 8-INCH (20-CM) CAKE; SERVES 12 TO 15

Make the
CARROT CAKE

1. Preheat the oven to 350°F (175°C). Grease and flour three 8-inch (20-cm) pans and set aside.

2. Sift together the flour, baking powder, baking soda, cinnamon, and salt and set aside.

3. In the bowl of a stand mixer fitted with the paddle attachment, beat together the oil and sugars for 2 minutes on medium. Turn the mixer to medium-low and add the eggs, one at a time. Stop the mixer and scrape down the bowl.

4. With the mixer on medium-low, add the flour mixture in two batches. Mix until just incorporated. Add the carrots and pineapple. Mix on medium-low for no more than 30 seconds, or until combined.

5. Evenly divide the batter among the prepared cake pans. Bake for 25 to 28 minutes, or until a toothpick inserted into the center of the cakes comes out clean. Let them cool on a wire rack for 10 to 15 minutes before removing the cakes from their pans.

Make the
LEMON CREAM CHEESE FROSTING

6. In the bowl of a stand mixer fitted with the paddle attachment, beat the cream cheese and butter on medium speed until smooth. With the mixer on low, gradually add the confectioners' sugar, lemon zest, lemon juice, and vanilla until incorporated. Turn the mixer to medium-high and mix until the frosting is fluffy.

ASSEMBLE THE CAKE

7. Tint the buttercream with the food coloring of your choice, if using.

8. Once the cakes have completely cooled, choose which layer will be at the bottom and place it on a cake plate or serving dish. Spread on half the lemon frosting with an offset spatula. Top with the next layer of cake and repeat with the remaining frosting, finishing with the final cake layer. Frost the top and sides of the cake with the vanilla buttercream. Make the spun-sugar nest just before serving, if using.

Make the
SPUN-SUGAR BIRD'S NEST, *if using*

9. Just before serving the cake, line the floors of your workspace with parchment paper. Secure a few wooden spoons to the edge of your countertop with painter's tape, leaving the ends sticking out over the covered floor. Alternatively, secure the spoons so that their handles hang over a large, dry sink.

10. Place the sugar, corn syrup, and ½ cup (120 ml) water in a heavy-bottomed saucepan. Swirl to combine. Heat over medium-high until the mixture reaches 300°F (150°C) on a candy thermometer, 10 to 15 minutes.

11. Meanwhile, prepare an ice bath in a large bowl and set aside.

12. As soon as the sugar reaches 300°F (150°C), immediately remove the saucepan from the heat. Carefully submerge the bottom of the pan in the ice bath to stop the cook-

ing process. Let it stand for about 1 minute before testing the sugar's consistency. The sugar is ready to use when long strands drip from a whisk or fork rather than drops of liquid sugar (see Baker's Notes).

13. Dip a wire whisk or the tines of a large metal fork into the hot sugar. Working quickly but methodically, wave the sugar back and forth over the spoon handles (at least 8 to 12 inches above). Test it out using large arm motions versus quick flicks of the wrist to see what creates the best sugar strands.

14. Working as you go, gather the strands and curve them into a nest shape.

BAKER'S NOTES

The sugar will be extremely hot at first, so use extra caution. The sugar nest tends to dissolve more quickly in humid climates. Do not refrigerate spun sugar. If strands of sugar do not appear right away, let the sugar cool slightly and try again. Once the sugar begins to cool, it will become unusable rather fast, so be sure to have everything prepared and work quickly. The cake will keep in the fridge for up to 3 days (see page 25).

DECORATE IT

Use a piping bag fitted with a round piping tip and filled with buttercream to create a simple design by piping dots (see page 37), like the scallop pattern shown here, on the surface of the cake. Finish the look by piping a pearl border (see page 37) around the base of the cake.

caramel apple cake

MAKES ONE THREE-LAYER 8-INCH (20-CM) CAKE; SERVES 12 TO 15

THE FALL MENU AT THE FROSTED CAKE SHOP was by far the most popular. Topping the list was this Caramel Apple Cake. It is incredibly moist, flavorful, and warms the soul even on the chilliest of autumn days. I used to pair it with a brown sugar caramel frosting, but I've stepped it up a notch for this version, with an ultra-creamy dulce de leche buttercream and a bold apple cider caramel sauce. Make this cake to celebrate the change of seasons or instead of traditional caramel apples at a Halloween festival.

For the
APPLE SPICE CAKE

Butter or nonstick cooking spray, for the pans

3 cups (375 g) all-purpose flour, plus more for the pans

2 teaspoons baking powder

2 teaspoons ground cinnamon

1 teaspoon ground ginger

1 teaspoon baking soda

½ teaspoon salt

½ teaspoon freshly grated nutmeg

½ cup plus 2 tablespoons (150 ml) grapeseed oil

1 cup (200 g) granulated sugar

1 cup (220 g) firmly packed brown sugar

4 large eggs

¾ cup (180 ml) unsweetened applesauce

1½ cups (240 g) finely diced peeled apples, such as Granny Smith, Honeycrisp, or Pink Lady

For the
DULCE DE LECHE BUTTERCREAM

1 large recipe Vanilla Swiss Meringue Buttercream (page 41)

½ cup (120 ml) dulce de leche (see Baker's Notes, page 252)

For the
APPLE CIDER CARAMEL

1 cup (240 ml) apple cider

½ cup (110 g) firmly packed brown sugar

1 teaspoon corn syrup

2 tablespoons unsalted butter, diced

For the
ASSEMBLY

Remaining Vanilla Swiss Buttercream

Make the
APPLE SPICE CAKE

1. Preheat the oven to 350°F (175°C). Grease and flour three 8-inch (20-cm) cake pans and set aside.

2. Sift together the flour, baking powder, cinnamon, ginger, baking soda, salt, and nutmeg and set aside.

3. In the bowl of a stand mixer fitted with the paddle attachment, beat together the oil and sugars on medium speed for 3 to 5 minutes. Turn the mixer to medium-low and add the eggs one at a time. Stop the mixer and scrape down the bowl.

4. Turn the mixer to low and add the flour mixture in three batches, alternating with the applesauce, beginning and ending with the flour mixture. Mix until just incorporated. Add the apples. Mix on low for no more than 30 seconds, or until combined.

5. Evenly divide the batter among the prepared pans. Bake for 24 to 26 minutes, or until a toothpick inserted into the center of the cakes comes out clean. Let them cool on a wire rack for 10 to 15 minutes before removing the cakes from their pans.

Make the
DULCE DE LECHE BUTTERCREAM

6. In the bowl of a stand mixer fitted with the paddle attachment, mix 2 cups (480 ml) of the buttercream until silky smooth. Add the dulce de leche and mix until combined.

ASSEMBLE THE CAKE

7. Once the cakes have completely cooled, level them and choose which layer will be at the bottom. Place it on a cake plate or serving dish. Spread on half the dulce de leche buttercream with an offset spatula. Top with the next layer of cake and repeat with the buttercream, finishing with the final layer. Frost the top and sides of the cake with the reserved vanilla buttercream.

Make the
APPLE CIDER CARAMEL

8. Place the apple cider in a saucepan and bring it to a boil. Reduce the heat to low and simmer until the cider reduces to ¼ cup (60 ml).

9. Add the brown sugar and corn syrup. Raise the heat to high and heat until the syrup reaches 240°F (116°C) on a candy thermometer. Remove the saucepan from the heat and stir in the butter. Pour the caramel into a heat-safe container and let it cool slightly, but use while still warm (see Baker's Notes). Carefully pour the caramel into the center of the cake and evenly spread with an offset spatula, letting it drip over the sides of the cake.

DECORATE IT

Use an offset spatula to create a swirl finish (see page 31) with the buttercream. Fill a pastry bag fitted with a petal tip with any remaining buttercream to pipe a ruffle border (see page 36) around the bottom of the cake.

BAKER'S NOTES

The recipe calls for store-bought dulce de leche, but if you'd like to make your own, bring a large pot filled with plenty of water to a boil. Remove the label from a can of sweetened condensed milk and carefully submerge the entire can in the water. Make sure that it is on its side. Boil for 3 hours, making sure the can is submerged in water the entire time. Very carefully remove the can from the hot water with canning tongs and let it cool completely before opening. Apple Cider Caramel cools much faster than regular caramel sauce and does not reheat as well. Be sure to assemble the cake first and pour on the apple cider caramel before it sets. Try practicing some "test drips" on the back of the cake to make sure it is not too hot. The cake will keep in the fridge for up to 4 days; it may also be frozen (see page 25).

pumpkin pie cake

MAKES ONE TWO-LAYER 10-INCH (25-CM) CAKE; SERVES 12 TO 15

THIS CAKE HARDLY NEEDS AN INTRODUCTION. All you really need to know is that it just may be my favorite cake combination of the entire book. Do I dare make such a bold statement? If pumpkin spice and brown butter are your things, then look no further. This cake is totally worthy of a front-row seat on the dessert table at your next Thanksgiving. Tired of tradition and the same sad pumpkin pie every year? Then I won't waste your time trying to convince you to make this and will just let the flavors speak for themselves.

For the
**BROWN SUGAR
PUMPKIN CAKE**

Butter or nonstick cooking spray, for the pans

3 cups (375 g) all-purpose flour, plus more for the pans

1 tablespoon baking powder

2 teaspoons ground cinnamon

½ teaspoon freshly grated nutmeg

½ teaspoon ground ginger

½ teaspoon salt

¼ teaspoon ground cloves

¾ cup plus 2 tablespoons (210 ml) grapeseed oil

1½ cups (330 g) firmly packed brown sugar

½ cup (100 g) granulated sugar

4 large eggs

2 cups (480 ml) pumpkin puree

For the
PIE CRUST DECORATIONS
(OPTIONAL)

1 store-bought rolled-dough pie crust

Freshly grated nutmeg, for sprinkling

For the
BROWN BUTTER FILLING

¾ cup (1½ sticks / 170 g) unsalted butter

2¾ cups (345 g) confectioners' sugar, sifted

2 tablespoons heavy cream or whole milk

½ teaspoon pure vanilla extract

For the
GRAHAM FROSTING

1 medium recipe Vanilla Swiss Meringue Buttercream (page 41)

1 cup (120 g) graham cracker crumbs

½ teaspoon ground cinnamon

For the
ASSEMBLY

Whipped cream, for garnishing (*optional*; or use ½ recipe Whipped Cream Frosting, page 185)

Make the
BROWN SUGAR PUMPKIN CAKE

1. Preheat the oven to 350°F (175°C). Grease and flour two 10-inch (25-cm) cake pans and set aside.

2. Sift together the flour, baking powder, cinnamon, nutmeg, ginger, salt, and cloves and set aside.

3. In the bowl of a stand mixer fitted with the paddle attachment, beat together the oil and sugars on medium speed for 2 minutes. Turn the mixer to medium-low and add the eggs one at a time. Stop the mixer and scrape down the bowl.

4. Turn the mixer to low and add the flour mixture in two batches. Mix until just incorporated. Add the pumpkin puree. Mix on low for no more than 30 seconds, or until combined.

5. Evenly divide the batter between the prepared pans. Bake for 23 to 25 minutes, or until a toothpick inserted into the center of the cakes comes out clean. Let them cool on a wire rack for 10 to 15 minutes before removing the cakes from their pans.

Make the
PIE CRUST DECORATIONS,
if using

6. Preheat the oven to 400°F (205°C). Line a baking sheet with parchment paper.

7. Unroll the pie crust and cut out the desired shapes. I like using a small star cutter, but any small shape will work. Place them on the lined baking sheet and sprinkle with a dash of nutmeg. Bake until the edges turn golden, about 5 minutes. Let them cool on a wire rack before using.

Make the
BROWN BUTTER FILLING

8. Melt the butter in a saucepan over medium heat, swirling occasionally, and cook until it is browned, about 8 minutes. The butter should be nutty and fragrant. It will start to foam and there should be flecks of brown at the bottom of the pan when ready. Remove the saucepan from the heat and pour the butter into a heat-safe container. Refrigerate it until it has the consistency of softened butter, 20 to 30 minutes.

9. Place the butter in the bowl of a stand mixer fitted with the paddle attachment and beat it on medium-low speed until smooth. Add the confectioners' sugar, cream, and vanilla and mix on low until incorporated. Turn the mixer to medium-high and beat until the filling is combined and creamy.

Make the
GRAHAM FROSTING

10. In the bowl of a stand mixer fitted with the paddle attachment, mix the buttercream until silky smooth. Add the graham cracker crumbs and cinnamon and mix until combined.

ASSEMBLE THE CAKE

11. Once the cakes have completely cooled, choose which layer will be at the bottom and place it on a cake plate or serving dish. Spread on the brown butter filling with an offset spatula. Frost the top and sides of the cake with the graham frosting and garnish with the whipped cream and pie crust decorations, if using.

DECORATE IT

Fill a pastry bag fitted with a medium star tip with whipped cream, if using, and pipe rosettes (see page 37) around the perimeter of the cake. To finish, add the pie crust decorations, if using, to the top of each rosette.

BAKER'S NOTES

The cake may be baked in two or three 8-inch (20-cm) cake pans. Adjust the baking time accordingly, about 22 to 26 minutes. The cake will keep in the fridge for up to 4 days; it may also be frozen (see page 25). Store the pie crust decorations separately.

pecan pear crunch cake

MAKES ONE TWO-LAYER 8-INCH (20-CM) CAKE; SERVES 10 TO 12

WHEN IT COMES TO BUSINESS and all things numbers, my father is the most intelligent man I know. However, he is a bit lost when it comes to food. He always picks obscure dishes at restaurants (once ordering a shrimp cocktail and an ice cream sundae together for a snack) and is like a one-man comedy show when trying to identify flavors in different foods. He claims that pears are his favorite fruit, so it's funny when he comes back from the grocery store with random papayas and things. In his defense, selecting pears can be difficult. And since dear Dad has such a difficult time pairing food together that he likes, I developed this Pecan Pear Crunch Cake for his November birthday.

  This cake is flavored with shredded pears that almost melt into the layers of moist spice cake. For fall, I wanted to incorporate nutty and aromatic flavors and knew this butter rum–pecan combination would make for a spectacular filling. Jazz up any fall birthday or gathering with the warm brown sugar frosting and the extra crunch of the pecan garnish. This year, try swapping out the pecan pie and serve this cake after your Thanksgiving meal.

For the
PEAR SPICE CAKE

Butter or nonstick cooking spray, for the pans

2½ cups (315 g) all-purpose flour, plus more for the pans

2 teaspoons baking powder

½ teaspoon baking soda

1 teaspoon ground cinnamon

1 teaspoon ground ginger

½ teaspoon ground cardamom

½ teaspoon salt

2 to 3 ripe pears, such as Bartlett, Concorde, or green Anjou

½ cup plus 2 tablespoons (150 ml) grapeseed oil

¾ cup (165 g) firmly packed brown sugar

½ cup (100 g) granulated sugar

1 teaspoon pure vanilla extract

2 large eggs

1 large egg yolk

½ cup (120 ml) sour cream

For the
BUTTER RUM PECANS

1½ cups (180 g) chopped pecans

1 large egg white

2 tablespoons dark rum

2 tablespoons firmly packed brown sugar

½ teaspoon ground cinnamon

1 tablespoon unsalted butter, melted

2 tablespoons granulated sugar

For the
BUTTER RUM PECAN CRUNCH FILLING

2 cups (480 ml) Vanilla Swiss Meringue Buttercream (page 41)

½ recipe Butter Rum Pecans (*see above*)

For the
BROWN SUGAR BUTTERCREAM

½ cup plus 2 tablespoons (150 ml) large egg whites

1 cup (220 g) firmly packed brown sugar

1 teaspoon pure vanilla extract

2 cups (4 sticks / 450 g) unsalted butter, at room temperature, cubed

For the
ASSEMBLY

Remaining Butter Rum Pecans, for garnishing (*see above*)

Make the
PEAR SPICE CAKE

1. Preheat the oven to 350°F (175°C). Grease and flour two 8-inch (20-cm) cake pans and set aside.

2. Sift together the flour, baking powder, baking soda, cinnamon, ginger, cardamom, and salt and set aside.

3. Peel and shred enough pear to make ¾ cup (115 g; see Baker's Notes). Drain by placing in a fine-mesh sieve and pushing out any liquids with a rubber spatula. Set aside. Peel and dice enough pear to make 1 cup (180 g). Set aside.

4. In the bowl of a stand mixer fitted with the paddle attachment, mix the oil and sugars together on medium speed for 2 minutes until combined. Stop the mixer and scrape down the bowl.

5. Turn the mixer to medium-low and add the vanilla, then add the eggs and egg yolk one at a time. Stop the mixer and scrape down the bowl.

6. Turn the mixer to low and add the flour mixture in three batches, alternating with the sour cream, beginning and ending with the flour mixture. Add the shredded pears and mix on medium-low for no more than 30 seconds after the last streaks of the dry ingredients are combined. Fold in the diced pears.

7. Evenly divide the batter between the prepared pans. Bake for 24 to 26 minutes, or until a toothpick inserted into the center of the cakes comes out clean. Let them cool on a wire rack for 10 to 15 minutes before removing the cakes from their pans.

Make the
BUTTER RUM PECANS

8. Reduce the oven to 300°F (150°C). Line a baking sheet with parchment paper.

9. Place the pecans in a bowl. Whisk the egg white until foamy and pour it over the pecans. In a separate bowl, stir together the rum, brown sugar, and cinnamon. Toss the rum mixture with the pecans until they are evenly coated. Spread the pecans on the lined baking sheet and bake for 20 to 25 minutes, stirring halfway through the cooking time, until fragrant and slightly toasted.

10. Toss the hot pecans with the butter and sprinkle them with the granulated sugar. Let cool to room temperature before using.

Make the
BUTTER RUM PECAN CRUNCH FILLING

11. In the bowl of a stand mixer fitted with the paddle attachment, mix the buttercream until silky smooth. Fold in half the butter rum pecans until combined.

Make the
BROWN SUGAR BUTTERCREAM

12. Place the egg whites and brown sugar in the bowl of a stand mixer. Whisk them together by hand to combine. Fill a medium saucepan with a few inches of water and place it over medium-high heat. Place the mixer bowl on top of the saucepan to create a double boiler. The bottom of the bowl should not touch the water.

13. Whisking intermittently, heat the egg mixture until it registers 160°F (70°C) on a candy thermometer.

Then carefully fit the mixer bowl onto the stand mixer.

14. With the whisk attachment, beat the egg white mixture on high speed for 8 to 10 minutes, until it holds medium-stiff peaks. When done, the outside of the mixer bowl should return to room temperature and no residual heat should be escaping from the meringue. Stop the mixer and swap out the whisk for the paddle attachment.

15. With the mixer on low speed, add the vanilla and butter, a couple of cubes at a time (see Baker's Notes). Once incorporated, turn the mixer speed to medium-high and beat until the buttercream is silky smooth, 3 to 5 minutes.

ASSEMBLE THE CAKE

16. Once the cakes have completely cooled, level them and choose which layer will be at the bottom. Place it on a serving dish. Spread on the butter rum pecan crunch filling with an offset spatula. Top with the second layer of cake. Frost the top and sides of the cake and decorate with the brown sugar buttercream. Garnish with the reserved butter rum pecans.

BAKER'S NOTES

To shred the pears, grate peeled pears with the large holes of a box grater, rotating around the core. If the buttercream starts to look "curdled" after adding in the butter, just keep mixing. The butter is probably too cold and will need more time to incorporate. The cake will keep in the fridge for up to 4 days; it may also be frozen (see page 25).

DECORATE IT

Use an offset spatula to create a rustic finish (see page 31). Fill a pastry bag fitted with a medium star tip with any remaining buttercream. Pipe stars (see page 37) around the top edge of the cake. Using a small handful at a time, scoop up and press the Butter Rum Pecans to the sides of the cake or sprinkle them on top.

winter peppermint cake

—

MAKES ONE THREE-LAYER 6-INCH (15-CM) CAKE; SERVES 8 TO 10

HAPPINESS IS A WARM CUP OF MULLED WINE, the scent of fresh pine, and roasted chestnuts being sold on the street corner. It is memories of skiing with my dad, covering the house with white twinkly lights, and building fires on chilly nights. And while I claim that fall is my favorite season, I think it is actually because fall precedes the winter holidays and the joy that that time of year brings.

This cake combines classic chocolate with fresh mint. It is rich, yet refreshing, like being bundled up on a crisp winter day. The white sanding sugar used to decorate the cake even shimmers like sun reflecting off fresh snow banks. It is best served with a cup of hot chocolate and peppermint marshmallows.

For the
WHIPPED FRESH MINT WHITE CHOCOLATE GANACHE

½ cup (120 ml) heavy cream

1 cup (50 g) lightly packed fresh peppermint

Scant 1¼ cups (7 ounces / 200 g) chopped white chocolate

¼ to ½ teaspoon pure peppermint extract (*optional*)

For the
SMALL CLASSIC CHOCOLATE CAKE

Butter or nonstick cooking spray, for the pans

1¾ cups plus 2 tablespoons (235 g) all-purpose flour, plus more for the pans

¾ cup (70 g) unsweetened cocoa powder

1½ teaspoons baking powder

1 teaspoon baking soda

¾ teaspoon salt

½ cup (120 ml) grapeseed oil

1½ cups (300 g) granulated sugar

1 teaspoon pure vanilla extract

½ teaspoon pure almond extract

2 large eggs

¾ cup (180 ml) whole milk

1 cup (240 ml) hot strong-brewed coffee

For the
VANILLA MINT BUTTERCREAM

1 small recipe Vanilla Swiss Meringue Buttercream (page 41)

Seeds of ½ vanilla bean

¾ teaspoon pure peppermint extract

For the
ASSEMBLY

1 to 1½ cups (220 to 330 g) white sanding sugar, for decorating (*optional*)

Fresh rosemary sprigs, for garnishing (*optional*)

Make the
WHIPPED FRESH MINT WHITE CHOCOLATE GANACHE

1. In a saucepan, slowly bring the cream to a simmer over medium-low heat. Meanwhile, gently muddle the mint. Remove the saucepan from the heat and add the mint. Let it steep for about 10 minutes. Transfer the mixture to a heat-safe container and continue to steep in the refrigerator for about 2 hours.

2. Strain the cream through a fine-mesh sieve set over a bowl and discard the mint. Place the white chocolate in a heat-safe bowl and set aside. Pour ⅜ cup (90 ml) of the cream into a medium saucepan. Slowly bring it to a simmer over medium-low heat. Pour it over the chocolate. Let stand for 30 seconds, then stir until smooth. Transfer the ganache to a heat-safe container and let it cool for about 2 hours. The ganache should be thickened but not solid.

3. In the bowl of a stand mixer fitted with the whisk attachment or with an electric whisk, whip the ganache until light, fluffy, and white in color. Add the peppermint extract (if using) for a stronger flavor.

Make the
SMALL CLASSIC CHOCOLATE CAKE

4. Preheat the oven to 350°F (175°C). Grease and flour three 6-inch (15-cm) cake pans and set aside.

5. Sift together the flour, cocoa powder, baking powder, baking soda, and salt and set aside.

6. In the bowl of a stand mixer fitted with the paddle attachment, beat the oil and sugar on medium speed for 2 minutes. Add the vanilla, almond extract, and the eggs one at a time. Stop the mixer and scrape down the bowl.

7. Turn the mixer to low and add the flour mixture in three batches, alternating with the milk, beginning and ending with the flour mixture. Stop and scrape down the bowl. With the mixer on low, stream in the coffee. Mix on medium-low for no more than 30 seconds, or until combined.

8. Evenly divide the batter among the prepared pans. Bake for 25 to 28 minutes, or until a toothpick inserted into the center of the cakes comes out clean. Let them cool on a wire rack for 10 to 15 minutes before removing the cakes from their pans.

Make the
VANILLA MINT BUTTERCREAM

9. In the bowl of a stand mixer fitted with the paddle attachment, mix the buttercream until silky smooth. Add the vanilla bean seeds and peppermint extract and mix until combined.

ASSEMBLE THE CAKE

10. Once the cakes have completely cooled, level them and choose which layer will be at the bottom. Place it on a cake plate or serving dish. Spread on half of the white chocolate ganache with an offset spatula or spoon. Top with the next layer of cake and repeat with the rest of the ganache, finishing with the final layer of cake.

11. Frost the top and sides of the cake with the buttercream. Cover the surface of the frosted cake with sanding sugar and garnish with fresh rosemary sprigs, if using.

DECORATE IT

Over a baking sheet or large piece of parchment, use handfuls of white sanding sugar to press against the sides and top of the cake. Continue around the cake, reusing the sugar that falls off as you go, until the cake is completely covered. Break sprigs of rosemary intro varying lengths and place them upside down on the top of the cake to look like a mini forest.

BAKER'S NOTES

The cake will keep in the fridge for up to 3 days; it may also be frozen (see page 25). Store the sanding sugar and rosemary separately.

IT WOULD NOT BE THE HOLIDAY SEASON at our house without a tin of Grandma's ginger crinkle cookies. Among my brother, cousin, and me, it is a tradition to fight over them. Soft yet chewy and sprinkled with sugar, they are always gobbled up much faster than the snowball, chocolate chip, and sugar cookies.

I could not write a cookbook—especially one about dessert—without mention of her famous cookies. No ginger cookie I have ever made could hold a candle to hers, so I must opt for the cake version instead. I've given an old-fashioned molasses cake a modern twist by pairing it with coffee buttercream and toffee sauce. The flavors are rich, yet creamy—something all generations can enjoy.

For the
GINGERBREAD CAKE

	Butter or nonstick cooking spray, for the pans
2½	cups (315 g) all-purpose flour, plus more for the pans
2½	teaspoons baking powder
2	teaspoons ground ginger
1½	teaspoons ground cinnamon
½	teaspoon salt
½	cup plus 2 tablespoons (150 ml) grapeseed oil
¾	cup (165 g) firmly packed brown sugar
½	cup (100 g) granulated sugar
1	tablespoon grated fresh ginger (*optional*)
½	cup (120 ml) molasses
2	teaspoons pure vanilla extract
2	large eggs
1	cup (240 ml) whole milk

For the
ASSEMBLY

1	recipe Coffee French Buttercream (page 69)
6	tablespoons (50 g) candy toffee bits
1	medium recipe Vanilla Swiss Meringue Buttercream (page 41)

For the
TOFFEE MOLASSES SAUCE

6	tablespoons (¾ stick / 80 g) unsalted butter, diced
¾	cup (165 g) firmly packed brown sugar
2	tablespoons molasses
½	cup (120 ml) heavy cream
	Seeds of ½ vanilla bean
¼	teaspoon salt

gingerbread coffee toffee cake

MAKES ONE FOUR-LAYER 8-INCH (20-CM) CAKE; SERVES 12 TO 15

Make the
GINGERBREAD CAKE

1. Preheat the oven to 350°F (175°C). Grease and flour two 8-inch (20-cm) cake pans and set aside.

2. Sift together the flour, baking powder, ginger, cinnamon, and salt and set aside.

3. In the bowl of a stand mixer fitted with the paddle attachment, beat the oil and sugars together on medium speed for 2 minutes. Stop the mixer and scrape down the bowl.

4. Turn the mixer to medium-low and add the grated ginger, if using, the molasses, vanilla, and eggs one at a time. Mix until combined. Stop the mixer and scrape down the bowl.

5. Turn the mixer to low and add the flour mixture in three batches, alternating with the milk, beginning and ending with the flour mixture. Mix on medium-low for no more than 30 seconds after the last streaks of the dry ingredients are combined.

6. Evenly divide the batter between the prepared pans. Bake for 24 to 26 minutes, or until a toothpick inserted into the center of the cakes comes out clean. Let them cool on a wire rack for 10 to 15 minutes before removing the cakes from their pans.

ASSEMBLE THE CAKE

7. Once the cakes have completely cooled, halve them horizontally with a long serrated knife to create four even layers (see page 25). Level the cakes and choose which layer will be at the bottom. Place it on a cake plate or serving dish. Spread on ¾ cup (180 ml) of the coffee buttercream with an offset spatula. Sprinkle the coffee buttercream with about 2 tablespoons of the candy toffee bits. Top with the next layer of cake and repeat twice with the coffee buttercream and candy bits, finishing with the final layer.

8. Frost the top and sides of the cake with the vanilla buttercream and refrigerate until set, 15 to 20 minutes.

Make the
TOFFEE MOLASSES SAUCE

9. In a saucepan, melt the butter over medium-high heat. Stir in the brown sugar and molasses until dissolved. Bring them to a boil and cook for 2 to 3 minutes. Remove the pan from the heat and whisk in the cream. Add the vanilla bean seeds and salt. Reduce the heat to medium-low and return the saucepan to the stove. Simmer, stirring, for 3 to 5 minutes, until the sauce thickens. Remove it from the heat and let cool.

10. Pour the toffee molasses sauce in the center of the top of the cake. Carefully spread it out with an offset spatula and let it drip over the edges.

DECORATE IT

Use a small offset spatula to create diagonals in the frosting for a slight rustic finish (see page 31) for the toffee molasses sauce to ripple over. Alternatively, use any of the buttercream finishes (see pages 30 to 35) to frost the cake before adding the sauce.

BAKER'S NOTES

Not sure if the toffee sauce is the correct temperature? Try a few practice drips on the side of the cake that will be turned to the back. The cake will keep in the fridge for up to 3 days; it may also be frozen (see page 25).

bittersweet chocolate orange spice cake

MAKES ONE THREE-LAYER 8-INCH (20-CM) CAKE; SERVES 12 TO 15

SINCE I AM SO CLOSE TO MY FAMILY, I feel fortunate to have a found a spouse everyone loves and gets along with. Over the years, my mom and husband, in particular, have bonded over helping me with cake deliveries, and taking the dogs out for their walks, and my mom has made great efforts to learn more about Brett's hobbies and interests. One thing that makes me laugh is my mom's ability to latch onto, and even exaggerate, someone's likes or dislikes. And when she found out about Brett's fondness for those chocolate-orange candies that are shaped like the real fruit, she started putting one in his Christmas stocking every year. I am not even certain that he likes them all that much, but I find the gesture too precious to question, and I even went so far as to make this cake in honor of it.

   I went with an orange-almond cake, spiced with cinnamon and cloves. It is incredibly tender and buttery, and the orange flavor really shines through. Paired with the most luscious bittersweet chocolate frosting, this winning combination is perfect for sharing among loved ones around the holidays and when winter citrus is available in abundance. Try serving slices with a sprinkle of sea salt flakes for an extra flavor note.

For the
ORANGE ALMOND CAKE

	Butter or nonstick cooking spray, for the pans
2½	cups (315 g) all-purpose flour, plus more for the pans
1	cup (115 g) almond flour
2	teaspoons baking powder
1½	teaspoons ground cinnamon
½	teaspoon ground cloves
½	teaspoon baking soda
½	teaspoon salt
1	cup (2 sticks / 225 g) unsalted butter, at room temperature
2	cups (400 g) granulated sugar
2	tablespoons finely grated orange zest

1	teaspoon pure vanilla extract
½	teaspoon pure almond extract
4	large eggs
1	cup (240 ml) buttermilk
¼	cup (60 ml) fresh orange juice (from 1 to 2 oranges)

For the
BITTERSWEET CHOCOLATE FROSTING

8	ounces (225 g) bittersweet chocolate
½	cup (1 stick / 115 g) unsalted butter, at room temperature
2	cups (250 g) confectioners' sugar, sifted
¼	cup (25 g) unsweetened cocoa powder
¼	teaspoon salt

1	teaspoon pure vanilla extract
¾	cup (180 ml) sour cream

For the
ASSEMBLY

	Flaky sea salt, for sprinkling (*optional*)

Make the
ORANGE ALMOND CAKE

1. Preheat the oven to 350°F (175°C). Grease three 8-inch (20-cm) cake pans (see Baker's Notes), then line the bottoms with parchment paper and set aside.

2. Sift together the flours, baking powder, cinnamon, cloves, baking soda, and salt and set aside.

3. In the bowl of a stand mixer fitted with the paddle attachment, beat the butter on medium speed until smooth. Add the sugar and orange zest. Turn the mixer to medium-high and mix until the butter is light and fluffy, 3 to 5 minutes. Stop the mixer and scrape down the bowl.

4. Turn the mixer to medium-low and add the vanilla, almond extract, and eggs one at a time. Stop the mixer and scrape down the bowl.

5. Turn the mixer to low and add the flour mixture in three batches, alternating with the buttermilk, beginning and ending with the flour mixture. Add the orange juice and mix on medium for no more than 30 seconds.

6. Evenly divide the batter among the prepared pans. Bake for 24 to 26 minutes, or until a toothpick inserted into the center of the cakes comes out clean. Let them cool on a wire rack for 10 to 15 minutes before removing the cakes from their pans.

Make the
BITTERSWEET CHOCOLATE FROSTING

7. Melt the chocolate in the top of a double boiler and set it aside to cool.

8. Meanwhile, in the bowl of a stand mixer fitted with the paddle attachment, beat the butter on medium until smooth and creamy. With the mixer on low, add the confectioners' sugar, cocoa powder, salt, and vanilla until incorporated. Turn the mixer to medium-high and mix until the frosting is light and fluffy. Stop the mixer and scrape down the bowl.

9. Once the chocolate has cooled, stir the sour cream into it. With the mixer on low, add the chocolate mixture to the frosting. Turn the mixer up to medium and mix until it is combined and creamy.

ASSEMBLE THE CAKE

10. Once the cakes have completely cooled, level them and choose which layer will be at the bottom. Place it on a cake plate or serving dish. Spread on ¾ to 1 cup (180 to 240 ml) of the chocolate frosting with an offset spatula. Top with the next layer of cake and repeat with the frosting, finishing with the final layer.

11. Frost the top and sides of the cake with the remaining frosting. Sprinkle a few pinches of sea salt around the top edge of the cake, if using.

DECORATE IT

Use an offset spatula to create a swirl finish (see page 31).

BAKER'S NOTES

The cake will keep in the fridge for up to 3 days; it may also be frozen (see page 25).

bonus: three-tier wedding cake

—

MAKES ONE THREE-TIER, THREE-LAYER CAKE; SERVES UP TO 65

NOW THAT WE HAVE EXTENSIVELY EXPLORED how to make a variety of awesome layer cakes, it's time to graduate! By adding a few supports here and there, you can turn a couple of stable and structurally sound layer cakes into a tiered cake.

When making a large celebration cake, there are certain items to consider. Not all cakes are created equal, and I do recommend using particular types of cakes over others, especially during the learning process. For tiered cakes, I would suggest starting with the Classic Chocolate Cake (page 49), Vanilla Bean Butter Cake (page 170), or any of the Buttermilk Cakes (pages 62, 65, 146, 173, 180, or 200). For now, I would stay clear of softer, less stable cakes and fillings like chiffon cake, carrot cake, pastry cream filling, whipped cream frosting, and the like. In addition, buttercream fillings, chocolate ganache, and fruit preserves work best for cakes that may be sitting out for long periods of time, as with wedding cakes. Many of the recipes throughout the book can be made into a tiered cake, but I am sharing just a few more to create this "naked" Three-Tier Wedding Cake.

For the
6-INCH (15-CM) ROUND LEMON GINGER CAKE

Butter or nonstick cooking spray, for the pans

2½	cups (325 g) cake flour, plus more for the pans
1½	teaspoons baking powder
¾	teaspoon baking soda
¾	teaspoon ground ginger
½	teaspoon salt
¾	cup (1½ sticks / 170 g) unsalted butter, at room temperature
1½	cups (300 g) granulated sugar
1	tablespoon plus 1 teaspoon finely grated lemon zest
½	teaspoon grated fresh ginger
¾	teaspoon pure vanilla extract
1	large egg
3	large egg yolks
1	cup (240 ml) buttermilk
1½	tablespoons fresh lemon juice
½	cup (85 g) diced candied ginger

For the
10-INCH (25-CM) ROUND LEMON GINGER CAKE

Butter or nonstick cooking spray, for the pans

4	cups (520 g) cake flour, plus more for the pans
2½	teaspoons baking powder
1¼	teaspoons baking soda
1¼	teaspoons ground ginger
¾	teaspoon salt
1¼	cups (2½ sticks / 280 g) unsalted butter, at room temperature
2½	cups (500 g) granulated sugar
1	tablespoon plus 2 teaspoons finely grated lemon zest
¾	teaspoon grated fresh ginger
1¼	teaspoons pure vanilla extract
2	large eggs
5	large egg yolks
1½	cups (360 ml) buttermilk
2½	tablespoons fresh lemon juice
¾	cup (125 g) diced candied ginger

For the
8-INCH (20-CM) YELLOW BUTTER CAKE

Butter or nonstick cooking spray, for the pans

3¼	cups (425 g) cake flour, plus more for the pans
1	tablespoon baking powder
¾	teaspoon salt
1	cup (2 sticks / 225 g) unsalted butter, at room temperature
2	cups (400 g) granulated sugar
1	tablespoon pure vanilla extract
6	large egg yolks
1½	cups (360 ml) whole milk

For the
WHITE CHOCOLATE BUTTERCREAM

1	large recipe Vanilla Swiss Meringue Buttercream (page 41)
5½	ounces (155 g) white chocolate, melted and cooled

For the
HONEY BUTTERCREAM

1	small recipe Vanilla Swiss Meringue Buttercream (page 41)
6	tablespoons (90 ml) honey

For the
ASSEMBLY

½	cup to 1 cup (120 to 240 ml) apricot preserves
	Fresh flowers (*optional; see page 39*)

For the
STACKING

	6-inch (15-cm) cake board
	8-inch (20-cm) cake board
	12-inch (30.5-cm) cake drum or serving dish
14	wooden dowels
	Serrated knife or small hand saw
	Nontoxic writing utensil or edible food writer
	Level (*optional*)

Make the
6-INCH (15-CM) LEMON GINGER CAKES

1. Preheat the oven to 350°F (175°C). Grease and flour three 6-inch (15-cm) cake pans and set aside.

2. Sift together the flour, baking powder, baking soda, ground ginger, and salt and set aside.

3. In the bowl of a stand mixer fitted with the paddle attachment, beat the butter on medium speed until smooth. Add the sugar, lemon zest, and grated ginger. Mix on medium-high until the butter is light and fluffy, 3 to 5 minutes. Stop the mixer and scrape down the bowl.

4. Turn the mixer to medium-low and add the vanilla, egg, and egg yolks, one at a time. Stop the mixer and scrape down the bowl.

5. Turn the mixer to low and add the flour mixture in three batches, alternating with the buttermilk, beginning and ending with the flour mixture. Add the lemon juice and mix on medium for no more than 30 seconds. Fold in the candied ginger.

6. Evenly divide the batter among the prepared pans. Bake for 22 to 24 minutes, or until a toothpick inserted into the center of the cakes comes out clean. Let them cool on a wire rack for 10 to 15 minutes before removing the cakes from their pans.

7. To make the 10-inch (25-cm) lemon ginger cake, follow steps 1 through 6 but use three 10-inch (25-cm) cake pans and bake for 24 to 28 minutes.

Make the
YELLOW BUTTER CAKE

8. Leave the oven at 350°F (175°C). Grease and flour three 8-inch (20-cm) cake pans and set aside.

9. Sift together the flour, baking powder, and salt and set aside.

10. In the bowl of a stand mixer fitted with the paddle attachment, beat the butter on medium speed until smooth. Add the sugar and mix on medium-high until the butter is light and fluffy, 3 to 5 minutes. Stop the mixer and scrape down the bowl.

11. Turn the mixer to medium-low and add the vanilla and egg yolks one at a time. Stop the mixer and scrape down the bowl.

12. Turn the mixer to low and add the flour mixture in three batches, alternating with the milk, beginning and ending with the flour mixture. Mix on medium for no more than 30 seconds after the last streaks of the dry ingredients are combined.

13. Evenly divide the batter among the prepared pans. Bake for 23 to 25 minutes, or until a toothpick inserted into the center of the cakes comes out clean. Let them cool on a wire rack for 10 to 15 minutes before removing the cakes from their pans.

Make the
WHITE CHOCOLATE BUTTERCREAM

14. In the bowl of a stand mixer fitted with the paddle attachment, mix the buttercream until silky smooth. Add the cooled chocolate and mix until combined.

Make the
HONEY BUTTERCREAM

15. In the bowl of a stand mixer fitted with the paddle attachment, mix the buttercream until silky smooth. Add the honey and mix until combined.

ASSEMBLE THE CAKES

16. Once the cakes have completely cooled, level all of them and choose which layers of each size will be at the bottom. For the 6-inch (15-cm) lemon-ginger cake, place the bottom layer on a 6-inch (15-cm) cake board. Spread on ¾ cup (80 ml) of the white chocolate buttercream with an offset spatula. Top with the next layer of cake and repeat with the white chocolate buttercream, finishing with the final layer. Use about ¾ cup (180 ml) of the white chocolate buttercream to crumb-coat the cake. Set it aside.

17. For the 10-inch (25-cm) lemon-ginger cake, place the bottom layer on a 10-inch (25-cm) cake board. Spread on 1½ cups (360 ml) of the white chocolate buttercream with an offset spatula. Top with the next layer of cake and repeat with the white chocolate buttercream, finishing with the final layer. Use the remaining white chocolate buttercream, about 1¼ cups (300 ml), to crumb-coat the cake. Set it aside.

18. For the 8-inch (20-cm) yellow butter cake, place the bottom layer on an 8-inch (20-cm) cake board. Fill a pastry bag fitted with a round tip with the honey buttercream. Pipe a ½-inch- (12-mm-) high dam around the top edge of the cake (see page 27). Fill the ring with half of the apricot preserves. Top with the next layer of cake and repeat with the buttercream and preserves, finishing with the final layer. Crumb-coat the cake with the remaining honey buttercream.

STACK THE CAKES

19. Place the crumb-coated 10-inch (25-cm) cake on a 12-inch (30.5-cm) cake drum or serving dish. Make sure that the top of the cake is as level as possible using the level tool. To support the cake, insert a wooden dowel in the center of the cake or at the highest point, if it is not completely level. Mark the dowel where it reaches the top of the cake using the nontoxic edible writer and remove it. Cut the dowel so that it will be flush with the top of the cake. For the 10-inch (25-cm) cake, you will need to cut nine dowels total, all of which are the exact same length. Place one dowel in the center of the cake, and the remaining eight evenly around the cake, making sure to put them within 1 inch (2.5 cm) of the edge of the cake.

20. Repeat the process with the 8-inch (20-cm) round cake using five dowels after carefully stacking the 8-inch (20-cm) round cake on top of the 10-inch (25-cm). Top the dowelled, 8-inch (20-cm) round cake with the 6-inch (15-cm) round cake. Fill in any gaps between the cakes and cake boards with buttercream or pipe on a bottom border around the cakes for a more finished look. Decorate with fresh flowers, if using.

BAKER'S NOTES

When transporting a large, tiered cake, you may pre-dowel each cake, then stack them upon arrival. Use an offset spatula to maneuver and stack the cakes. Cake drums and dowels may be found online or in the baking section of your local craft store. To fully cover the cakes in buttercream, you will need an additional 12 to 13 cups of buttercream, or two large recipes Vanilla Swiss Meringue Buttercream (page 41). The cake will keep in the fridge for up to 4 days; it may also be frozen (see page 25).

MIX AND MATCH

—

My intention for writing *Layered* was not only to provide recipes and instructions for how to make some of my favorite cakes at home, but also to invite you to create your own combinations! Now that you've accumulated an arsenal of cakes, fillings, frostings, and garnishes, feel free to mix and match the recipes and decorating techniques to create your own one-of-a-kind confections. I've provided a few examples to help get you started:

NEW CREATION	CAKE	FILLING	FROSTING	NOTES
Vanilla Cappuccino Cake	vanilla bean butter cake	espresso ganache	espresso buttercream	*Top the cake with swirls of whipped cream and a dusting of cocoa powder.*
Summer Basil Peach Cake	polenta olive oil cake	basil whipped cream	fresh peaches	*This is your go-to for a backyard barbeque at the height of summer.*
Chocolate Malt Cake	devil's food cake	chocolate malt filling	fudge frosting	*Garnish with whole or chopped-up malt balls.*
Peanut Butter Banana Cake	roasted banana chip cake	peanut butter cream cheese frosting	meringue frosting	*With its marshmallowy icing, this cake is like the ultimate Fluffernutter sandwich. Bake cake in three 8-inch round pans for about 25 to 28 minutes.*
Strawberry Champagne Cake	white chocolate cake	strawberry cream	champagne buttercream	*Garnish with white chocolate curls.*
Baked Alaska Cake	classic chocolate cake	ice cream of choice	meringue frosting	*Follow the directions for building the Banana Split Cake and frost with meringue. Freeze for 30 to 60 minutes, then lightly toast with a kitchen torch.*
Pink Lemonade Cake	lemon butter cake	strawberry cream	vanilla Swiss meringue buttercream	*For an extra blast of flavor, brush limoncello over the cake layers before assembly.*
Victoria Sponge Cake	chiffon cake	raspberry jam and whipped cream	whipped cream frosting	*Leave the sides unfrosted and pile on your favorite berries on top.*
Pumpkin Latte Cake	brown sugar pumpkin cake	caramel cream cheese frosting	espresso ganache	*Double the ganache recipe to frost the entire cake.*
Chocolate-Dipped Strawberry Cake	classic chocolate cake	strawberry cream	strawberry rose buttercream	*Smoothly frost the cake then drizzle with chocolate glaze.*
Milk and Cookies Cake	vanilla bean butter cake	brown butter filling	vanilla Swiss meringue buttercream	*Fold 1 cup mini chips into the cake batter before baking.*
Spumoni Cake	classic chocolate cake	cherry jam and pistachio buttercream	vanilla Swiss meringue buttercream	*Top the cake with chocolate glaze, buttercream rosettes, and candied cherries.*
Key Lime Pie Cake	lime cake	lime filling	graham frosting	*Finish off the cake with swirls of whipped cream and fresh lime zest.*
Lemon Blueberry Cake	blueberry buttermilk cake	lemon curd	vanilla Swiss meringue buttercream	*Decorate the cake with a pile of fresh blueberries or candied lemon slices—perfect for spring!*

ACKNOWLEDGMENTS

—

I never thought writing my first cookbook would be a simple feat, but the process has proved to be much more involved and laborious than I could have imagined. I certainly could not have done it alone, and I want to thank everyone who helped bring *Layered* to life, one page at a time. I am so grateful to have you all in my life.

To my agent, Melissa Server White—thank you for your encouragement and faith in this project from day one. Thank you for helping this first-time author navigate through the publishing world and always making me believe I could succeed.

To my editor, Laura Dozier—thank you for your unyielding support and guidance throughout this entire process. Thank you for helping me develop my ideas and providing such a positive environment for me to create. To Sally Knapp, Deb Wood, and the team at Abrams Books—thank you for transforming my words and photographs into something beautiful and tangible. Thank you for giving me the creative freedom to make this book my own and for your expertise for making it better than I could have ever dreamed possible.

To my husband, Brett—thank you for your patience and unconditional love. Thank you for your tireless hours spent washing dishes, running out to pick up last-minute ingredients, and endless taste-testing. Thank you for being the voice of reason, even in the middle of the night, and never ever letting me doubt myself.

To my mom and dad—thank you for always encouraging me to follow my dreams and for being my biggest cheerleaders in all that I do. Thank you for helping me establish my former bakery—down to getting the plans approved by the city, painting the walls, and even making sugar flowers.

To my brother, Ryan—thank you for my camera, which turned out to be a major turning point in my career. Thank you for our long chats about finding our passions while remaining business-minded and for keeping me grounded.

To Bob and Pink—thank you for being the most supportive in-laws I could have ever asked for and for polishing up the very first drafts of my recipes and anecdotes.

To my friends and family—thank you for shaping the stories and inspiring many of the cakes throughout this book.

To my baby boy, Everett—thank you for literally being with me from the very first photograph taken and recipe tested all the way until I submitted the first manuscript, just days before you were born. Thank you for reminding me what is really important in life and for teaching me a love that I never knew existed.

SOURCES

———

Over my years as a pastry chef, cake decorator, and food stylist, I have accumulated a lot of baking equipment and have built a serious collection of cake stands, props, and decorations. I enjoy picking up unique serving pieces and browsing antique stores for just the right utensil, but have easily found some of my favorite pieces at more commercial home goods and baking stores. You may find many of the products and brands I use in my own kitchen and styling at these retailers.

Anthropologie:
anthropologie.com
Cake stands, dessert plates, glassware, and linens

Bob's Red Mill:
bobsredmill.com
Wide array of specialty flours; also available in many fine grocery stores

Callebaut Chocolate:
callebaut.com
Premium dark and white chocolate; also available in many fine grocery stores

Crate & Barrel:
crateandbarrel.com
Baking tools, cake stands, dessert plates, and more

The Cross Decor and Design:
thecrossdesign.com
Cake stands, dessert plates, linens, and decorations

The Flair Exchange:
theflairexchange.com
Party décor, including confetti and paper garlands

Food 52:
food52.com/shop/
Beautifully curated baking tools, cake stands, dessert plates, and decorations

Global Sugar Art:
globalsugarart.com
Baking tools, cake pans, sprinkles, and more

The Gourmet Warehouse:
gourmetwarehouse.ca
Vancouver-based restaurant supply and specialty foods store

Herriott Grace:
shop.herriottgrace.com
Beautiful handmade goods, candles, and cake flags

Kate Spade New York:
katespade.com
Modern dinnerware and dessert plates

King Arthur Flour:
kingarthurflour.com
Wide array of flours, cocoa powders, and sugars; also available in most grocery stores

KitchenAid:
kitchenaid.com
Heavy-duty stand mixers

Michaels:
michaels.com
Wide array of sprinkles, cake pans, baking tools, and more

Nielsen-Massey:
nielsenmassey.com
Vanilla bean paste and other extracts

The Perfect Purée of Napa Valley:
perfectpuree.com
Passion fruit concentrate and other fruit purees

Pier 1 Imports:
pier1.com
Cake stands, dessert plates, linens, and more

Sur La Table:
surlatable.com
Baking tools, cake pans, sprinkles, and more

West Elm:
westelm.com
Baking tools, dinnerware, flatware, linens, and more

Whole Foods Market:
wholefoodsmarket.com
Organic and specialty foods

Williams-Sonoma:
williams-sonoma.com
Equipment, baking tools, cake pans, and some specialty foods

INDEX

Page numbers in *italics* refer to photographs.

Published in 2016 by Abrams

Text and photographs copyright © 2016 Tessa Huff
Photographs on pages 1, 28, 29, 31, 32, 33, and 34 copyright
© 2016 Ryan Lindow

Library of Congress Control Number: 2015949316

ISBN: 978-1-61769-188-1

Editor: Laura Dozier
Designer: Deb Wood
Production Manager: Denise LaCongo

The text of this book was composed in Brandon Grotesque
and Domaine

Printed and bound in China
10 9 8 7 6 5 4 3

Abrams books are available at special discounts
when purchased in quantity for premiums and promotions
as well as fundraising or educational use. Special editions
can also be created to specification. For details, contact
specialsales@abramsbooks.com or the address below.

ABRAMS The Art of Books
115 West 18th Street, New York, NY 10011
abramsbooks.com

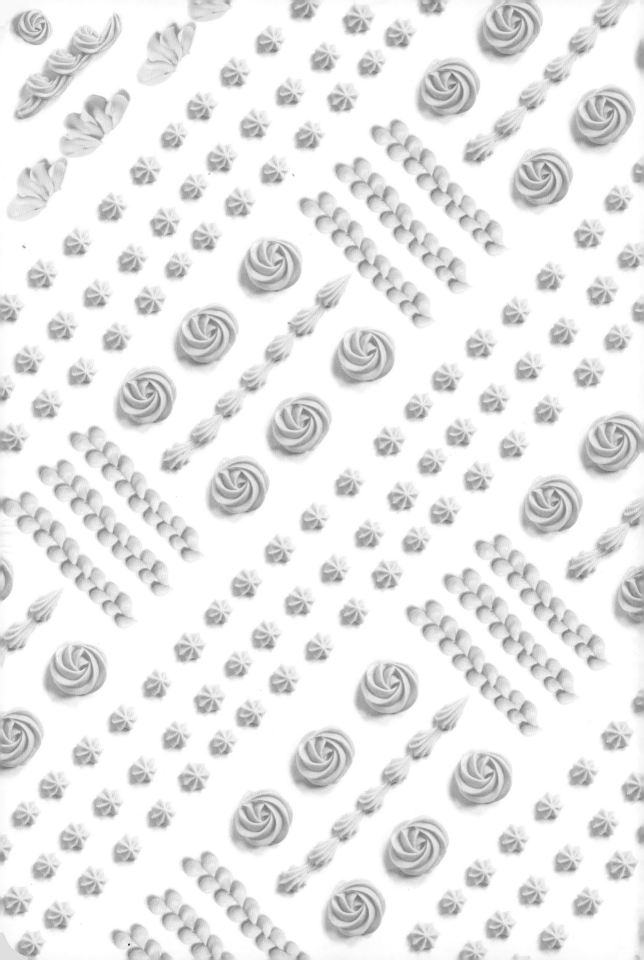